Women writing childbirth

Until recently, the story of childbirth has been a marginalised one. In this lucid and challenging book, Tess Cosslett brings childbirth centre stage.

Her detailed readings of birth-stories – both literary and medical – reveal deeply embedded assumptions about how women are viewed, and how we view ourselves. The current debates about 'natural' childbirth, as advocated by Sheila Kitzinger, Grantly Dick Read and others, are examined alongside key literary works by writers such as Doris Lessing, Margaret Atwood, Fay Weldon, Toni Morrison.

Cosslett's case for a re-evaluation of motherhood in today's society presents a challenge as much to feminists themselves as to the medical and scientific world. This will prove an essential book to students of women's studies as well as to lay readers and childbirth professionals.

For Alice and Greg

Women writing childbirth

Modern discourses of motherhood

Tess Cosslett

Manchester University Press
Manchester and New York
Distributed exclusively in the USA and Canada by St. Martin's Press

Copyright © Tess Cosslett 1994

Published by Manchester University Press
Oxford Road, Manchester M13 9NR, UK
and Room 400, 175 Fifth Avenue, New York, NY 10010, USA

Distributed exclusively in the USA and Canada
by St. Martin's Press, Inc., 175 Fifth Avenue, New York,
NY 10010, USA

British Library Cataloguing-in-Publication Data

A catalogue record for this book is available from the British
Library

Library of Congress Cataloging-in-Publication Data

Cosslett, Tess.
    Women writing childbirth: modern discourses on motherhood/
Tess Cosslett.
        p. cm.
Includes bibliographical references.
ISBN 0–7190–4323–9. — ISBN 0–7190–4324–7 (pbk.)
1. English literature—Women authors—History and criticism.
2. English literature—20th century—History and criticism.
3. Mother and child—Literary collections. 4. Childbirth—Literary
collections. 5. Motherhood—Literary collections. 6. Mother and
child in literature. 7. Childbirth in literature. 8. Motherhood in
literature.   I. Title
PR116.C64   1994
820.9′354—dc20

ISBN 0 7190 4323 9 *hardback*
     0 7190 4324 7 *paperback*

Printed in Great Britain by Biddles Ltd, Guildford and King's Lynn

Contents

I felt I'd been *tricked*, actually *tricked*, by the health visitor, by the books I'd read. . . . And somebody had said well it's not like it is in the films or something. And I thought well it's exactly like 'Gone With the Wind' – it's *exactly* like those old movies when they're all writhing about in agony . . .

(A woman describes childbirth,
Ann Oakley, *From Here to Maternity*)

Grantly Dick-Read drew attention to culturally induced fear of the childbirth process current in our own society, in which stories relating to pain and endurance are handed down from mother to daughter . . . stories which find a place in our literature and films . . .

(Sheila Kitzinger,
The Experience of Childbirth)

Acknowledgements

I would like to thank the Lancaster University Centre for Women's Studies Research Seminar, the Women's Studies Network Conference, the Northern Network Seminar, and the Lancaster University English Department Staff Seminar, all of whom have heard and commented usefully on several parts of this book. Thanks to Penny Summerfield and Elizabeth Roberts for an Oral History Workshop. Thanks to Carole Rhodes, for telling me about *The Squire*, and Michael Wheeler, for telling me about *Still Life*; to Antonia Byatt, for listening patiently and reacting helpfully to my interpretations of her novel, and to Laurel Brake for organising the day school at which this could take place. Thanks to all the women who listened to my birth-story and gave me theirs. Thanks to Greg and Alice, without whom this book would not exist.

Introduction

Childbirth, as an experience belonging to the private sphere of womanhood, has long been marginalised as a subject for public representation. In particular, accounts of childbirth from the perspective of the birthing woman herself have been relegated to private diaries, or anonymous letters to magazines (Huff 1991). Before the twentieth century, childbirth did not often appear in fiction, and when it did it was nearly always seen from an audience point of view – the father's, the attendants' (Kreppel 1984; Poston 1978). The distaste of some male critics for the subject is voiced by H. G. Wells, reacting to Enid Bagnold's 1938 novel, *The Squire*, whose plot is constructed round a birth, seen from the perspective of the mother, a strong, central female character. Wells felt as if 'I'd been attacked by a multitude of many-breasted women . . . and thrown into a washing basket full of used nursery napkins' (Sebba 1987 xvii). Wells attempts to dismiss Bagnold's subject as something both monstrous (many-breasted) and trivial (nursery napkins). A contemporary feminist critic, on the other hand, can celebrate the power of her attack, an early example of the transgressive and subversive activity of writing the female body, without reference to approved male constructions of the feminine. As Hélène Cixous says, 'For if there's one thing that's been repressed, here's just the place to find it: in the taboo of the pregnant woman' (Cixous 1981 261). Bagnold's novel is one of the earliest attempts to inscribe the experiences of pregnancy and childbirth into the culture; since the 1930s, an increasing stream of women's accounts of childbirth, fictional and non-fictional, has been published. Doris Lessing, also the first to put menstruation into fiction in *The Golden Notebook* (1962) (however one may criticise her rather negative attitude to it), is another pioneering figure in this story, with her account of hospitalised childbirth in *A Proper Marriage* (1956). In another context, these novels might be called 'seminal'; here I prefer to see them as mothers of the childbirth-story.

As a central, life-changing event for many women, childbirth needs to be made visible, written about, from a woman's perspective. Too often, the story has been taken away from women by the 'audience perspective' accounts of fathers, or, more influentially, doctors. A 'medicalised' version of childbirth, in which women are objectified as machines for producing babies, has become increasingly dominant in the twentieth century. This medical discourse has taken institutional shape in the routines of hospitalised birth. Medical versions of childbirth reduce the woman to an object: to restore her subjectivity is the aim of the women writers in this study. Their work, and my own interest in them, I see as part of the recovery of maternal subjectivity, which Marianne Hirsch, in *The Mother Daughter Plot* (1989), identifies as a new, belated subject for feminist criticism. As Maureen T. Reddy puts it, 'feminism was largely a daughter's critique', with a suspicion of mothers and motherhood, until in the second half of the 80s a number of studies, including Hirsch's, began to draw attention to the mother's subjectivity (1991 81).

In the recovery of maternal subjectivity in the birth-story, the natural childbirth movement plays an ambiguous part. As the medical 'story' has been gaining credence and power, an oppositional discourse of 'natural childbirth' has been taking shape. This discourse can be seen to lie behind both Bagnold's celebration of natural motherhood, and Lessing's critique of hospitalised birth. The 'story' of natural childbirth, with its emphasis on the birthing woman's *consciousness* as the key to the process of giving birth, seems to offer women writers a powerful plot within which to write women-centred accounts of childbirth. And yet the discourse is in many ways anti-feminist, dependent on prescriptive myths of primitive, essential motherhood.

In their concern to free women from 'medicalised' versions of childbirth, feminist critics have often not realised how profoundly women's opposition to the medical establishment is informed by natural childbirth rhetoric. Emily Martin, for instance, in *The Woman in the Body* (1987), dissects textbook descriptions of women's bodies, and shows how their mechanistic language is behind the treatment of women in hospitals; she presents women's resistance to this treatment as a spontaneous, revolutionary activity. Similarly, Cynthia Huff, in her article 'Delivery: the cultural re-presentation of childbirth', discusses American women's accounts of birth in the *Ladies Home Journal* in the 1950s, presenting them as attacks on the dehumanising hospital system. But she does not notice how their wish to make childbirth 'the easy natural thing it should be', or their protests at the exclusion of fathers and the denial of 'the opportunity to share an experience which should be the culmination of all a man and woman have hoped and planned for in an honest-to-goodness marriage', are products of the prevailing natural childbirth rhetoric (1991 116–18; see also Wertz and Wertz 1979). The Victorian women whose diaries she also quotes from had no idea that childbirth should be easy and natural, nor that fathers should be present: these notions, as much as the hospital birth system itself, are cultural products of particular historical moments.

This suggests that in investigating women's accounts of birth we are not suddenly going to find 'authentic' (Poston 1978 20–2) voices, liberated as the 'false' stories of the doctors are lifted off. I find myself in a characteristic post-modern dilemma: both wanting to affirm women's voices, the inscription of their hitherto marginalised subjectivities, and needing to show how these voices, those subjectivities have been culturally constructed by prevailing discourses and cultural practices. A way through this dilemma is suggested by Paul Smith when he writes, 'a person is not simply an *actor* who follows ideological scripts, but is also an *agent* who reads them in order to insert him/herself into them – or not' (1988 xxiv–xxxv). Similarly, Sidonie Smith, following Judith Butler, has defined identity as 'a practice of working within and against the rules' (1991 189). Thus the consciousness of a birthing woman, whether constituted in an autobiographical account, or as a 'character' in a fiction, involves a process of *negotiation* with prevailing ideologies (see Cosslett 1988 1–15), whose aim is, I would argue, power: in terms of writing, the power to take over the story, in terms of childbirth, the power to control the experience; or, in both cases, the power to protest, or celebrate, lack of control.

An earlier formulation which also captures what I think is going on in contemporary women's accounts of childbirth is Nancy

Cott's words about nineteenth-century women's writings: 'The meaning which women ascribe to their own behaviour is reducible neither to the behaviour itself nor to the dominant ideology. It is derived from women's consciousness which is influenced by the ideas and values of men, but is nevertheless uniquely situated, reflective of women's concrete position within the patriarchal power structure' (in Anderson *et al.* 1990 103). It is always easier to see the traces of dominant ideologies in the writings of the past: it is very difficult to see their workings around and in us now, when we naively assume we are talking (and writing) in our 'own' voices. To disentangle *all* the cultural echoes in childbirth accounts would be an impossible task, like a cat trying to catch its own tail. In this book I am concerned to trace the workings of two opposing 'official' stories of childbirth: the story of the medical experts, and the story of the natural childbirth experts. I want to show how the woman's story of childbirth makes use of, is overwhelmed by, or resists these two powerful stories.

I have characterised medical discourse and natural childbirth discourse as the two dominant or 'official' discourses about childbirth in our culture, since both of them have had power to shape the way childbirth is conducted and organised. As Paula Treichler points out, controversies about the conduct of childbirth – where it takes place, who is in charge, how much intervention is used – are at the core controversies about 'meaning'. It is by defining childbirth as a 'medical event', and by getting official acceptance of that definition, that the medical institution has been able to gain a monopoly over the treatment of childbirth and make hospitalisation almost universal (Treichler 1990 116). But the competing definition of childbirth as a 'natural' event has also been gaining in public power, and has actualised itself in developments like home births, birth centres, and more power for midwives. These ways of talking and writing about childbirth have a practical effect on the institutions within which birth takes place.

There is also a third, marginalised, unofficial popular discourse whose echoes can be heard in women's accounts: the 'old wives' tale' – the oral tradition of women telling each other about childbirth, whose unstructured, ghoulish horror stories challenge the simple, optimistic structures of our modern myths of birth. I am also concerned to show how other cultural stories of race and class, which are largely omitted from the official discourses, nevertheless leave their mark when women write the experience from their point of view. Finally, at the risk of essentialism, I want to suggest that the body itself, the physical condition of maternity, challenges all our cultural scripts, and resists a unifying definition.

In investigating women's attempts to write childbirth, I have looked mainly at 'literary' accounts, both novels and poems. Many of these, however, are susceptible to autobiographical as well as fictional interpretations. The lines are not clearly drawn: so-called 'real life' accounts of childbirth are also constructed in negotiation with other discourses, and even with literary patterns. Moreover, actual childbirth practice can be seen as governed by the power of the various stories about childbirth, their construction of the woman as agent or patient, chief actor or part of the scenery (Treichler 1990). Recognising a certain arbitrariness in generic definitions, I have included two contrasting collections of 'real life' stories among my literary examples: *Giving Birth, How It Really Feels* (1987), edited by Sheila Kitzinger, and *From Here to Maternity* (1981), edited by Ann Oakley. Kitzinger's accounts provide examples of the stories of natural childbirth converts; Oakley's explicitly illustrate the disillusionment of many mothers with the cheerful official books and talks on childbirth, and are nearer to the oral tradition.

I have also, briefly, looked at the books of some 'experts': *Natural Childbirth* (1933) by Grantly Dick Read, the founding 'father' of the twentieth-century natural childbirth movement, and *The Experience of Childbirth* (1962, 1984) by Sheila Kitzinger, one of the movement's most powerful present-day advocates. As I have suggested, feminist critics often seem unaware of the provenance and implications of the natural childbirth-story and its accompanying images. Kitzinger provides an example of a woman writer struggling, with partial success, to take over Dick Read's story for a woman-centred point of view. She parallels and influences other women writers' attempts in the same direction. The medical story of childbirth has been extensively analysed and criticised by feminist writers in recent years (e.g. Donnison 1977; Martin 1987; Mitford 1992; Rich 1977; Rothman 1982; Towler and Bramall 1986). I did not feel it necessary for me to reiterate this criticism in any detail; instead, I have provided one illustrative example, O'Driscoll and Meagher's *Active Management of Labour* (1980), of a recent obstetric textbook in which the medical story

both is and is not present. I want to show how even this story has
begun a negotiation with the natural childbirth-story, and how hard
it is to find a 'pure' form of either story: Read himself turns out
to support the medical institution, and Sheila Kitzinger's followers
are adepts at medical terminology. Even the idea that there *are* two
competing birth-stories could be seen as a powerful, simplifying
cultural myth, within which many of the stories I discuss work.

This book is in no way meant to be a history of obstetrics in
the twentieth century: such studies have been ably written by other
women, to whom I refer. The experts' books I have analysed are
meant to stand as examples of particular types of birth-story,
highly influential on the women's texts that are my main concern.
My main focus is on women writing as women giving birth, even
if both of those 'women' are read as identities constructed in
negotiation with ideological norms. As a feminist I am concerned
to assert, though also to question, this identity of 'women'. The
scope of this study includes writers from America, Britain and
the Commonwealth. I have used texts by both 'canonical' women
writers, such as Margaret Atwood, Doris Lessing, Toni Morrison,
Sylvia Plath, and less well-known writers who deserve to be
more widely read. Childbirth is, as I have said, a relatively new
subject for literature, and it has been quite difficult to track
down instances; in the American context, I have been particularly
grateful for the anthology *Cradle and All* (1989), edited by Laura
Chester, which is full of interesting writing. Poems from Chester's
collection by Toi Derricote, Sharon Doubiago, Sharon Olds, and
Alicia Ostriker have been especially useful to my argument.

The movement of this study is from a consideration of women
writers' negotiations with the official stories of childbirth, to more
complex issues that undermine the totalising effect of the official
discourses. The first two chapters detail negotiations, first with the
natural childbirth-story, and then with the medical story. I begin
the book by investigating the language of natural childbirth, as it
has been so central to an oppositional, potentially woman-centred
account of childbirth. In particular, I concentrate on the stereotype
of 'the primitive woman', who is still regularly referred to in
antenatal classes and books. I trace her transformations from her
appearance in Grantly Dick Read's *Natural Childbirth*, through

Sheila Kitzinger's attempts to appropriate and change her, and her various fictional appearances, idealised, satirised or subverted. The next chapter concentrates on women writers' negotiations with medical discourse and medical institutions, often represented as both repressive and masculine, in opposition to the ideal of the primitive woman. Technological intervention in birth can be presented as an emanation of a patriarchal science and its need to control women's bodies. Nevertheless, medical discourse can also be used by women to empower themselves in surprising ways, and it too can be subverted.

The third chapter introduces the notion of 'other' women, differences between mothers and non-mothers, women of different classes and races. As these differences are dramatised in women's birth-stories, the unifying 'woman' of the official stories is fractured. Natural childbirth writers see motherhood as the essential attribute of womanhood; in the discourse of medical expertise, all women are reduced to their bodily functions. In birth-stories, these definitions are questioned by contrasts with other women: contrasts with non-mothers bring out the mother's status as woman, the social meaning of motherhood; contrasts with other mothers often highlight differences of class and race. In this chapter I also look at representations of the 'old wives' tale', the stories women tell each other about childbirth. This oral tradition, we will find, is reviled by medical experts and natural childbirth enthusiasts alike. Its sometimes gruesome stories are contrasted with the optimistic stories of the official discourses: efficient, anaesthetised, pain-free, technological birth, or ecstatic, drug-free, painless, natural birth. As presented in written accounts, the old wives' tales articulate the unacceptable side of childbirth in our culture. So bad is their reputation that many fictional accounts are also concerned to distance themselves from this oral, woman-centred tradition, and yet I see many of these accounts as belonging to it, in so far as they go beyond or around the official discourses and present unassimilable and unacceptable aspects of childbirth.

In the last chapter, I look at the perplexing questions of individuality and identity that are raised by writing the birth-story from the woman's point of view, perplexities and complexities that are ironed out in the official stories. An 'inside' view of the particular physical condition of maternity – two in one, one becoming two

– can radically challenge the idea of the autonomous individual subject. Here, the challenge to the notion of 'identity' comes not from the ideologies and discourses of culture, but, however 'essentialist' it may sound, from the body itself. Our culture has no way of formulating the intersubjectivity between mother and foetus/baby without reducing one to the object of the other: witness the polarised debate on abortion. While some women writers express the relation of mother and foetus/baby in simplified terms of devourment or a benign extension of being, others present it as both at once. The pronoun for the foetus also shifts ambiguously: s/he, it, you. There is also no adequate language for the physical process of giving birth, as an 'individual' splits to produce another individual, and the subsequent formation of two new identities. Women writers struggle with organic and mechanical imagery, metaphors of rebirth and death. Finally, the autobiographical conclusion analyses some versions of my own birth-story, in the context of three other women's stories, recorded during a project in which I was collecting oral birth narratives.

1

Natural childbirth and the 'primitive woman'

There have always been advocates, male and female, of a non-interventionist, more 'natural' approach to childbirth. In the twentieth century, this opposition to interventionism has crystallised into the natural childbirth movement. This loosely-constituted movement is usually traced back to the work of the British doctor, Grantly Dick Read, in the 1930s. Read's work became popular in the USA in the 40s, along with the slightly different approach of the French doctor, Fernand Lamaze. Read not only favoured a more 'natural', non-interventionist approach, he also argued that pain in childbirth was not 'natural', and could be eliminated by inducing the right state of mind in a birthing woman (Donnison 1977; Read 1933; Towler and Bramall 1986; Wertz and Wertz 1979). Thus the focus for natural childbirth discourse becomes not the woman's objectified body, but her subjective state of mind. This makes natural childbirth discourse particularly relevant to my purposes in this book: to show what happens when the birth-story is told from the woman's point of view. The discourse of natural childbirth would seem to be offering a powerful model to writers exploring the consciousness of the birthing woman; yet, as we will see, it has an anti-feminist, traditionalist legacy that is hard to shake off.

A powerful image in the natural childbirth-story has always been 'the primitive woman': anyone who has been to antenatal classes will probably recognise the stereotype. Often identified as 'African', she goes into the bushes on her own, gives birth painlessly and without fuss, and returns immediately to her work in the fields. In various forms, she haunts Western women's birth-stories – as an instinctive power in their own bodies, as a learned ideal to be lived up to, as a delusion shattered by experience, or, revised and reversed, as a representative of the primitive *pain* of childbirth. The primitive woman is, however, not nearly so primitive as she seems: she is a cultural construct, incorporating the maternal ideals of a particular society, and, paradoxically, her instinctive wisdom has to be learnt from books by 'civilised' women. She begins as very much a male ideal, allowing domination of the birth-scene by the charismatic male obstetrician; taken over by women writers, she is used to assert female power and autonomy, though she still carries with her some anti-feminist implications. Other women writers are concerned to explore and explode the paradoxes she encodes, and to rediscover her in a new form.

The primitive woman as a male construct

Grantly Dick Read, the 'father' of the modern natural childbirth movement, is credited with introducing the ideal of the primitive woman into obstetric theory (Freedman and Ferguson 1950 363), though she probably has a long history, and must be descended ultimately from the 'Noble Savage'. In a key scene in Read's pioneering 1933 book, *Natural Childbirth*, he watches a 'native' woman leaving her work to give birth painlessly and joyfully in a thicket by herself (Read 1933 40). Anthropological research has suggested that painless childbirth is by no means universal or even common among so-called 'primitive' cultures. Instead, a wide range of different cultural beliefs and practices surround childbirth, providing parallels with almost every approach, interventionist or non-interventionist, male- or female-centred, to be found in the West (Freedman and Ferguson 1950; Mead and Newton 1967). Read, however, is working within a simplistic, pseudo-evolutionary opposition of nature and culture, primitive and civilised; 'primitive' women, for him, are not the product of *different* cultures, but those 'whose natural development has not yet attained a state of civilisation', they are 'without culture' (Read 1933 22). In this model, culture has corrupted civilised women from their natural state of painless and joyful motherhood.

How does Read know this, one is tempted to ask? Partly, because he is working with some rather old-fashioned nineteenth-century ideas of social evolution, and even Natural Theology: that is, the idea that the natural is inherently good, and well-designed. In his book he repeatedly refuses to accept that pain in childbirth can be part of what he sees as a divinely designed Nature. The passage in which he observes the primitive woman is made to fit into these assumptions: he does not speak to her, so we learn nothing about her consciousness. It is all inferred by Read from her facial expressions and actions: 'her face became set, not with pain or fear, but *almost* with a sense of expectancy. . . . The child appeared when she was in a half-sitting position. It *seemed* that she smiled almost immediately. . . . She wrapped the baby in the cloth that was round her own shoulders and then looked at me and laughed' (Read 1933 40; my italics). Surely there could be several different reasons for her to have 'laughed' at the watching alien doctor? Especially interesting in the scene are the power relations: the woman giving birth so efficiently by herself seems a symbol of female autonomy and power, yet the meaning of her actions is immediately appropriated by the male doctor observing her, and made to fit into his theories. The primitive woman is taken over and made to serve the ends of a particular culture, especially its agenda for women.

So Read sees motherhood as women's natural and essential role, obscured by the distortions of civilisation: 'among the primitive races a girl is brought up from the point of view of survival. Sexual life and the reproduction of her kind are the fulfilment of her highest ideals' (Read 1933 42). This idealisation of motherhood has, however, some very 'civilised' ends in view, namely the strength and efficiency of the nation as a whole:

> A healthy and happy parturition is not just the delivery of the mother of her child. It is the making of a mother who will in every way be fitted to carry out the duties of motherhood, which is not only to bear children, but to be the corner-stone of the temple of Home, without which no nation can produce a family of worthy citizens. . . . Children born in pain, born of fear . . . cannot . . . be expected to produce a high level of national efficiency.
>
> (99)

Thus a particular ideology about women as domestic angels contributing to the strength of the nation-state is being promoted under the label 'Nature'. Read is participating here in a prevailing ideology of his time – the campaign to produce a better imperial race by improving childbirth education and facilities (Lewis 1980). We can find his idealisation of motherhood in Enid Bagnold's nearly contemporary novel, *The Squire* (1938, 1987).

In Read's interpretation, the painlessness of 'primitive' childbirth is not to do with the primitive woman's physical way of life, nor with her cultural practices, but with her uncorrupted state of mind. She is not afraid, and she experiences no pain, because she has not been taught to be afraid or to expect pain. It is fear that tenses up the body and produces pain. 'Civilised' women have been taught fear by false cultivation. But all this, while seeming to value women's subjectivity, still reduces their consciousnesses to the innocent or duped objects of the knowledgeable male expert observer. So, in Read's scheme, it is only the highly-trained, charismatic obstetrician who can counter the women's 'civilised' fears and restore them to their 'natural' state. He writes himself back as principal character into a scene – primitive painless childbirth – that would seem to have no place for him at all. The silencing of women enacted in his book is reflected in the way it is addressed, not to pregnant women, but over their heads to other male obstetricians. In dealing with women patients, writes Read, 'it is necessary to create the atmosphere that can give confidence in *our* teaching and that can allow *us* the influence essential for the control of their emotions' (26; my italics). 'Control' is an interesting word here – just as in the medical model the doctor tries to 'control' the woman's body, so here he tries to 'control' her emotions.

Read is helped in this project by another concept of female 'nature', derived from Freud. Though I have said that some of his theoretical frameworks are rather out of date – social evolutionism and Natural Theology – he also latches onto Freudianism, a much more fashionable twentieth-century development. Freud also was interested in recovering the primitive, located for him in the subconscious. He too exercised powers of interpretation and control over his female patients' states of mind. This is how Read makes use of Freudianism:

> In spite of the emancipation of woman, in spite of her having attained equality in many paths of life, in her normal state she is found subconsciously to look upon man as the protective sex of the genus. Some psychologists go so far as to say that the seeds of resentment in women can sometimes be traced to the sense of

something lacking in them that man possesses. . . . these references
are to the normal woman, that is, the woman whom Nature made
most fitted for natural purposes.

(Read 1933 102)

So, paradoxically, 'Nature', which has just shown that women can
give birth entirely on their own, is now brought in to show their
necessary dependence on men.

The reactionary basis of Read's thought can perhaps be brought
out by reference to another 1930s novel, Vera Brittain's *Honourable Estate*. Here, the ideas of motherhood as woman's proper
role, and childbirth as a 'natural' event not requiring medical
attention, are put into the mouth of an ignorant Victorian patriarch:
'The trouble with women nowadays . . . was that they were too
pampered; they made such scenes about these natural processes
that you'd think having a baby was a major operation' (Brittain
1936 41). This optimism is shattered when he witnesses his
wife's parturition: 'the sanguinary spectacle which every poorly-
conducted birth relentlessly offers to those who behold it' (46). He
is forced to reassess his view of Nature's relation to the birthing
woman, 'the tormented body through which he had watched
Nature's purposes being so ruthlessly accomplished' (48). Here
we again have a man as observer of a woman's experience of
childbirth – but the scene has been set up by a woman writer
to educate him. We also have the woman's own voice indirectly
present: just before the birth, her husband reads and is shocked
by her diaries, which record what he calls her 'sinful rebellion
against motherhood' (40) – in fact a longing for emancipation only
to be fulfilled later in the novel by her daughter-in-law, Ruth, who
successfully combines motherhood and career.

The ironic contrast set up in *Honourable Estate*, between naive
pronouncements about 'natural' birth and the shock of the actual
experience, is one that later women writers make much use of,
often to comic effect. In these later accounts, as we will see, the
target is not Victorian patriarchy, but the twentieth-century natural
childbirth movement, though the comparison with *Honourable
Estate* suggests how far Read may have been merely reformulating
old anti-feminist positions. Nevertheless, his idealisation of the
primitive woman does contain possibilities of empowerment for
birthing women: if we remove the watching male doctor, she

is a strong, autonomous figure; and if we likewise spirit away the charismatic male obstetrician, women's own consciousness becomes the centre of the birth-process. This is what Sheila Kitzinger has attempted to do with Read's ideal of natural childbirth. But even before Kitzinger, women began to take more control of the process of natural childbirth as practised by Read.

Read got nowhere with his attempt to persuade his fellow obstetricians in the medical establishment of the value of his approach; his biographer comments again and again on the professional jealousy that hampered his career (Thomas 1957 65, 71, 84, 98, 107, 112, 133). But midwives and birthing women did begin to take up his ideas: women reading the book may have seen a way to greater control of the birthing process themselves. Be that as it may, it was among women, as midwives and patients, that Read found his greatest support. The second edition of his book, now called *Revelation of Childbirth*, takes some account of this. Read explains how women educated in natural childbirth ideas 'became interested in the performance of their own parturition. . . . They were able to criticise their own sensations during labour, and to differentiate between hard work and pain' (Read 1942 94). A more active participation by women themselves is being recognised. Read appeals for more first-hand accounts from *women*, in order to persuade other *women*: 'Woman cannot be persuaded by mere man, but only by members of her own sex. . . . Let women speak who have borne their children naturally, and who know the truth' (226). The third edition, *Childbirth Without Fear*, goes even further in the direction of addressing itself to women. It claims to be written 'for the mothers of the rising and succeeding generations' (Read 1954 v). Read writes of the thousands of letters he has received from mothers, confirming his theories, and he presents his philosophy of natural childbirth as originating from the *voice* of a woman in Whitechapel, who said, after giving birth, '"It didn't hurt. It wasn't meant to, was it, doctor?"' (10). The book is presented as both written for and originating from women. Aiming at women's support might also, of course, indirectly achieve his goal of persuading the medical profession to his position: 'if enough women could be awakened to the possibility, they themselves surely would set up such a clamour for natural methods, that the doctors would be forced, willy-nilly, to give them what they demanded' (Thomas 1957 116).

Female appropriation

Nowadays, although natural childbirth in France is still associated with charismatic male figures – Michel Odent, Frédérick Leboyer – in Britain it is associated with a charismatic *female* figure, Sheila Kitzinger. Moreover, Kitzinger is not a qualified obstetrician, and is herself a mother. Her work has done much to reclaim natural childbirth for a female-centred approach, which can empower women against institutionalised medicine and its mostly male practitioners. The shift to a female point of view is marked in her pioneering book, *The Experience of Childbirth*. Rather than being addressed by one male medical expert to others, as Read's first book was, Kitzinger's book is 'written by a layman [sic] for laymen [sic]' (Kitzinger 1962 11). In the 'Author's Note', Kitzinger describes herself as someone who has been preparing mothers for childbirth, and who has had four babies herself. Women's experience – her own and her pupils' – lies behind her claim to authority, but she also lays claim to 'male' medical knowledge and terminology, which she wishes to make accessible to and empowering for other women. Kitzinger's multiple, shifting role, combining medical expert, teacher and confidante of birthing women, and woman who has given birth herself, is reflected in the shifting point of view and addressee of her writing: sometimes it is the experiences of a generic 'woman' that are being described; sometimes 'the woman' shifts into 'one', which includes the author as a possible participant in the experiences; sometimes a 'you' is introduced as addressee, as direct instructions are given to the reader as pregnant woman, and occasionally the author comes in in the first person, either describing her own experiences, or relaying those of her pupils. Kitzinger is both sympathetic observer and participant.

As we have seen, one central, potentially liberating, feature of the natural childbirth model is that it draws attention to the subjective experience of the birthing woman, not just to her objectified body. Her state of mind is the key to a successful birth. As we saw, Dick Read took the consequence to be that the male obstetrician must *control* that state of mind. Kitzinger, on the other hand, seeks to give control to the woman herself – to listen to her account, to let her make decisions: 'She is no longer a passive, suffering instrument. She no longer hands over her body to doctor and

nurses to deal with as they think best. She retains the power of
self-direction, of self-control, of choice, and of voluntary decision'
(1962 20). As we might expect, this empowering of the woman
leads to a rather less glamorous view of the obstetrician than
Read gives us. Kitzinger discredits the idea that 'natural childbirth
implies a sort of hypnotic relationship between the doctor and
patient', and insists that a woman can put the method into practice
'even if the obstetrician or midwife knows nothing about it at all'
(24). Women who are over-dependent on their doctors are seen as
immature types looking for father-figures.

The way in which Kitzinger is taking over centre-stage for
women from doctors can be seen in her use of the metaphor of
'conducting'. She refers in a footnote to Lamaze's recording of 'a
labour conducted by himself. It is interesting to compare this with a
record of a birth by Dick Read' (Kitzinger 1962 144). Presumably,
she means the *record* is by Dick Read, but the alternative reading, a
birth by Dick Read, neatly conveys how far these male obstetricians
have become the central figures, the creative artists, in the birth
scene. A paragraph on the same page then advises 'one' on how
to push out one's baby: 'One pushes exactly when and as long as
and as strongly as each [contraction] indicates. It is a little like the
orchestra responding to the conductor's baton. The contracting
uterus is the conductor' (144). We see here how the conductor
is no longer Lamaze, or Dick Read – but, surprisingly, neither
is it 'one' – 'one' is the orchestra, responding to the conducting
uterus. Here a rather different model puts the woman's body,
with its involuntary urges and rhythms, not her prepared and
knowledgeable conscious mind, at the centre of the process. This
is where the 'nature' of natural childbirth comes in, and we are
returned to Read's primitive woman.

So far in my argument it may have seemed as if Kitzinger
has dispensed with 'nature' altogether – her emphasis on the
conscious, informed, active woman is similar to that of the Lamaze
method, which presents itself as *better* than nature (Karmel 1959
42). In *The Experience of Childbirth*, Kitzinger claims to be
taking her ideas from both Read and the Frenchmen Vellay and
Lamaze (Kitzinger 1962 13), adapting both and adding elements
of her own. The Lamaze method of 'childbirth without pain' (as
opposed to Read's 'childbirth without fear') involves learning
specific breathing techniques, and is based on a Pavlovian model

of conditioning the body to ignore pain (Lamaze 1958). The method became popular in the 1950s, especially through the efforts of Marjorie Karmel, an American woman, who had used the method for her first birth in Paris, and then returned to America and attempted to put it into practice there. In her book, *Babies Without Tears*, Karmel presents herself as originally excited by Read, but put off by his 'mystical' attitude to motherhood (Karmel 1959 42). The Lamaze method cuts this out, and offers her a practical route to power and control over her own labour. Her book shows a woman making use of natural childbirth techniques to assert herself as central actor in her own drama – though Lamaze is still present in the background as all-wise, semi-magical guru, Karmel goes beyond him in using the method by herself in an unsympathetic American hospital setting. Karmel's brisk dismissal of Read's 'mystical' notions frees her from traditional notions of motherhood and Read's accompanying anti-feminism: her self-image is not as 'primitive woman', but as a highly trained sportswoman, and athletic achiever (22, 49, 67, 92, 140).

We often find Kitzinger too using this kind of image. The highly trained sportswoman, in control of her body and the environment, has nature tamed, unlike the primitive woman giving in to her 'natural' urges. Thus Kitzinger, like Karmel, sees the husband, midwife and woman forming a 'team' (Kitzinger 1962 44), and advises that a birthing woman should take no drugs 'that a car driver would not take before setting out on a night journey in fog, or an athlete before taking part in a race' (121). She also tells us stories about pupils of hers who practised birth-relaxation on a motorbike or in the cockpit of an aeroplane (75). The introduction of cars, motorbikes and aeroplanes here takes us even further from the primitive woman: these women are successful achievers, in control of machines and bodies. Yet, despite her own use of these metaphors, Kitzinger feels she has to attack both the emphasis on 'athletic skill' in the Lamaze model, and its 'mechanistic' aspect, and reinstate Read's 'spiritual' dimension (21, 23, 141, 144). She sees the Lamaze approach as too dangerously like the objectifying mechanical model, and the way in which Lamaze breathing techniques have been easily co-opted into the dehumanising routines of American hospitals may prove her right. As Barbara Katz Rothman describes it, 'A woman who maintains a fixed, if somewhat glazed, cheerful expression and

continues a regular pattern of breathing is said to be "in control",
as she is carted from one room to another and literally strapped
flat on her back with her legs in the air' (Rothman 1982 177).
The 'control' the woman seemed to have gained from the Lamaze
method is illusory.

In attempting to restore the 'spiritual' dimension to birth,
Kitzinger, like Read, goes to Freud, producing a pseudo-Freudian
account of the unconscious and its primitive urges, to which
women must learn to conform. As in Read, we have the paradox
of civilised women learning to be 'natural': 'she must, above all,
have learned to trust her body and its instincts. We are seeking
to achieve a functional harmony of the woman's body which to a
few civilised women comes naturally, but which most of us have
to learn painstakingly' (Kitzinger 1962 21). So while Kitzinger, as
we saw, gives primacy to the birthing woman's state of mind, her
account of what she calls 'the psychology of pregnancy' turns out
to be a very oppressive pseudo-Freudian account based on the idea
of 'adjustment' – the woman's adjustment (or failure to adjust) to
her 'natural' roles both as mother and wife. Well-adjusted women
give birth easily; poorly-adjusted women have difficulty. As with
much psychological explanation, this relies on the concept of the
normal, and implies *blame* for deviance from that norm. While
Read used Freud to discover natural dependency in women's
subconscious, Kitzinger uses him to discover sexuality as woman's
basic 'natural' urge. So giving birth naturally is depicted as an
adjustment to heterosexual sexuality, involving an acceptance of
'primitive instinctual pleasures' (105). A women stuck in a long
labour, it is implied, is maladjusted, 'for some reason which may
have its origins in her own childhood and which is probably linked
to the quality of her marriage relationship' (105–6), since there
'remains in the process of giving birth a sexual element of which
women are dimly aware and which tends to frighten some' (97).
It is very interesting that later, in another context, Kitzinger insists
that a long labour can be pleasurable, to a well-prepared woman
(119) – here the model is of the woman in control, making
what she wants out of her experience. But in the psychological
section, Kitzinger is carried away by the logic of her model of
the inhibited woman unable to adjust to her primitive sexual
urges. In this second model, the primitive woman is located in
the woman's body/subconscious, as a powerful, though still silent,

dictatorial force. Because she is necessarily silent, Kitzinger, like Read, can read her own interpretations into the primitive woman's actions.

Central to Kitzinger's interpretation of natural, well-adjusted womanhood is, as in Read, the notion that women are essentially *mothers*: 'A woman expresses herself in childbearing. Without this experience she feels that she has missed something, that she is incomplete, in some way, wasted' (1962 68). Moreover, motherhood is seen in the context of a traditional marriage relationship: the last page of the book insists that birth is essentially 'part of a marriage, and can enrich or deprive it according to how the experience is lived through by both man and woman' (192). As we have seen, the quality of the marriage relation is alleged to affect the woman's ability to give birth, and the husband's participation and presence throughout is insisted on. The natural childbirth movement's emphasis on the birth as the couple's experience fitted in very well with the culture of the 50s, with its emphasis on marriage and the 'feminine mystique' (Wertz and Wertz 1979 181–9). Kitzinger's 1962 book retains a lot of this 50s ideology, as well as anticipating the sexual 'liberation' of the 60s in its frank discussion of sexual relations and impulses – this also can lead to a very traditional model of women's role. As with Read, we have the impression that 'natural' can easily be made to mean whatever is culturally sanctioned at the time – and, when applied to women, can be used to reinforce reactionary prescriptions about their role. The primitive woman is easily transformed into the conformist housewife.

Interestingly, Kitzinger is a little more aware than Read of the culturally conditioned aspect of the mother and wife role she holds up as 'natural' – she discusses the difficulties of sustaining these roles in face of 'the general lack of clarity in masculine and feminine roles within our society at this time. ... a general lack of acceptance of the roles of wife and mother as they have been known for centuries in Western society', so that women now 'are required to take on all men's tasks and characteristics without relinquishing any of their femininity and charm' (1962 55–6). All this suggests a nostalgic harking back to times when roles were clearer, but a later section points out that different difficulties arose under the old system, when an over-devoted mother could stunt her children's psychological growth (191). As in the discrepancy about long labours, we have the impression of Kitzinger pulled in different directions by the different models she is using.

This ambivalence is reflected in a more recent book of Kitzinger's, *Giving Birth, How It Really Feels* (1987). Here she explicitly mocks Read's ideal of the primitive woman: natural childbirth does not mean teaching 'women that they can go out and squat in the woods with the squirrels and other wild creatures and have their babies on a pile of leaves' (Kitzinger 1987 27). The very word 'natural' in this context is questioned; instead, she uses a new metaphor: childbirth is an *art*, whose techniques have been so well learnt and practised that when put into action it *seems* 'natural' (26). Playing the piano, dancing, or skiing are the analogies she draws. She also wants her pupils to be aware of medical terminology and of 'the way the medical system works' (29). Highly trained and fully informed, these far from primitive women are to be in control of their own birth processes, yet the primitive is still incongruously present in another analogy she makes – birth as orgasm, a profound sexual experience. How can one have an orgasm whilst also remaining aware of the medical technicalities and the social and political context? It is interesting that in her introductory chapters Kitzinger gives two quite different, parallel but separate, accounts of birth – one is a lyrical 'fantasy' describing her own experience of childbirth 'in terms of imagery of water and its movement' (23–4) – the 'natural' narrative; the other is a standard medical description of 'the usual pattern of labour', in terms of first stage, transition, second stage, and what the cervix and the uterus are doing at each stage (53–4).

I'm not at all suggesting that Kitzinger *should* be able to give a single, self-consistent account of childbirth – in the last chapter, I will be exploring how birth can never be represented by any one type of discourse or narrative, or even from a consistent, unified point of view. Here, I want to suggest the problems and advantages of the ideal of the primitive woman for women wanting to wrest control of the experience from male doctors and male-centred accounts. Though Kitzinger appears to dismiss the primitive woman in *Giving Birth*, she still needs her in the background as a validation for what she is doing, as a goal towards which her women strive. All their techniques and information are directed towards attaining the primitive woman's 'flowing' presence in their own bodies.

That the primitive woman may be an unrealisable but necessary ideal is suggested by her appearance in Margaret Atwood's novel, *Surfacing* (1973, 1979). Towards the end of the novel, the alienated heroine's rediscovery of her lost, authentic self is figured as a pregnancy, and a vision of a totally 'natural' birth, clearly related to Dick Read's description: 'This time I will do it by myself, squatting, on old newspapers in a corner alone; or on leaves, dry leaves, a heap of them, that's cleaner. The baby will slip out easily as an egg, a kitten, and I'll lick it off and bite the cord, the blood returning to the ground where it belongs'. This picture contrasts with her previous abortion, when she was victim of 'the death machine, emptiness machine'. The figure of the primitive woman giving birth provides a powerful image of female autonomy – but it is clear that this is only a fantasy: she imagines the resulting baby 'will be covered with shining fur' (Atwood 1979 156). While the heroine does go on to enact a return to the primitive, retreating into the woods and discarding all the trappings of civilisation, the point of the novel is that she has to return eventually to civilised 'reality': the baby won't really be born in the woods, and she may not even be pregnant. The natural birth is a powerful fantasy that the heroine carries away with her, that will affect her attitude to herself and to her possible pregnancy and childbirth, but not one that will actually take place.

On the other hand, the primitive woman, while not actually giving birth in the bushes, can be rediscovered in one's own body, through metaphor and simile, even in a modern institutional setting. This is powerfully put in Sharon Doubiago's poem, 'South America Mi Hija':

> She took my clothes, put me
> on that hard board in that tiny green cell,
> tied a paper to my neck.
> He sat at my feet. Silent. But there.
> An occasional grin. The consummate moment
> of our teenage marriage.
> . . . .
> In the bursting of your coming, muscle, skin, walls,
> the smock untied. I leaned back on my hands,
> my stretched, engorged breasts exposed, laughed,

entered a strange stream, a sexual
stream, the ecstasy of time and place, a churning
like mountains, like seas at the risen continents.
I could hear time, a machine sound.
I could feel creation, myself in place
for the first time.

(Doubiago 1989 102)

As in Atwood's image, the birth puts the heroine in touch with her
'real' self, through a harmony with Nature. The nature imagery is
strongly reminiscent of Kitzinger's description of birth in terms of
'water imagery': 'The birth of the baby has come as if on a tide
which streamed through me . . . the swelling wonder of creation
as the womb-fruit ripens, tilts, and feels almost bursting in its
strength. . . . My body is like an island fretted by waves, like
a widening bay filled by a swollen tide' (Kitzinger 1987 23–4).
Streaming water, bursting, sexual ecstasy, natural creation are
the terms of these descriptions. Doubiago's teenage mother is
presumably innocent of any knowledge of medical terminology or
the medical account of the birth process, so, unlike for Kitzinger,
there need be no parallel medical story. Is this then how birth
'really' feels? Well, for some women perhaps, but, as we have
seen, Kitzinger and her pupils only reach this experience through
long training. Could the descriptions of Atwood's and Doubiago's
'natural' births have been created without Read's promotion of the
primitive woman, and the natural childbirth movement's subsequent popularisation of the idea of 'natural' birth? What is
interesting is that both Atwood and Doubiago present the primitive
woman as arising spontaneously from the woman's subconscious
or body, as an innate power – her cultural origins are suppressed
or not acknowledged.

In doing this, women writers could be seen as paralleling
Kitzinger in her attempts to wrest natural childbirth from its male
cultural origins, and use it to make women central to the birth
process. The earliest use of this strategy pre-dates Kitzinger, and,
interestingly, is nearly contemporary with Read's first book: Enid
Bagnold's novel, *The Squire*. The heroine, known as 'the squire',
gives us a description of childbirth in terms of water imagery which
would not be out of place in Kitzinger's book:

> there comes a time, after the first pains have passed, when you
> swim down a silver river running like a torrent, with the convulsive,

corkscrew movements of a great fish, threshing from its neck to
its tail . . .
   Now the first twisting spate of pain began. Swim then, swim with
it for your life. If you resist, horror, and impediment! If you swim,
not pain but sensation! . . . Keep abreast of it, rush together, you
and the violence which is also you! Wild movements, hallucinated
swimming!

                                    (Bagnold 1987 101, 145)

As in Read and Kitzinger, it is only tension and resistance that
produce pain: but how did Bagnold come by these ideas? She
presents it, through the squire, as a matter of learning through
personal experience: 'the first time is all panic. The second half-
panic, but at the third and fourth times something began to dawn
on me. I said, "Is this really *pain*?"' (100). Through her experience
of several births, she has come upon 'the secret of childbearing in
the past, when women had eleven and fifteen children and learnt
how to have them' (102). Personal experience leads to ancient
wisdom.
   But is 'natural' childbirth really 'natural', or is it a cultural
practice that we learn from books? Read's *Natural Childbirth*
appeared in 1933, before the publication of *The Squire*, though
after Bagnold's last child was born in 1930. But in 1923, Bagnold
had met Harold Waller, a progressive doctor with advanced ideas
about childbirth and child-care. 'Harold Waller influenced Enid's
ways and views of life more completely than anyone she had met
since Antoine [Bibesco, her second lover]', writes her biographer,
and when she gave birth to her second child, 'With Dr Waller's
constant advice and the help of an excellent nurse, Ethel Raynham
Smith [the original of the midwife in *The Squire*], Enid thoroughly
enjoyed this baby' (Sebba 1986 84, 90). This contrasts with her
first birth, which she describes '"as though an outside power
was forcing you through a sausage machine"' (Sebba 1986 81).
The change in her experience of childbirth *may* have been due
to experience, but more likely was due to Waller.
   This conclusion is reinforced by the way Bagnold rewrites culture
as nature in her descriptions of both the birth itself, and the
breast-feeding that follows. Standard medical practice at the time
was to administer chloroform to the woman as the final stage, the
actual pushing out of the baby, began. This is presented in *The
Squire* without comment, as the climax of a totally *natural* birth:

'The corkscrew swirl swept her shuddering, until she swam into a tunnel – the first seconds of anaesthesia'. Four stars across the text represent her unconsciousness – then the baby cries, and 'out of her river the mother was drawn' (Bagnold 1987 146). The anaesthetic is the climax of her watery journey, unconsciousness her natural goal. Such an assumption would be anathema to Kitzinger, who stresses repeatedly the importance of being conscious during the actual emergence of the baby, the supreme sexual and spiritual moment of the whole experience. What to Bagnold is natural, to Kitzinger is unnatural interventionism. The same process of culture being transformed into nature is glaringly obvious in Bagnold's description of breast-feeding. In an idyllic first feeding scene, 'The squire, bending over the baby, her watch in her hand, would have given him ten minutes' (151). Feeding at fixed intervals, which is now seen as rigid and unnatural, is presented as a *natural* rhythm: 'Strange, concentrated life, that no man knows, shared with the cat in the stable and the bitch in the straw of the kennel. . . . The regularity of her milk, as always, astonished the squire. At six and ten and two and six and ten, to the tick, to the instant, her breasts swelled and reminded her' (169–70). In A. S. Byatt's novel *Still Life* (1985, 1986), we get a contemporary critique of this practice as carried out in a 1950s hospital, and now seen as an institutional tyranny imposed by unsympathetic nurses:

> Babies must feed steadily for the prescribed ten minutes – no more, or mother's nipples would be sore, no less, or they might not put on. . . . Those who asked to feed frequently, or enjoyed sleeping in their mother's arms, were designated 'spoiled' and frightful warnings were uttered about not letting these helpless human scraps get the upper hand. Nurses dehumanised babies.
>
> (Byatt 1986 100)

I do not think we can say that Kitzinger and Byatt are right, and Bagnold wrong, but only that fashions in anaesthesia and breast-feeding have changed. What is important is the way Bagnold co-opts cultural practices for her powerful, autonomous 'natural' woman.

In later accounts, it is less easy for heroines to be presented as totally innocent of natural childbirth as a cultural practice – Atwood's heroine has to retreat beyond culture, Doubiago's has extreme youth, and in *Still Life* Byatt presents her heroine,

Stephanie, as purposely *ignoring* the books on natural childbirth; she has in fact read 'a book about natural childbirth', but had

> made no effort to perform the relaxation exercises prescribed by the book. She had always been confident in her self-possession in her own body. She imagined women were not so civilised that they had no natural sense of what to do with things that happened to everyone as imperatively as eating and excreting. If it was natural to relax, she would relax, when the time came.
>
> (Byatt 1986 85)

As in *The Squire*, 'natural' childbirth is being presented as innate and primitive. However, Stephanie is giving birth in a hostile institution, the 1950s NHS hospital, while the squire was able to actualise her ideal of a natural childbirth in the setting of her home, helped by a sympathetic midwife. The hospital nurses are presented as working *against* what Stephanie's body is telling her to do. They stop her walking about the room in the first stage of labour, and force her to get into bed. As she goes into the final stages, the nurses lay hands on her: 'She wished the women dead for holding her so uncomfortably in an unnatural position' (92). 'Unnatural' routines destroy her chance of a 'natural' birth, but when the nurses do leave her alone, we are shown Stephanie 'obeying some powerful instinct', walking rhythmically up and down, working *with* the rhythms of the pain (90–1). The pain is imaged as 'singing', not hurting, when she relaxes into it (87).

But could Byatt have written this without having read the literature of natural childbirth? In both Byatt's and Bagnold's novels, however, we can say that there is a great *need* to present cultural practices as natural and instinctive, to assert that women have access to some ancient wisdom of the body during childbirth. I do not want to imply that women writers have somehow been brainwashed into accepting 'natural' childbirth as natural; instead, it seems to me they are creating empowering solutions to the paradox presented by a book on 'natural childbirth' written by a man. In *The Squire* the idea of a non-resisting, pain-free childbirth is presented as occurring spontaneously to the mother herself, as a product of her personal experience, and as a recovery of past female wisdom, and we are shown her putting the idea into practice on her own initiative and with her own encouragement. Similarly, Stephanie ignores the books and trusts to her own body, which gives her the right messages in spite and not because of institutional intervention. Both women claim natural childbirth as a woman's unaided power, and marginalise or render invisible its male cultural origins. This laying claim to female centrality and power is also evident in another way Bagnold may have rewritten Dick Read: he ends *Natural Childbirth* with water imagery – specifically, an image of doctor and midwife standing on the shore, encouraging the frail bark of the baby through the waves of labour. Lest this image might seem to put the doctor into too marginal a position, Read adds a final image implicitly likening him to Christ walking on the water, calming the fears of the disciples. Bagnold too uses water imagery to describe labour – the flowing river and the swimming fish – but here the mother is at the centre of the process, she is the fish who knows how to swim with and within the currents.

Another way in which Bagnold revises Read's 'primitive woman' is by using imagery of heroic *male* action to describe her heroine and her attitude to giving birth. This imagery exists incongruously with the 'natural' water imagery, rather as Kitzinger uses both 'athletic' and 'natural' images. Read also sometimes uses 'military' imagery – civilised woman's extreme terror at childbirth is compared to the extreme terror Read has witnessed and experienced in the First World War. The alleviation of this terror is a military campaign for the obstetrician:

> The work of readjusting the minds of women occupied in the primitive functions of childbirth requires as much skill, precision and foresight on the part of those who are concerned with it as the counter-measures against bombs from aeroplanes, gas attacks, magnetic and acoustic mines, submarines and all the improvements of modern warfare demand from those whose business it is to understand these things.
>
> (Read 1933 51)

Here, the intelligent military strategist becomes *not* the woman herself, but the male medical expert, 'whose business it is to understand these things'. This appropriation by the obstetrician of the central, active role in childbirth is essential to Read's approach, as we have seen. Bagnold, in contrast, takes over the military role for her birthing woman: the squire will bear her baby like 'a soldier', thinks the nurse approvingly. The squire also describes her relationship with her midwife as 'like a boxer with his trainer. . . . we gather together as for a race' (Bagnold

1987 100), prefiguring Karmel and Kitzinger's 'athletic' imagery. The 'male' role taken by the squire is emphasised by the absence of her husband during the whole book, allowing her to take the title and function of 'squire', the 'master' of the house. The 'male' language casts her as a heroic and controlling figure, not the silent and passive primitive woman.

The primitive woman discredited

While all these women writers are concerned to take over the primitive woman for women, obscuring her male cultural origins, other writers are equally concerned to discredit her, often emphasising the contrast between 'primitive' painless childbirth as an ideal, and the pain and confusion of the 'real' experience. In these accounts, the cultural origins of natural childbirth, the fact that it is a theory learnt from books, are ironically pointed up. In Fay Weldon's novel *Puffball*, natural childbirth rhetoric is fiercely satirised. Just as the heroine, Liffey, is about to haemorrhage, her husband fatuously repeats the old chestnut about the 'primitive' woman:

> 'It's an entirely natural process,' said Richard. 'Nothing to worry about. African mothers go into the bush, have their babies, pick them up and go straight back to work in the fields.'
> They all looked at Liffey, to see how she would take this.
> 'And then they die,' said Liffey, before she could stop herself.
> (Weldon 1980 244)

In this case, Liffey does not die, though she nearly does, but Weldon also shows death resulting from this kind of naive acceptance of the natural childbirth position. Liffey and her husband Richard have let their London flat to a group of drop-outs, one of whom, Lally, is pregnant. Her sister, Helen, believes in an extreme version of natural childbirth and denies her any medical attention whatsoever. Helen says confidently, '"All that stuff about pain is part of the myth. Having a baby is just a simple, natural thing"' (92). Weldon fastens gleefully on the clichés of natural childbirth rhetoric. Predictably, the baby is eventually stillborn.

Stupid pronouncements about primitive women are also sent up by Doris Lessing in *A Proper Marriage*, a novel set in Rhodesia just before and during the Second World War. The heroine's 'friend' Stella repeats received wisdom about the natives: 'They're not civilized, having babies is easy for them, everyone knows that. . . . everyone knows they are nothing but animals, and it doesn't hurt them to have babies' (Lessing 1977 27). The colonial assumptions behind the myth of the primitive woman are exposed here. Margaret Drabble also punctures the received wisdom in a scene in an English antenatal clinic where the pregnant heroine of her novel *The Millstone* sees 'a black woman who sat there not with the peasant acceptance of physical life of which one hears, but with a look of wide-eyed dilating terror' (Drabble 1966 57). There is, however, a rather racist distancing and condescension here: like Dick Read, Drabble reads the silent woman's feelings from her face, and begins to construct a new stereotype – the primitive bottom-line is not painlessness and joy, but pain and terror.

False stories about painless childbirth are what 'one hears', what 'everyone knows', but, more specifically, they come from books. Ann Oakley's collection of interviews, *From Here to Maternity* (1981), is based on this sort of irony. 'What many of the women who were interviewed said was that they were misled into thinking childbirth is a piece of cake and motherhood a bed of roses. . . . I have constructed the book around this conclusion' (Oakley 1981 6). In her accounts there are continual contrasts between the hopeful predictions of natural childbirth books, and what actually happens: 'You're not allowed to call them pains, are you? They're contractions. It always makes me laugh when I read that because I *knew* they bloody well hurt. . . . Also the breathing wasn't working – it's a load of old codswallop, that breathing' (87). A lot of discontent focuses on the semantic sleight of hand that redefines 'pains' as 'contractions': 'I felt I'd been *tricked*, actually *tricked*, by the health visitor, by the books I'd read – by the Gordon Bourne book, because he said that the word pain should *not* be applied to labour contractions' (109). The naive self-righteousness set up by these book-learned expectations is satirised by the American writer, Doris Betts, in her short story 'Still Life With Fruit': 'Surely the sister knew enough to say "contraction" and never "pain". For some women – not Gwen of course – that could be a serious psychological mistake' (Betts 1974 337). Not surprisingly, the description of Gwen's experience punctures this complacency: 'The next pain hit her and this one was a pain – not a "contraction" at all. One more lie in a long line of lies' (351). This contradiction between theory and experience can be summed up by the ironic epigraph to the chapter describing the heroine's painful childbirth in *A Proper Marriage*: '*You must remember that having a baby is a perfectly natural process.* FROM A HANDBOOK ON HOW TO HAVE A BABY' (Lessing 1977 123).

Protagonists who are naively dependent on books, and who, paradoxically, also cling to the ideal of the primitive woman, are presented in Toi Derricote's poem, 'Natural Birth' (1983), and Margaret Atwood's short story, 'Giving Birth' (1977, 1984). Like Fay Weldon, Atwood exploits the comic possibilities of a confrontation between naive, book-learned natural childbirth enthusiasts and the uncontrollability of the real experience of childbirth. Thus, in the prenatal class, the only woman who has actually given birth before significantly insists she wants 'a shot this time', to stop the pain. The others disapprove of her 'wrong attitude': 'The books talk about "*discomfort*". "It's not discomfort, it's pain, baby," the woman says. The others smile uneasily' (Atwood 1984 231). Like one of Oakley's informants, the experienced woman here substitutes 'pain' for the euphemistic 'discomfort' of the textbooks, implying an unrealistic naivety in the natural childbirth version the other women have swallowed. Jeanie, the protagonist, is fully clued up on the natural childbirth version of birth – the narrator makes gentle fun of her devotion to 'handbooks'. On the way to hospital, she is 'doing her breathing exercises and timing her contractions with a stopwatch' (228–9). This emphasis on intelligent control is, however, mixed with myths about 'primitive' painlessness: later, sitting in a hospital wheelchair, she guiltily tells herself about 'peasant women having babies in the fields, Indian women having them on portages with hardly a second thought'. The primitive woman is an image of strength for Jeanie: her worry is that she may 'collapse after all. . . . After all her courageous talk' (233). But, ironically, Jeanie is mostly reliant on the printed word, not on primitive instincts, to get her through the experience: '"I think I have back labour", she says to A [her accompanying male]. They get out the handbook and look up the instructions for it. It's useful that everything has a name' (233). The distance between the primitive woman in the fields, and the modern woman consulting her handbook brings out the contradiction in modern natural childbirth discourse.

Toi Derricote's heroine has also accepted the natural childbirth version of birth beforehand – a combination of Lamaze and Read, it seems. She

> wanted lamaze (painless childbirth) – i
> didn't need a husband or a trained doctor – i'd do it
> myself, book propped open on the floor, puffing
> and counting . . .
>   . . . when the time came, i
> would not hurt like all those women who screamed and
> took drugs. I would squat down and deliver just like the
> peasants in the field, shift my baby to my back, and
> continue . . .
>
>   (Derricote 1983 109)

Of course, the birth is nothing like this: '*it hurts   i can't help it   oh/ it hurts so bad!* ' (111); not only is there an ironic contrast between theory and experience, but also between the peasants squatting in the field and the heroine squatting over her Lamaze textbook. Appearing to contrast, both are part of an unworkable, self-contradictory theory.

While all these writers send up the contrast between natural childbirth rhetoric and the 'real' experience, Elizabeth Baines shows up how natural childbirth practices, the myth of 'control', have been co-opted by the medical establishment. In her novel *The Birth Machine* (1983), we see the heroine, Zelda, using natural childbirth breathing techniques to 'control' her labour, with the approval of the hospital personnel. As several commentators have pointed out, some natural childbirth techniques have been easily co-opted by the hospital, since they make 'patients easier to manage' (Wertz and Wertz 1979 192). Breathing techniques in particular have been encouraged, since 'the method keeps the woman quiet by giving her a task to do, making being a "good" – uncomplaining, obedient, cooperative – patient the woman's primary goal' (Rothman 1982 92). The desire to be a good patient goes along with a false sense of being in 'control':

> Much is made in childbirth preparation circles of the woman's
> being in control during labor, but all that is meant by that is

control over her expressions of pain. A woman who maintains a fixed, if somewhat glazed, cheerful expression and continues a regular pattern of breathing is said to be 'in control', as she is carted from one room to another and literally strapped flat on her back with her legs in the air.

(177)

The Birth Machine dramatises these ironies:

It was a technique, to be learned. . . . until very recently taught in only the most progressive hospitals, still not available everywhere, so you were lucky to have it. . . .
Now, on the day, four o'clock in the afternoon, at long last they have Zelda's contractions under control. . . . A roll of graph paper records them, a clean tongue protruding out of the machine.
Zelda practises the technique. She is in control.

(Baines 1983 66)

'Control' of the contractions is really in the hands of the hospital authorities, operating the 'machine'. Her sense of being 'in control' is illusory. Her breathing exercises are rewarded by patronising praise from the authorities: 'That's a good girl' (68). The obverse of this appeal to duty is the threat of blame: 'you'd a duty to take advantage of it [the breathing techniques]; if you didn't there'd be no excuse, no cause for complaint on the day' (66). As Rothman says, 'According to the rules of the game, if the laboring woman chooses to deal with her pain by crying or calling out, she has entirely forfeited her right to make demands' (Rothman 1982 177).

Rediscovery and revision

Nevertheless, what is surprising about Baines and other writers – Lessing, Weldon, Atwood and Derricote can be included here – is that having sent up natural childbirth, they then go on to rediscover the primitive woman, transformed in various ways, as a female power to be reckoned with, deeply involved in the birth process. In some cases, a specifically female wisdom or magic is involved. To understand what is going on here it is necessary to introduce another stereotype. Related to the primitive woman is what Adrienne Rich has called the stereotype of 'the filthy peasant crone'. In Rich's formulation, she is the tradition of midwifery, whose opposing stereotype is 'the aseptic male obstetrician' of modern medicalised childbirth (Rich 1977 145). The history of childbirth involves the gradual encroachment of men – male doctors, male midwives – upon an originally wholly female preserve. The men are associated with the increased use of instruments – from forceps to foetal monitors – and consequentially increased intervention. From their point of view, this process represents a victory over the ignorance and superstition of 'peasant crones'. But feminist historians have wanted to revalue the peasant crone and her ancient female wisdom, a more 'natural', instinctive approach, a faith in the female body and its power, rather than a will to regiment and control it (Donnison 1977; Jordanova 1989; Oakley 1984; Towler and Bramall 1986). Unlike the silent, accepting primitive woman, the peasant crone cannot easily be made into a male ideal. To the 'aseptic male obstetrician' she represents the unacceptable side of the primitive and the feminine: ignorant, dirty, interfering. She has her own ideas, a competing tradition, a knowledge or 'witchcraft' which can challenge male domination of the birth-scene. Women writers represent her as a midwife or birth-companion, but also as a 'magic' power in a woman's own body, in the same way as the primitive woman can be internalised.

In Bagnold's *The Squire*, the midwife who helps the heroine achieve her 'natural' birth has some of the ancient intuitional wisdom of the peasant crone; she is the latest in 'the medieval line of priestesses, wise-women, gamps, midwives', and she uses 'her mysteriously developed instinct' to predict correctly the time of birth (Bagnold 1987 121, 123). In Lessing's *A Proper Marriage*, the peasant crone also appears as a birth-helper, but, unlike Bagnold's midwife, one unsanctioned by the medical establishment. The heroine, Martha, is giving birth in a nursing home, presented as a rigid, unsympathetic institution. She has been left alone, struggling in a difficult and painful labour, when a native cleaning woman comes into the room. With the touch of her 'wet dirty hand' on Martha's stomach, and her incantation, 'let the baby come, let the baby come, let the baby come', she releases Martha's tension (Lessing 1977 209). Though Lessing has mocked Stella's idea that the natives give birth easily because they are primitive animals, she makes clear here that their culture has its own wisdom about childbirth.

But this is not all: Martha has a powerful attraction towards native women, who seem for her to symbolise 'natural' womanhood, an ability that she lacks to accept the reproductive function. Martha partly knows this is her own sentimental projection: seeing a native woman with her children (the same woman who prompts Stella's ignorant remarks), Martha thinks,

> This easy, comfortable black woman seemed extraordinarily attractive, compared with the hard gay anxiety of Stella and Alice. Martha felt her as something simple, accepting – whole. Then she understood she was in the process of romanticising poverty; and repeated firmly to herself that the child mortality for the colony was one of the highest in the world. All the same . . .
>
> (Lessing 1977 26)

The possibilities suggested in that 'All the same . . .' are developed in the childbirth scene. The cleaning woman is frightened off by the arrival of someone Martha thinks of as 'the pink nurse': her 'aseptic', colonial antithesis. But the rhythms of the native woman have become incorporated into Martha's own body, and help her to resist institutional interference and rigidity. Martha listens to the sound of the cleaning woman's brush 'as if it were the pulse of her own nature, and did not listen as the pink nurse lifted her legs, levered them energetically up and down, and said, "That's the stuff, push!"' (166).

In Baines' *The Birth Machine* too, an external 'peasant crone' provides an image for a 'primitive' force in the woman's own body that resists the coercion of the medical establishment. In this case, the peasant crone is not the 'native woman' but the 'witch'. The heroine, Zelda, is the victim of an experimental 'convenience' induction. As she lies in the hospital, attached to her 'machine', reminiscences of childhood come into her mind. These centre on the den in the woods where she and her friends played games of witchcraft. Zelda's induction doesn't work, and leads to an emergency Caesarean. During the operation she hallucinates, and an equivalent of the 'filthy peasant crone' appears in the form of Hilary, one of her childhood friends: 'She steps forward, craning, her cardigan hanging, her knee-socks wrinkled, unscrubbed, gownless . . . "What's she doing here?" says Roland irritably. "Look, she isn't scrubbed up, she isn't aseptic, she's a hazard, send her home"' (Baines 1983 75–6). In contrast to Hilary here, the gleaming, aseptic appearance of the male obstetrician in charge is often stressed: 'He's so white, his coat shining, no other hospital laundry has this glow' (69). Here an opposition is being set up not only in terms of witchcraft versus technology, but, very precisely, in terms of filth versus asepsis, 'natural' dirt versus technological purity.

Towards the end of the book, Zelda suddenly realises the power of the 'witch', the power to be female, filthy, guilt-free, autonomous: 'To eat alone, to have it all to yourself, to shuffle carefree in the woods, to need no approval, to be free of the trap of the cold glass case. And to suffer no guilt' (Baines 1983 118). All through the book there have been references to fairy-tales: here, Snow White's glass coffin brings together the imprisoning definitions and institutions of male obstetrics and technology, with the impossible 'perfection' demanded of women in a male-centred society. Zelda breaks out from this composite glass case when, at the end of the book, she runs away from the hospital with her baby. Earlier, we have seen her beginning to realise this power, breaking out from the 'control' of the breathing exercises and the approval of authority, into noise, animality, filth, that turn out to be magical power, not disabling shame: 'She's their baby, their goody, their Frankenstein beauty. Oh, no, she's not, here's the urge: her mouth howling, frog-legs flexing: they flinch back. She can make them flinch back, hold them off from her own magic circle' (72). Just as Martha takes the rhythms of the native woman into her own body, so Zelda finds the magic power of the witch in hers.

A more fully developed witch figure appears in Weldon's *Puff-ball*. Here, she is in no way a birth-helper, as she is working against the pregnant heroine, but the heroine herself eventually gains some of the witch's 'magic' power, as an attribute of her pregnant body. As we have seen, Weldon makes fun of naive female believers in natural childbirth. A more formidable representative of the 'natural' woman is Liffey's neighbour, Mabs, a kind of earth-mother who actually practises witchcraft. Like Hilary in *The Birth Machine*, she can be read as the 'filthy peasant crone' who opposes the interventions of the 'aseptic male obstetrician' in this novel. Specifically, she nearly prevents Liffey from getting to the hospital in time when she starts to haemorrhage from a *placenta praevia*, and though the narrator gives us precise scientific reasons for this complication, she does not discount the possibility that it is caused by Mabs's spells and potions. Mabs could be taken as a satire on the 'natural' mother – she is only happy when pregnant, and she produces her babies 'like loaves from a greased tin' (Weldon 1980 219). Mabs, as a mature woman, has some female power that the immature Liffey lacks – unlike Liffey, who flaunts her shape in trousers, Mabs wears skirts, to hide 'the power and murk' beneath (43). She uses her powers malevolently against Liffey and her baby only because she herself is unable to conceive at the moment, and she suspects (wrongly) that her husband Tucker is the father of Liffey's baby. Her use of her 'female' powers, however, rebounds on herself – the pin she sticks into an effigy of Liffey produces appendicitis in her own daughter – and as soon as she *does* become pregnant her power subsides. She is now satisfied, and gives in to the doctor and his medicine on various counts:

> She allowed the doctor to put Eddie on a course of antidepressants, and Audrey on the pill, and she herself on valium to cure the rages she now admitted to, and Tucker on Vitamin B because he drank so much home-made wine. With every act of consent, every acknowledgement of his power, her own waned. She felt it. She didn't much mind.
>
> (Weldon 1980 265)

The 'filthy peasant crone' gives in willingly to modern male medicine, the beneficent enemy of uncontrolled 'natural' powers.

Barbara Katz Rothman points out that the contemporary home birth movement in America consists of an alliance between two rather different groups: feminists, with a highly developed critique of patriarchal institutions, and 'traditional' women, who want to get back to family-centred values (Rothman 1982 24, 32, 49, 94, 97, 109). This tension between different ideologies seems always to be present in any attempt to create a female-centred natural childbirth movement. By caricaturing *both* the naive feminist opponents of the male medical institution *and* the malevolent earth-mother, Weldon has covered the spectrum of natural childbirth stereotypes. Nevertheless, the maternal 'power' that Mabs represents is *not* entirely discredited – it comes to work also within Liffey, to her advantage. The progress of Liffey's pregnancy is mostly described in scientific, technical language, with, seemingly, no room for magic or witchcraft. But all this changes in a surprising chapter called 'Annunciation', in which, quite simply, Liffey's baby speaks to her from inside the womb and tells her, '"It's me. . . . I'm here. I have arrived. You are perfectly all right"', and she feels 'a presence; the touch of a spirit, clear and benign' (Weldon 1980 138–9). The conversation with the baby is associated with a new ability in Liffey to read the realities of the situation around her – to hear what people really mean, to see Mabs's real malevolence. Newly in tune with nature through her biological and spiritual link with the baby, 'Liffey now has powers of her own', to withstand Mabs's witchcraft (142). So here Weldon validates the 'natural' mother, introducing elements of maternal magic and witchcraft that seemed to have been banished by her use of medical terminology and her fierce satire of the natural childbirth movement.

The issue of whether natural childbirth can be painless does not really come up for Weldon and Baines, as both their heroines are delivered by Caesarean section. But Atwood and Derricote, in their rediscoveries/revisions of the primitive woman, concentrate on her *pain*. They invert Read's equation, primitive equals painless. Derricote's heroine has to give up all her naive 'peasants in the field' optimism in the face of relentless pain, but at its extremity, she recognises inside herself

> another
> woman's body. Some other woman, all muscle and nerve, is
> tearing apart and opening under me.
>
> i move with her like skin, not able to do anything else,
> i am just watching her, not able to believe what her
> body can do, what it *will* do, to get this thing accomplished.
>
> this muscle of a lady, this crazy ocean in my teacup.
> she moves the pillars of the sky. i am stretched into
> fragments, tissue paper thin. The light shines through
> to her goatness, her blood-thick heart that thuds like
> one drum in the universe emptying its stars.
>
> (Derricote 1983 113)

This powerful, goddess-like woman dwarfs the primitive woman of natural childbirth rhetoric. She is like the innate rhythms that Stephanie, Byatt's heroine, finds in her own body, with the difference that she does not banish pain, and she cannot be stopped by institutional interference. Like the 'witches' in Baines and Weldon, she is both natural and supernatural; but she is elemental – not so much the witch as perhaps the goddess the witch serves. Women, excluded from culture, have often been identified with both the natural *and* the supernatural, both beyond culture in different ways. But claiming the power of the supernatural gives women much more power than the purely 'natural' primitive woman of Dick Read.

In 'Giving Birth', however, Atwood makes no such claims: 'primitive' pain belongs to the powerless and underprivileged, not to the elemental and supernatural. The heroine of the story has gone to all the proper classes and read the right books to prepare for a natural childbirth, and is fully educated in the beliefs of the modern natural childbirth movement. Nevertheless, she is accompanied through her birth experience in hospital by a more 'primitive', uneducated, alter-ego, who is terrified, unprepared, unwilling and screams with pain. Just like the wise African cleaning woman in *A Proper Marriage*, this alter-ego belongs to a different, less privileged group than the heroine – but an interesting reversal has taken place. Natural childbirth is now the province of books and culture, a difficult technique learnt by the educated and privileged; it is the uneducated 'foreign' woman who goes through the experience in more 'natural' pain and agony. She is being used to represent a part of the heroine's psyche, the 'natural' anxiety and terror that will surface, despite her natural childbirth training.

The 'other woman' is described as 'not real in the usual sense' (Atwood 1984 232). She is lower class, possibly a foreign immigrant. She has not, of course, attended the prenatal classes: she is not clued up as to the correct exercises and attitude, or the absence of pain; as Jeanie enters the hospital, she hears screaming and 'knows that the woman screaming is the other woman and she is screaming from pain' (232). This is the underside, the obverse, of the cheerful natural childbirth version of birth. Later, Jeanie imagines she catches sight of the other woman on an emergency trolley – soon after, Jeanie is having 'some of the apprehensive feelings she associates with planes, including the fear of a crash' (234). Again, the other woman objectifies her worst fears. Jeanie has a vision of the other woman's 'face, distorted with pain and terror' (236). The agonised face, the screams, are the traditional outward signs of the inward pain of childbirth, the props of the

audience-point-of-view account. These outward signs haunt the
consciousness of the birthing woman as she strives to imagine
what her own experience will be like: "Will I sound like that?"
she asks, as she has difficulty with her breathing technique (236).
Here we see that the other woman's behaviour would also represent
an ultimate slipping from the standards Jeanie has set herself. At
the end of the story, Jeanie imagines the other woman 'leaving
the hospital now that her job is done. She has seen Jeanie safely
through, she must go now to hunt through the streets of the city
for her next case' (240). The woman is seen as a benign helper,
like Doris Lessing's African cleaning woman. But rather than
embodying the 'primitive' instinctual wisdom of natural childbirth,
she embodies the 'primitive' terror that every woman, no matter
how well instructed in natural childbirth, undergoes.

Do these revised primitive women then evade the ideological
prescriptions about natural motherhood that natural childbirth
seems to carry along with it? As I have suggested, the 'peasant
crone' stereotype seems to carry other, less purely 'natural' connotations. Doris Lessing's native woman is a product of culture, not
nature. Nevertheless, she provides for Martha a happy image
of motherhood as women's destiny. Lessing, however, guards
against the prescriptive implications of this by recognising Martha's
'romanticising' projections at work, and she also offers a powerful,
negative image of traditional motherhood in Martha's mother,
Mrs Quest. Martha has a great horror of being engulfed in the
traditional female role by her body and its reproductive instincts,
a horror which is usually externalised by the appearance of her
suffocating, overbearing, unfulfilled mother, who is delighted by
the pregnancy. Martha dreads becoming like her. Mrs Quest
represents perhaps the 'institution' of motherhood in Martha's
white colonial society. The native woman represents an alternative
model of 'traditional' womanhood that briefly reconciles Martha
to her female body: like Stephanie's brief intuitions of a natural
childbirth in *Still Life*, she stands for a happy 'experience' of
motherhood that the heroine's cultural institutions will not allow.

What is interesting about Elizabeth Baines' version of the peasant
crone, the 'witch', is not just the power of her witchcraft, but the
fact that she is not a mother at all. She has the power 'to eat

alone, to have it all to yourself'. While Baines' opposition of female witchcraft and male technology in *The Birth Machine* falls neatly into the 'spiritual' feminist division of nature/science as female/male domains, her 'nature' is not necessarily maternal, even when giving birth. The heroine ends the novel by escaping from the hospital with her baby: we do not know what new definitions of motherhood her autonomous witchlike power will give birth to. Fay Weldon, on the other hand, has been accused by the feminist critic Paulina Palmer of reinstating 'mystical' notions about motherhood in *Puffball*, adopting a 'viewpoint identifying women with nature and the body', which 'may be criticised as ideologically regressive' (Palmer 1989 99). But Weldon's viewpoint is very hard to pin down in this novel: as we will see in the next chapter, she also endorses the scientific description of Liffey's condition, and the technological intervention that saves her life. And while Liffey finds identity and maturity through producing her baby, there are also hints that the baby, and 'Nature', may have been using Liffey as a pawn all along. Weldon seems to be playing with a number of different, contradictory ways of envisaging childbirth, rather than prescribing any one way.

What, then, of Toi Derricote's powerful natural/supernatural woman? It seems to me that she has nothing to say about the rightness or wrongness of motherhood: she is just there, as a power to be called on in extremity. No amount of 'adjustment' to female role expectations will make her any easier or harder to contact. Moreover, everything about her is not harmonious, not 'flowing' as in Kitzinger's description, but incongruous, revolutionary, 'this ocean in my teacup'. It would be very hard to read her as any endorsement of the 'housewife' role. Finally, Atwood's 'primitive' woman in 'Giving Birth' restores the cultural dimensions of race and class to the 'natural' stereotype. Moreover, as well as being unprepared by natural childbirth classes, her 'primitive' woman is an *unwilling* mother. She 'did not wish to become pregnant . . . did not choose to divide herself like this . . . did not choose any of these ordeals, these initiations'. The foreign woman, in her unwillingness to have a baby, defeats the resources of language: she cannot be said to 'give' birth, and while 'the word in English for unwanted intercourse is rape', 'there is no word in the language for what is about to happen to this woman', unwanted childbirth (Atwood 1984 230). The stereotype of the primitive woman with her happy adjustment to motherhood has been completely inverted. In so far as the heroine's childbirth and motherhood are successful, it is because of cultural privilege and cultural instruction.

The 'primitive woman' in Black women's writing

In this section, I want to look at some African births described by the Nigerian-born writer, Buchi Emecheta, and then at Toni Morrison's description of an Afro-American slave woman giving birth in her novel, *Beloved* (1987). As we have seen, the 'primitive woman' is most frequently located as 'African', and the racism implicit in this designation is made clear in Lessing's *A Proper Marriage*. How, then, do Black women writers make use of, or react against, the stereotype in their representations of childbirth? In Emecheta's utopian novel, *The Rape of Shavi* (1983, 1985), she appropriates the story for an idealised picture of African culture untouched by Western ideas. But in her realist novel, *The Joys of Motherhood* (1979, 1988), also set in Africa, we are shown that African mothers can have difficult, painful births, and motherhood is a false goal for women. Morrison explodes the myth of the 'primitive' Black woman in other ways. Her heroine does give birth in the open, and carries straight on with her flight from slavery, but all this is presented as an almost unbearably cruel situation, forced on her by her treatment as slave, as 'primitive' in the sense of less than human.

Emecheta's *The Rape of Shavi* creates the fantasy African kingdom of Shavi, as a utopian ideal, stumbled upon by white intruders who are confident in the superiority of their own culture. One of the intruders is a white woman doctor, who, itching to intervene, watches a 'primitive' birth. While Ista, the Western doctor, is all for 'natural' birth, and the squatting position that the woman adopts, this is a breech birth, and she is convinced a Caesarean is necessary. The only help the woman is getting is the rhythmic singing of the midwives. But the birth is successful after all, and 'Ista's Western arrogance had never suffered such a deflation' (Emecheta 1985 142). Like the birth in Vera Brittain's *Honourable Estate*, this scene is set up to shock and deflate the attitudes of a prejudiced observer: not the Victorian patriarch this time, but the female believer in Western medicine (a position Brittain herself seems to take up).

The scene has some resemblances to Read's primitive woman: the Western expert watches and learns from the primitive woman. But there are several important differences. One is that the woman has female helpers (peasant crones?) who know very well what they are about; the other is that pain is not minimised or written out of the account: the woman 'screams', and 'went on in agony for a long time' (139, 140). Non-intervention, rather than painlessness, is being argued for. Non-intervention is of course the position of some Western women obstetricians, notably Wendy Savage, criticised and penalised for refusing to order routine Caesareans in cases of breech birth and other complications. It is impossible to say how far Emecheta's ideal birth scene may have been influenced by Western notions of what non-interventionist birth *should* be like; and *The Rape of Shavi* is of course a utopian fantasy, not claiming to show us what birth in Africa is really like.

Like Read, Emecheta does not let us into the consciousness of the birthing woman here: the point is the effect of the scene on the Western observer. But in one of her realist novels she does give us the experience of childbirth from the point of view of a Nigerian mother. Nnu Ego, the heroine of *The Joys of Motherhood*, has nine children in all; not all the births are described, and some are said to be 'without pain', but the two which are described seem far from ideal. When she goes into labour with her first child:

> she slipped out and went to the cook's wife next door. Between them they managed to stifle her labour cries, and Nnu Ego agonized for hours there in the back of their shared kitchen so as not to wake their sleeping husbands and the Madam in the main building. It was only after the baby was born that Nnaife would be woken from his masculine slumber.
>
> (Emecheta 1988 67–8)

This picture of masculine privilege and indifference is rather different from Shavi, where ancient religious tradition keeps the men away from the birth house (141). When Nnu Ego's final baby arrives, she is too proud to ask for any help, so 'she knelt in the middle of her room, holding on to the bed post, and, with her teeth dug right into her lower lip to prevent herself from screaming, she gave birth to a baby not bigger than a kitten' (245). The implication is that as this is her ninth baby, she should be too experienced to need help. These two birth experiences are both distorted from the traditional cultural pattern in some way (interestingly, in both cases the babies die), one by Nnu Ego's proud attitude, one by the near presence of the white mistress, who also must not be disturbed. We are given no details of the painless births, or those Nnu Ego undergoes back at her father's village. Nevertheless, it is clear that birth experiences in this book are as different for African women as for white women: Africans have no special 'primitive' magic for uniformly painless or successful births. In a fantasy text like *The Rape of Shavi*, Emecheta can make use of the stereotype of the primitive woman – as Margaret Atwood does in her heroine's fantasy in *Surfacing*; in a more realist text, Emecheta gives her short shrift, as Atwood also does in 'Giving Birth'. Emecheta's texts once more illustrate how the ideal of the primitive woman can go along with traditional ideas about motherhood. In *The Rape of Shavi*, the women happily play traditional roles, though they are endowed with a lot of power. But the whole point of *The Joys of Motherhood* is to show how Nnu Ego has wasted her life by devoting it entirely to motherhood, and the ideal of being a 'good' mother. Ironically, she dies alone, her children only rewarding her too late with an expensive funeral.

Morrison's novel *Beloved*, however, decisively severs the connection between the 'primitive woman' stereotype and traditional ideas of motherhood. It is precisely because of her categorisation as 'primitive' that Sethe's rights as a mother are denied to her. The novel is set in the mid-1800s, and can be seen as exploring some of the oppressive history behind the 'primitive' stereotype, and its connections to motherhood. Sethe, the slave woman, is observed and categorised by her master, the 'schoolteacher'. She overhears him telling his pupils to list her 'human' and 'animal' characteristics in separate columns (Morrison 1987 193). The schoolteacher with his notebook, observing and writing up Sethe's behaviour, makes an illuminating parallel to Dick Read, observing his 'primitive woman' giving birth. Schoolteacher's assumption that Sethe is subhuman also parallels Stella's colonialist assumptions about black women as 'animals' who give birth painlessly, in Lessing's *A Proper Marriage*. The context of slavery reveals how useful it is to those in power that 'primitive' women not only give birth painlessly, but also go straight back to *work* afterwards. It is interesting that Dick Read's 'primitive woman' turns out to be based on a Belgian peasant woman, not an African at all, and that he sees 'primitive' characteristics in British working class women (see p.90 below). In all cases, it appears very convenient that *working* women are not hindered from work by childbirth. A different perspective, such as Morrison gives us, reveals how constant work, and separation from their children, is *imposed* on these women.

Schoolteacher's view of Sethe as partly 'animal' has devastating effects on her ability to perform the role of mother. She can be experimented upon and abused: Schoolteacher's nephews take her breast-milk and flog her while she is pregnant. The taking of the milk has complex and horrifying implications. On one level, they treat her like a cow, to be milked; on another, the incident figures their extreme dependence on her, and refers to the fact that Black slave women often wet-nursed white children, to the detriment of their own children. Yet if they do suck at her breasts, they are affirming a *human* kinship. Schoolteacher himself, in retrospect, chides the nephews for going too far in their abuse, rendering Sethe as 'creature' mad and intractable. He appropriates her maternity in another way: for him she is a breeding machine, and her children become his wealth. The pregnant Sethe is 'the breeding one' and the baby 'her foal' (Morrison 1987 227). They represent a valuable 'property that reproduced itself without cost' (228). A similar attitude to motherhood is evident in Sherley Anne Williams' *Dessa Rose* (1988); here, the pregnant heroine, who has taken part in a slave revolt, is saved from hanging till her baby is born, so that this valuable piece of property is not wasted.

Slave women's children could be sold away from them: this has been the fate of most of the children of Sethe's mother-in-law, Baby Suggs. In the face of this deprivation, she has cultivated indifference: 'it wasn't worth the trouble to try to learn features you would never see change into adulthood anyway' (Morrison 1987 139). Sethe, on the other hand, is pushed to the other extreme, and develops a fierce, 'thick', protective love for her children, and a determination to hang onto them and to preserve them from the horrors of slavery. This obsessive love culminates in her murder of one of her baby daughters, to save her from being recaptured by Schoolteacher. Neither Baby Suggs' indifference, nor Sethe's murderous love, are 'natural': both are reactions to the oppressive way motherhood was constructed for the slave woman. As Morrison puts it:

For Sethe for instance the condition under which she has lived
i.e. slavery is such that when her children are threatened with
re-enslavement, murder becomes an act of mother love. 'I took
my babies and put them somewhere they'd be safe.' Motherhood
was her identity. She lived in a world that tried to deny her
responsibility for her children. So she protected them with the
ferocity of a lioness.

(Morrison 1988, quoted in Walters 1993 180)

Susanna Walters helpfully comments on this passage, in the context
of mother/daughter relations: 'The exigencies of oppression help
construct a multitude of survival mechanisms, often manifesting
themselves in a toughness that less aware daughters might read as
a repudiation of maternal love but that these writers interpret as a
sign of womanly struggle in a world that has repudiated their very
existence' (Walters 1993 180). Yet another 'survival mechanism'
described in the novel is that of Sethe's own mother, repeatedly
raped by white men, who 'threw away' all her babies except Sethe,
conceived with a Black man. In all sorts of ways, motherhood is
restricted, distorted and appropriated by the institution of slavery.
So whatever is 'primitive' in Sethe's behaviour is an effect of her
treatment. While Schoolteacher sees her murder of her baby as
a reversion, caused by freedom, to 'the cannibal life' her people
'preferred' (Morrison 1987 151), the abolitionists manage to
turn around the 'cry of savagery' (260), presumably onto the
slaveholders. As Stamp Paid, another ex-slave, puts it, whatever
'jungle' the white people see in the Black people is one they have
put there themselves; it is the whites' own 'jungle' (198).

All these considerations bear on the way the novel's birth-scene
can be read. On her way to freedom in the North, where her three
other small children already are, Sethe gives birth to her fourth
child, Denver, in a boat on the Ohio River. She spends the previous
night in labour in a shed, lying on a pile of leaves. An exemplary
'natural' birth by a 'primitive' woman, it might seem. The birth-
scene is presented in the narrative as a story, shaped by Sethe
and told to Denver, as explanation of her 'miraculous' birth. It is
Denver who later saves her mother from her destructive, obsessive
relationship with the ghost of Beloved, the baby she killed. The
birth of a miraculous child on the dividing line between freedom
and slavery is obviously loaded with symbolic resonance. We are
to read it in one sense as a triumph, a great achievement. Sethe sees

her escape, her rescue of her children, and her giving birth to them, as evidence of agency – her power, her ability to act:

> I did it. I got us all out. Without Halle too. Up till then it was the only thing I ever did on my own. Decided. And it came off right, like it was supposed to. We was here. Each and every one of my babies and me too. I birthed them and I got em out and it wasn't no accident. I did that. I had help, of course, lots of that, but still it was me doing it . . .
>
> (Morrison 1987 162)

The particular help Sethe gets during the birth of Denver is from Amy, a white girl, running away from a life as an indentured servant. While Sethe's ability to give birth in 'natural' surroundings is celebrated, that she should be forced to this is part of her oppression. Her pain – from the swollen feet of a runaway, from her cut-open back, and from her labour – is vividly described. In previous labours, Sethe has always had expert attendance, from an 'Aunt Phyllis' Mr Garner, her previous owner, always sent for (160). Sethe stresses her own inexpertness, her need for advice from women like Aunt Phyllis or Baby Suggs. Her mothering instincts are not innate, and her 'natural' birth is in no way her choice. Reflecting back from *Beloved* to Dick Read, I wonder what terrible circumstances drove his 'primitive woman' to give birth unaided in the bushes.

And yet, despite the pain and degradation, Morrison does create a sense of 'natural' magic in the scene. The emergence of Denver's head is described, through Amy's eyes, in natural terms: 'here come the head, as Amy informed her as though she did not know it – as though the rip was a breakup of walnut logs in the brace, or of lightning's jagged tear through a leather sky' (Morrison 1987 84). Amy's attitude is both devalued by Sethe's implied irritation – 'as though she did not know' – and validated by the poetic elaboration of the images of logs and lightning. But these are not soothing images – this is nature being violent. Nature imagery comes largely through Amy, as she searches out spider-webs to lay on Sethe's wounded back, demonstrating in this and other ways her skill with 'sick things' (82). Sethe focuses on the strength and skill of Amy's hands in her telling of the story: Amy's healing powers are a matter of skill in dealing with the 'natural'. In my terms, she is more of a 'peasant crone' (though a very young one) than a 'primitive woman'. Wrapping up the baby after the birth, the two women do their 'work' 'appropriately and well' (85). The ambivalence of the 'natural' in the context of childbirth is indicated by the imagery of the bluefern spores:

> Spores of bluefern growing in the hollows along the riverbank float toward the water in silver-blue lines hard to see unless you are in or near them, lying right at the river's edge when the sunshots are low and drained. Often they are mistook for insects – but they are the seeds in which the whole generation sleeps confident of a future. And for the moment it is easy to believe each one has one – will become all of what is contained in the spore: will live out its days as planned. This moment of certainty lasts no longer than that; longer, perhaps than the spore itself.
>
> (Morrison 1987 84)

Maybe Denver is a miracle; maybe she will just become another 'throw-away' person, as Sethe and Amy are described (84). The bluefern spores cast a magical, but possibly deceptive light over the birth-scene.

Beloved challenges the 'primitive woman' stereotype in a very fundamental way, by giving us an account of birth and motherhood from the perspective of a woman who has been unwillingly cast as 'primitive'. The stereotype is not just a construct of white people's fantasy, to be ridiculed, dismissed, enjoyed, appropriated; a particularly terrible kind of oppression is encoded in her construction. Morrison, like the other women writers I have discussed, creates opportunities for women's power, agency and skill in the act of giving birth, but almost despite its 'primitive', 'natural' setting.

Institutions, machines and 'male' medicine

The discourse of medical expertise has its roots in the scientific revolution which began in the seventeenth century, which conceptualised Nature as a machine that could be controlled by human intervention. In the history of childbirth, the use of a medical discourse is parallelled by and legitimates increasing intervention, and the take-over by men – male midwives and doctors – of the originally wholly female role of the midwife. The power of male obstetricians over female bodies has been convincingly likened to the power scientific discourse claimed over a passive, 'female' Nature. In the twentieth century, the preconceptions of this objectifying medical discourse have led to the increased hospitalisation of childbirth and increased use of technological intervention: foetal monitoring, epidurals, inductions, Caesareans (Donnison 1977; Jordanova 1989; Martin 1987; Rich 1977; Rothman 1982; Towler and Bramall 1986).

Existing in a symbiotic relationship with the figure of the primitive woman, is the image of the oppressive medical institution. Either the two are seen as mutually exclusive, or as opposites that must be somehow united. They define each other: medical science celebrates its triumph over the primitive and natural, while the ideal of the primitive woman provides a standpoint for a critique of the institution. When women write about institutionalised childbirth, they speak as victims, but they protest against this treatment. Their accounts focus obsessively on certain scenes of ritual medical humiliation: the shaving and enema, the strapping down of arms and legs. Adrienne Rich is not alone in seeing the way birthing women are treated by the medical institution as emblematic of their oppression in society at large: 'No more devastating image could be invented for the bondage of woman: sheeted, supine, drugged, her wrists strapped down and her legs in stirrups, at the very moment when she is bringing new life into the world' (Rich 1977 170–1). Yet, as we will see, other women find ways to turn their own knowledge of medical discourse against the institution, or to subvert it for their own purposes.

The oppressive institution

Criticism of the medical institution begins to surface in mid-century, when the hospitalisation of births is on the increase, and becoming the norm. Imagery of industrialisation and mechanisation are often used to describe the hospital and its procedures, contrasting with the 'natural' imagery that surrounds the primitive woman. The 'mechanical' hospital is represented as simultaneously super-efficient *and* hopelessly chaotic in the mixture of neglect and violence it visits upon its female victims. Certain focal scenes of suffering and indignity recur in these descriptions: the mother left to labour alone, or displayed before a crowd of male students; shaving of the pubic hair; fastening down of arms and legs; and, in later novels, actual technological interventions like inductions or Caesareans. Rigidly efficient but totally unsympathetic staff preside over all these rituals. In Doris Lessing's *A Proper Marriage*, set in the 40s, it is neglect and isolation that are stressed, despite the rigid 'efficiency' of the nursing home. The receptionist is 'a long white gleaming pillar of efficiency' (Lessing 1977 158), and the labour ward is 'another gleaming white room'(162). But when Martha first enters, it is chaos and confusion that are stressed, as mysterious doors open and close, no one has time for her, and she is parked in a corridor. In A. S. Byatt's *Still Life*, set in a 50s NHS hospital, rather than the private nursing home of *A Proper Marriage*, the picture is much darker. Not just neglect, but indignity and violence are stressed. Stephanie's entry into the world of the hospital is explicitly presented in hellish terms: 'it was written over the entrance, gold letters on purple gloss on red brick. Gynaecology and Obstetrics. Inside the archway an archetypal hand, the first of a series, pointed on a placard. Ante-natal Clinic, First Right. It was dark in there' (Byatt 1986 11). Although, or perhaps because, rigid routines are imposed, ridiculous and barbaric indignities abound.

The gown Stephanie has to put on is much too small, leaving her half-naked: 'She was used, but not reconciled, to such indignities' (14). The patients become dehumanised: Mrs Owen, a new patient, is too intimidated to tell anyone she is about to have a miscarriage. Stephanie is especially distressed, because she didn't help: 'We taught her to stand in line. . . . This place puts you in line. You stay in it' (16). When Stephanie arrives at the hospital in labour, she suffers the indignities of the ritual shaving and enema. As we have seen, the nurses hold her in 'unnatural' positions as she tries to give birth. After the birth of her second child, as she is stitched, 'She thought they could not be aware of the cruelty of hoisting her fat, forked legs into their meat hooks and canvas slings' in a room described as a 'butchery' (249). The woman is reduced to a piece of meat.

Institutional violence against women reaches its peak in Elizabeth Baines' *The Birth Machine*, set in the early 70s. The title of the novel is richly ambiguous, bringing together several related complexes of ideas. Most immediately it refers to the actual machine, the infusion unit, which is used to induce labour in Zelda, the pregnant heroine. In a metaphorical sense, it also describes the hospital within which the birth takes place, with its efficient, dehumanising routines. Finally, it also suggests the way Zelda's body is regarded and treated by these two 'machines' – as another machine, in need of mechanical attention to get it started, a machine for giving birth. Emily Martin, in her book *The Woman In The Body*, has pointed out that modern obstetric techniques result from an underlying image of body as machine (Martin 1987 54), and Martin Richards sees the obstetric profession as founded on an ideal of 'intervention, seeing most clinical problems in terms of a kind of engineering' (Richards 1975 597). The depersonalising routines that Zelda suffers under are part of this 'mechanical' approach. The book begins with the shaving and enema: degrading rituals focused obsessively on by women writers. They are administered by an 'expressionless' nurse, and described in terms of 'coldness': 'the razor slaps, coldly, briefly. The job is done'; 'the cold intrusion of the enema'; 'everything is cold' (Baines 1983 7). Patients are stripped of their individuality and given numbers: 'Sister reports: Single Ward Number Fourteen. Patient Four-Five-Oh' (14). Not just routines, but actual machines eliminate personal contact: 'in cases like these, where there's so little happening, the machine can take over the observing and measuring, leaving staff free for other things' (56).

The ultimate depersonalising indignity is of course the induction itself, which turns out to have been entirely unnecessary. The 'machine' in this case is probably the Cardiff infusion system, in which 'the rate of infusion can be controlled automatically by feedback from the intra-uterine pressure, measured with an intra-amniotic catheter and pressure transducer' (Howie 1977 85). The obstetrician in charge celebrates this combination of two machines into one: 'most medical advances have turned on just that kind of creative connection' (Baines 1983 12) – as he connects up Zelda to the machine, under the eyes of his admiring students. Ann Oakley comments on another such innovative technical combination: 'modern monitoring equipment combines a tracing of uterine contractions with one of the fetal heart-rate: thus, it has been possible for obstetricians to see at one glance both the condition of the uterus and the condition of the fetus (but not the condition of the mother)' (Oakley 1984 192). Similarly, the induction machine in Baines' novel is focused on a disembodied uterus, and the emotional reactions of the patient, as they try to connect her to the machine, are an irrelevant nuisance: 'Mrs Harris's fingers are trembling just a little. What's she got to be afraid of?' (Baines 1983 13).

The novel, published in 1983, is very precisely set in the early 1970s. At this time, the number of inductions was increasing dramatically, and 'convenience' inductions for non-medical reasons were making their first appearance. In the mid-70s, protests were made about this trend, and controversy raged – the new public awareness of the situation is reflected in the novel. But the heroine is presented as unaware of the possibility of 'routine' induction, especially as she is given inadequate and misleading information by her doctors. As a woman, and as a 'lay' person, Zelda feels doubly excluded from the world of medical expertise and explanation, and only gradually pieces together evidence that reveals the real motive behind her induction. Though some consultants were willing to admit they performed 'non-medical inductions', this was not widely admitted, and, as Martin Richards points out, there was a 'grey area' where 'medical' and 'non-medical' indications overlapped (Richards 1975 596, footnote). It is in this 'grey area' that Zelda's induction takes place; there are some medical indications, derived from a misreading of her symptoms, but it is only when she manages secretly to get hold of her own hospital notes that she sees the truth: 'Clinical Trial: Convenience Induction' (Baines 1983 113). In the event, the whole process goes disastrously wrong, and she ends up having a Caesarean.

The same fate awaits the heroine of Caroline Bowder's novel, *Birth Rites* (1983), but in her case it is planned and necessary, as she is suffering from *placenta praevia*, a life-threatening complication that can only be avoided by surgical intervention. While not, therefore, protesting against mechanical intervention as such, Bowder shows that the indignities, rigid rituals, and mechanical approach of earlier decades are still flourishing in the early 80s. Her book concentrates obsessively on the rituals of hospital life: her heroine, Xenia, has been admitted early because of complications, and the first 106 pages describe in detail her first day in hospital. The hospital is seen as a machine, 'the baby-producing plant' (Bowder 1983 205), and a prison. Indignities proceed from and lead to further depersonalisation: after the initial shaving and enema, a new patient is 'now hospital property' (12). Xenia sees herself transformed into 'a unit of administration, the embodiment of a file full of information and instructions for treatment' (86). In this depersonalisation, the patients' names are lost: 'Now Mrs. ... er ... (the sister moved to the end of Mrs. Long's bed to get a glimpse of the name on her label)' (4). Labelling is also stressed in Sharon Doubiago's poem, as part of a process of depersonalisation in a rigid institution: 'She took my clothes, put me/ on that hard board in that tiny green cell,/ tied a paper to my neck' (Doubiago 1983 102). In *Birth Rites*, another 'label' given to Xenia is 'an interesting case', to be stared at by a crowd of medical students (Bowder 1983 28). This scene of helpless exposure to the male gaze, like the shaving and enema, is recurrently focused on by women writers representing hospitalised birth. For instance, in Buchi Emecheta's novel, *Second-Class Citizen* (1974, 1987), the heroine bursts into tears when she sees 'all those men with hungry eyes, like vultures, looking on' (Emecheta 1987 28). Racial as well as sexual oppression is going on here: the only person to sympathise with the Black heroine is 'the Indian woman in the group', who 'looked as if she was being forced to eat shit' (126). The *Birth Machine* also has a scene where the heroine is displayed before a group of students (Baines 1983 142). The objectification of women that results from mechanised hospital childbirth is perhaps best summed up by Sheila Kitzinger, in an attack on 'the baby factory', where women are treated 'as if they were so many fish on a slab' (Kitzinger 1962 59).

While mothers' individualities are erased in these institutions, the active protagonists become an equally nameless, depersonalised 'They', who make all the decisions and inflict the routines and treatments. In several of Anne Oakley's 'real life' accounts in *From Here To Maternity*, we can see this happening. Typically, the account by 'Alison Mountjoy' (the names are all fictitious) is a narrative of decisions and actions taken by medical authorities; it begins with the words 'The doctor had said at the hospital. . . .', with occasional protesting or triumphant interventions by the mother. So, although threatened with an induction, 'there I was starting off by myself: I felt so proud of myself, and I didn't tell anybody for about an hour. I can't *tell* you how pleased I was that I started off by myself'. The not telling is interesting – the woman keeps control and knowledge of the story to herself for a while here. But 'they' soon take over again: 'So when they did take me upstairs, they didn't do anything. Until about twelve when they decided they wanted to monitor the baby which apparently they do *routinely* there. And the bag [membranes] hadn't broken by then so they had to do it – I said why, what for? But of course they didn't listen' (Oakley 1981 87). While this woman manages to stick to her own critical and resistant view of what 'they' are up to, other women are totally taken over by the point of view of the medical authorities: 'I always thought you could push when you wanted to push, but you don't: you have to wait for their command. They feel your tummy and your face is all crinkled up with agony and they say oh you've got a pain, you can push now' (93). Here, the woman has moved over into 'their' point of view, observing her own face 'crinkled up with agony', and deducing from this that she must be having a pain. The context of this slippage in the perspective – 'their' control of 'your' pushing – suggests that this woman's own version of events is being taken over by the powerful official one of the hospital staff, so much so that she takes on their point of view, and allows herself to be constructed by their narrative perspective.

This complete surrender of autonomy to 'them' is more self-consciously commented on by the fiction writers. As Bowder's heroine puts it, 'They do the doing, I do the suffering (patient means that)' (Bowder 1983 151). Baines' heroine similarly renounces the active mode: 'The body that she has renounced, they have infused. They have preserved it, improved it. They take care. They make checks' (Baines 1983 103). The power of the institutional 'They' is summed up by Doris Lessing in *A Proper Marriage*, when the woman in the next bed to Martha advises her, 'You'd better do as they want, dear. It saves trouble. They've got their own ideas' (Lessing 1977 167).

Good words for the medical institution

It is, however, possible to find writers who endorse the medical institution and hospitalised birth. Interestingly, it is the writers of the 30s, before hospitalisation had really got under way, and those of the 80s, when some of its worst practices were beginning to be mitigated as a result of criticism from the natural childbirth movement, who find good words to say for the system. The novels of the 30s show an attitude of acceptance towards the hospital and the medical establishment. While *The Squire* shows an idyllic home birth, the midwife also has plans for a 'palisaded' maternity clinic 'where mothers could be set apart from the world, for more than a month, for two, for three' (Bagnold 1987 161). The clinic is seen as a retreat and refuge from the demands made on women by the family. It is interesting that working-class women at this time were campaigning for more hospitalisation, to allow women just this period of rest from housework (Lewis 1980 120, 129). In the squire's upper-class home, the midwife recreates a version of her ideal nursing home, holding her patient to rigid routines, and keeping the family at bay. All this is seen as good and restful by the squire. While the squire is presented as achieving a 'natural' birth, the advances of medical science are incorporated into this, as we have seen with her acceptance of the use of chloroform. The midwife, too, though possessing the ancient wisdom of the peasant crone, also has a modern scientific training. There is an important historical difference here between Britain and North America: while in the United States and Canada midwives were hounded out of existence, in Britain they became state registered in 1902, and the amount of training required to practise as a midwife was steadily increased. In the nineteenth century there had been attempts to register midwives on the same footing as doctors, but these failed, and the 1902 Act gave them a position subordinate to doctors, yet with more independence than nurses. Bagnold can thus present her midwife as a highly trained expert, approved by the medical establishment, while she is also a close and sympathetic female friend of the pregnant heroine. The close, personal relationship between the squire and her midwife is what the later critics of hospitalisation find missing, and what the contemporary home birth movement is trying to recreate.

Vera Brittain, in *Honourable Estate*, also validates medical science, though from a different angle. While her Victorian heroine suffers from a botched home birth, the life of her 1930s heroine, Ruth, is saved by a hospital birth, with 'every alleviation that science could provide' (Brittain 1936 539). Ruth sees this as a triumph over the ways of Nature, 'the feeling of helplessness, of being completely under Nature's control' (547). While these two novels show pro- and anti-natural childbirthers both in favour of hospitalisation, Dick Read, another contemporary, is somewhat critical of hospital practices, particularly the isolation and neglect suffered by patients, especially in the second edition of his book, *Revelation of Childbirth* (1942). By this time, hospitalisation was becoming more common. This edition also contains an attack on the 'mechanisation' of birth, and the tendency of certain obstetricians to write about women as machines: 'the woman concerned becomes a machine, without consciousness or volition; things happen in the reproductive mechanism' (Read 1942 67). Disconcertingly, however, Read later uses the same sort of language himself: 'The mother is the factory, and by education and care she can be made more efficient' (228). The only difference between Read and his opponents seems to be that he advocates 'education and care', while they advocate technical interference, to produce this mechanical efficiency. Read is also always very keen to prove his *scientific* credentials, explaining the basis of what he is up to in chapters of daunting scientific terminology. While he generally attacks the administration of drugs to ease pain, like Bagnold he condones it in small amounts in the second stage as 'sound and right' (Read 1933 94). In addition, the unnecessary administration of drugs is not seen so much as a feature of hospital management of childbirth, as what the patients themselves have been led to expect and demand: it is part of their faulty conditioning in fear of pain. Those chiefly responsible for this conditioning are not the medical establishment, but *novelists* (he actually gives *Honourable Estate* as an example), and *mothers*, as I shall show in the next chapter. Read is only too eager to assert the authority of the medical establishment against untrained women's meddling with his patients' minds.

We have to wait until the 80s to find fiction writers, and even natural childbirth advocates, willing once more to speak well of the medical establishment's role in childbirth. Fay Weldon, in *Puffball*, endorses the life-saving power of the medical institution. Her heroine Liffey, like Xenia in *Birth Rites*, is suffering from *placenta praevia*: intervention is absolutely justified. Her life is saved by the benign expertise of the hospital authorities, 'the gentle, powerful concern of authority, and the dramatic indications of its existence – masks and lights and drugs and ministering hands' (Weldon 1980 259). Margaret Atwood's short story, 'Giving Birth', gives a more tentative, mixed account of the institution; while most other writers dramatise oppositions between Nature and the medical institution, 'Giving Birth' shows a 'natural' (= learnt from books) birth in a medical setting that is not nearly so hostile as the heroine supposed. Jeanie discovers that the hospital is not the authoritarian, unsympathetic institution she was prepared for: 'She intends to put up a struggle over her pubic hair. . . . but it turns out the nurse doesn't have very strong feelings about it' (Atwood 1984 233). Later, the hospital holds her to her natural childbirth choice, while she begins to have second thoughts:

> They pass another doctor.
> 'Need me?' she asks.
> 'Oh no,' the nurse answers breezily. 'Natural childbirth.'
> Jeanie realises that this woman must have been the anaesthetist.
> 'What?' she says, but it's too late now . . .
>
> (Atwood 1984 238)

The earlier part of the labour is presided over by 'a fat old woman dressed all in green', with 'tribal hands' that have surely 'presided over a thousand beds, a thousand kitchen tables' (234–5). Here Atwood momentarily evokes the ancient female birth-wisdom of the peasant crone, but in an institutionally approved setting. In this story Atwood, like Weldon, questions the extremist line on the efficacy of natural childbirth, but she does not go so far as to discredit natural childbirth entirely – it does work to some extent for her protagonist. She dramatises the process of negotiation between expectations and experience, patient and hospital, autonomy and intervention. Jeanie has to go through discrepancies between the hospital version of what is happening to her and what she imagines: '"Only *four?*"' she exclaims, feeling cheated, and 'they must be wrong', when the doctor says she is four centimetres dilated (237); 'This is absurd', she thinks, when asked not to push yet; and finally she does score a victory, 'The baby is being born when Jeanie said it would, though just three days ago the doctor said it would be at least another week, and this makes Jeanie feel jubilant and smug' (238).

This picture of birth as a negotiation with a possibly sympathetic medical institution is, surprisingly, very strong in Sheila Kitzinger's book, *Giving Birth, How It Really Feels*. Though her whole approach is based on an opposition to the medical institution, she here exhorts her followers to sympathise with and understand the feelings of the medical personnel, instead of 'wondering what "they" will think, what "they" will do to her, and even – worst of all, if "they" will interfere' (Kitzinger 1987 28). As we saw, this characterisation of the medical personnel as a faceless, all powerful 'they' is an important extension of hostile representations of the hospital. Kitzinger tells us about one of her students having a necessary vacuum extraction: the obstetrician tells Kitzinger, who is present, that 'he always relied on the informed participation of the mother, and worked with her to get the baby born' (41).

A mixed picture of the institution also comes across, from an opposite perspective, in a 1980s obstetric textbook, *Active Management of Labour*, by the Irish obstetricians, Kieran O'Driscoll and Declan Meagher. Just as Kitzinger is willing to negotiate with the medical institution, so they show themselves willing to incorporate some of the ideals of the natural childbirth movement into what seems at first a highly 'mechanised' model of hospital birth. Emily Martin has shown how medical textbooks set up models of women's reproductive systems as machines or factories, models which are then actualised in the ways birthing women are treated in hospitals (Martin 1987 54–67). I expected O'Driscoll and Meagher's book to be a straightforward tract in support of this 'mechanised' approach. The very title of their book enacts the 'factory' metaphor: reproduction is recast in terms of production, relations between Management and Labour. I hopefully turned to the section entitled 'Visual Representation of Labour', expecting to find photographs of women giving birth: in fact, I found pages of graphs. Women's experience is reduced to mathematical representations. Moreover, these graphs are supposed to represent a 'norm' to which women *must* conform: O'Driscoll and Meagher lament that 'the parameters of normal labour, to which all should aspire, are seldom, if ever, defined' (O'Driscoll and Meagher 1980 46), and they go on to define them. This is not just an abstract definition, it has practical consequences: their method of 'active management' means that *no* labour is allowed to go on for more than twelve hours. If it seems to be going too slowly, oxytocic drugs are administered to 'accelerate' the contractions. While natural childbirth writers insist that every labour is different, O'Driscoll and Meagher have only one model, in which it 'proceeds in a straight line' (34). Much of the book is taken up with instructions on how to administer this 'active' system. The language of 'management' is blatantly used: there must be 'clear direction from the top', and 'the chain of command must be sharply defined', while 'details of procedure' must be 'standardised' (82–3).

On the other hand, all this is not as mechanistic and inhuman as it seems. O'Driscoll and Meagher are against the use of inductions (as opposed to 'accelerations') and Caesareans, and the use of pain-killing drugs. Having been accelerated through the first stage of labour, the mother is to take over again in the second stage, 'in full control of her faculties . . . permitting her to deliver her own child', with a 'sense of dignity' (63). Interventionism is not the main goal of 'active management': 'the word "active" refers to the nature of the involvement of the consultant obstetrician, and is not intended to convey to the reader that he intervenes more often' (3). The argument is that intervention to shorten the early stages, and efficient organisation, will leave the staff with much more time for personal contact with the patients. O'Driscoll and Meagher show themselves very much alive to patients' complaints of isolation, 'deplorable lack of sensitivity', and 'affronts to personal dignity' (78). Their nurses are 'trained to develop close personal relationships with patients', and never to leave them alone, while consultants are to be frequently present on the wards (88, 83). 'Medical efficiency and human compassion can exist side by side', they insist (5).

What is going on here is partly that O'Driscoll and Meagher are trying to take the wind out of the sails of the home-birth movement, which they see as inspired solely by the emotional damage done to mothers by impersonal and badly organised hospital systems (O'Driscoll and Meagher 1980 79). They are advocating a kind of benevolent despotism by the hospital instead. The contradiction between their professed respect for mothers' autonomy, and their ideal of direction 'from the top' surfaces in the section on antenatal education. They insist that mothers must be treated as adults, not as children, but this involves advising them 'of what their role is and how best to achieve it' (91). While they stress the importance of this role, they use the language of prescription and enforcement to describe it: a woman must 'be *made* to face the fact that childbirth is primarily a mother's responsibility', and 'be *made* to feel the proper custodian of her own health' (89, my italics). This is followed by sharp criticism of the 'outrageous conduct' of deviant mothers, who do not want to fit into the system, and 'learn how to behave with dignity and purpose during the most important hours of their lives', resulting in 'degrading scenes' (91). Some kinds of patient choice are not to be allowed. On the other hand, as we will see in the next chapter, the discourse of natural childbirth also makes sharp distinctions between 'good' and 'bad' mothers and their attitudes to birth. The tension between ideals of patient autonomy and of medical control is neatly dramatised when O'Driscoll and Meagher tell us how mothers at antenatal classes are encouraged to believe 'they are well able to give birth to their own children', by instruction in the correct pattern of labour, after which they 'are given a copy of the partograph to take home' (60).

Active Management of Labour suggests the range of different interpretations that can be put on to the hospitalisation of birth, from benevolent paternalism to rigid hierarchy. The book reveals the male desire to regiment and control female bodies that many women writers criticise and object to; at the same time it is alive to many of these criticisms, particularly the criticism of mechanisation and disorganisation at the level of personal interaction.

Institutionalised birth as emblem of women's oppression

The paradigmatic example of hospitalised birth as violence against women is perhaps described in Margaret Atwood's *Surfacing*:

> they shut you up into a hospital, they shave the hair off you and tie your hands down and they don't let you see, they don't want you to understand, they want you to believe it's their power, not yours. They stick needles into you so you won't hear anything, you might as well be a dead pig, your legs are up in a metal frame, they bend over you, technicians, mechanics, butchers, students clumsy or sniggering practice on your body, they take the baby out with a fork like a pickle out of a pickle jar. After that they fill you up with red plastic, I saw it running down through the tube. I won't let them do that to me ever again.
>
> (Atwood 1979 74)

The passage sums up the details provided by writers like Byatt, Bowder and Baines. The shaving of the pubic hair and the fastening of hands and legs are focused on as humiliating rituals, symbolic of women's powerlessness. The woman is treated as both a machine and a piece of meat, experimented on by 'mechanics, butchers'. She has become a spectacle for a crowd of male onlookers: instead of escaping from the audience point of view of childbirth, she has merely become aware of it as what defines her. Things are done to her by a faceless, all-powerful 'They': the third person plural removes the blame from any individuals, and attaches it to the institution as a whole, which is presented as an irresistible power. The companion passage to this is the later fantasy of natural birth, squatting on the leaves. And this earlier description, too, is a fantasy: the heroine had an abortion, not a birth, and she comes to realise that the powerless-victim mentality of those days is another falsehood she must escape from. The description functions as an emblem of her loss of selfhood to an alienating, mechanised male society. Adrienne Rich, too, sees hospital birth as an emblem of the social oppression of women: 'No more devastating image could have been invented for the bondage of woman: sheeted, supine, drugged, her wrists strapped down and her legs in stirrups, at the very moment when she is bringing new life into the world' (Rich 1977 170–1). Hospital birth provides a symbol for women's oppression; women's oppression also explains *why* hospital birth is like it is: it is a blatant physical enactment, a concentration and focusing, of forces that are better concealed in other social situations.

This symbolic resonance is carried by many of the fictional representations of hospital birth. Lessing, in *A Proper Marriage*, presents the nursing home as representative of insensitive white colonial society. The hospital in *Still Life* is linked to the family as one of the repressive social institutions that prevent Stephanie actualising her potential: after the birth, she is 'ground between two communities, the ward and the family, both it seemed intent on forming her and William to their own rites and classifications' (Byatt 1986 99). *The Birth Machine* presents mechanised birth as part of a wider male technological conspiracy against women. At the end Zelda, clutching her baby (symbol, it seems, of her recovered past, and her recovered self), escapes in disguise from the hospital, and also, it is implied, from her oppressive marriage. She breaks free of Snow White's 'cold glass case' (Baines 1983 118), an image which brings together the imprisoning institutions of male obstetrics and technology, with the impossible 'perfection' demanded of women in a male-centred society. Caroline Bowder's *Birth Rites* shows the hospital as a machine for turning individualised women into standardised mothers. The culture of the ward is founded on an image of mindless motherhood: there are no mirrors 'to remind us who we are', but there are flower arrangements, implying that 'Mother, to whom these offerings were made, equalled Child in mentality' (Bowder 1983 34). Robbed of their individuality by the institution, women can be re-labelled as generic 'mothers', as Nikki Giovanni describes in 'Don't Have A Baby Till You Read This' (1971): 'The nurses all said, "You're fine now, Mother," and I said, "My name is Nikki," and they said, "Yes, Mother"' (Giovanni 1971 105). In *The Birth Machine* too, standardised maternal responses are assumed: a nurse asks, '"thinking about your baby?" No, Zelda is not thinking about her little baby. No, she is having no maternal feelings' (Baines 1983 55).

How far, then, is the hospital as instrument of social control identified as a *masculine* power? In *A Proper Marriage* it is 'the pink nurse' who embodies rigid hospital efficiency (Lessing 1977 166); in *Still Life* too, it is 'nurses' who hold Stephanie in 'unnatural' positions, and impose rigid feeding routines: 'nurses dehumanised babies' (Byatt 1986 100). Doctors are evasive and embarrassed, rather than powerful: 'he did not meet her eye: this was usual' (15). The powerful men at the top of the hierarchy are not investigated. In Margaret Drabble's *The Millstone*, the male consultant, Mr Prothero, is seen as an enlightened ally for the heroine in her fight against the stupid, rigid, nurses of the NHS (Drabble 1966). *Birth Rites* provides a less favourable picture of the male consultant, in Mr Whitechapple, who is remarkable chiefly for his expensive car, the infrequency of his visits, and his abstracted air: 'There were various things Xenia had been meaning to ask him but they had all disappeared from her mind. In any case his manner was so abstracted she felt he would inevitably ignore her if she attempted to address him' (Bowder 1983 118). Kieran O'Driscoll and Declan Meagher's injunction that consultants should visit the ward frequently and be 'actively' involved with their patients seems very much to the point here. Sheila Kitzinger, too, stresses the unapproachability of male obstetricians: 'I know that one obstetrician who prides himself upon his sympathy is described by more than one patient as "unapproachable" and "always so rushed". His skill does not extend to any deep understanding of his relationship with his patients' (Kitzinger 1962 59). She attacks the

> tradition that there must exist a social distance between doctor and patient which serves to maintain his dignity and status *vis-à–vis* the layman and to make his pronouncements worthy of respect. The 'bedside manner' disappeared with the doctor who acted the part of kindly father confessor and avuncular adviser − a role which itself served to maintain this distance by its assumption of implicit authority and superior status − and in his place has come the clinician, the foreman and manager of the baby factory who treats the women lying on the examination tables as if they were so many fish on a slab.
>
> (Kitzinger 1962 59)

Here, both the Dick Read-type father-figure and the unsympathetic proponent of the mechanical model are attacked as remote and authoritarian. Elsewhere, male doctors get off more lightly: in discussing women who are overdependent on their birth attendants Kitzinger describes the woman dependent on a male doctor, who needs and − it is implied − gets 'a father figure who must care for

her and let her come to no harm – who will be firm, authoritarian
and kind, like a loving father'. But the woman who needs a
mother is criticised for 'girlhood dependence', especially if she is
the daughter of a 'mother-dominated home' (108). A portrait is
provided of an 'over-motherly midwife' who may 'use her kindness
in order to get power over her patient', exercising 'a will of iron
that must not be thwarted' (109). 'Wilful' midwives here come in
for criticism that 'authoritarian' doctors escape, perhaps because
of their remoteness.

In these representations the powerful men are absent, or busy
and abstracted, like fathers in traditional nuclear families, while
the nurses and midwives, like mothers, get on with the business
of enforcing the patriarchal order on to the children/mothers. The
infantilisation of the patients is commented on by several writers.
In *Still Life* the nurses speak to the patients 'as one speaks to
distracted children or incapable old people' (Byatt 1986 14).
'Everything is reduced to physical needs', complains Xenia in
Birth Rites, 'and they treat us like children!' (Bowder 1983 196).

Different formulations are used by the two 1930s novelists,
Bagnold and Brittain, who both see the medical institution as
benign, and as gendered, though in different ways. Bagnold presents her idealised midwife in *The Squire* as a perfect blend of
ancient female wisdom *and* male scientific training. The midwife
speaks up for male science, and the male take-over of childbirth:

> 'I care so much,' said the midwife, sitting up straighter, 'that I am
> prepared to give up the baby – the victim of centuries of women –
> to the attack of man!'
>
> The squire's eyes opened.
>
> 'The book of instinct has long, long been closed,' said the
> midwife.
>
> 'But what do we get instead?' said the squire. 'The science-guided
> baby! Labelled, its tears and stools in bottles, its measurements on
> a chart, its food weighed like a prescription!'
>
> 'Better than muddle,' said the midwife.
>
> (Bagnold 1937 182–3)

Bagnold sees scientific advance and its application to obstetrics
as *male*: this is not an insight exclusive to later feminist writers.
But because it is male, it is not therefore oppressive: it can
be appropriated by women. Vera Brittain's *Honourable Estate*
shows approval of the medical institution in a different way.

Brittain opposes Bagnold's idea of 'natural' birth, and instead
provides a technological hospital birth that saves the life of her
1930s heroine. The earlier, mismanaged Victorian home birth is
presided over by a male doctor; the efficient 1930s hospital birth
is presided over by 'Dr Geraldine Vane', fulfilling the hopes of
Janet, the Victorian heroine, whose only comment in her diary
on her experience of childbirth was '"Women doctors? YES!!"'
(Brittain 1936 50). Technology, science and women's emancipation
go together, against Nature and patriarchal ignorance.

Women doctors are not, however, seen as the solution by
Elizabeth Baines, in her much later *The Birth Machine*. Here,
cruel caricature is used to emphasise that women in obstetrics are
imitation men, striving to emulate and even outdo the men in their
technological expertise and lust for power. Thus the decision to
induce Zelda is broken 'briskly' to Zelda by a female consultant:
'She was tall and broad-shouldered, her hair barbered at the neck,
an imitation man' (Baines 1983 34). And the Professor's star pupil
is the symbolically named super-efficient Arleen Manning, who
plans to outdo her mentor: 'These are the days of opportunities for
women. She'll be better than any of them, mere men, pretend gods,
who have gone before her' (57). So female doctors are definitely
not an alternative: like natural childbirth techniques, they can be
co-opted, only too willingly, into the patriarchal system.

In *The Birth Machine*, the impersonality and violence of mechanised hospital birth is traced back unequivocally to a powerful
male figure, Professor McGuirk, an embodiment of Adrienne
Rich's stereotype of the 'aseptic male obstetrician'. Not only is
he responsible for the hospital system, but he represents the 'male'
scientific/technological project, encoded in scientific language,
dedicated to the control of women's bodies. The Professor is the
consultant who has decided that Zelda should be induced, but,
significantly, we do not first see him in the clinic or on the ward:
he appears giving a lecture to an international conference, and
later we also see him lecturing to medical students, his successors.
Martin Richards, speculating on why induction for non-medical
reasons has become so widespread, despite lack of evidence for
its advantages or its safety, locates the cause in the 'belief system'
of the obstetric profession, with its preference for technological
intervention and control (Richards 1975 597). By presenting the
Professor first and most importantly as lecturer, as disseminator

of a certain world-view, Baines prioritises the professional 'belief system' that lies behind what her heroine has to undergo. Richards also points out that professional status is at stake: 'High status within obstetrics seems to go with the use of the most up to date technical innovations' (600); it is the Professor's status as international celebrity that is stressed, a status dependent on his enthusiastic publicity for the 'machine' – the infusion unit which is being used to induce Zelda's birth.

The connection between the Professor's enthusiasm for induction, and a coldly objective scientific world-view, is made explicit in the parallels drawn between the research being conducted by Zelda's husband, Roland, and her own predicament. Attached to the hospital is the Centre for Medical Research, where Roland, a pupil of the Professor, conducts experiments on rats to test the effects of oestrogen. Zelda, a drip attached to her arm, 'half-lies, half-sits, her legs splayed . . . Within lies the placenta, past its maximum efficiency'. At the same time, upstairs, 'The rat lies, cruciform. Inside is the liver, which will reveal new truth, and provide the world with scientific data' (Baines 1983 22). Roland's research is on contraception – it is also male experimentation on the female reproductive system. The parallel between Zelda's induction and the rat experiments turns out to be even closer than it at first appears: by the end of the novel, Zelda realises that the induction was totally unnecessary, its only point was to test out and demonstrate the Professor's new techniques. She has indeed been experimented on.

The whole process is presented as a conspiracy against the heroine, by male-directed science and technology. A crucial scene is where the heroine re-interprets the medical textbook she had turned to for information earlier, and sees, hidden beneath its bland, impersonal language, the rationale for what has been done to her:

> *Any condition may be an indication for induction if it is considered safer for the mother, or for the foetus, or for both, that the pregnancy does not continue any longer.* Any condition. Any undefined condition. If for any undefined reason it is considered safer. Her healthy body may be a condition. Their lack of faith in her healthy body may be an indication.
>
> It was there, between the lines, and she hadn't seen it.
>
> (Baines 1983 70)

The ambiguous and sinister passage from the textbook has, in fact, appeared earlier in the book – a clue laid for the discerning reader. It appears in the Professor's lecture to his students. The Professor is neatly listing indications for induction on the board, under headings and sub-headings: 'The horizontal headings begin to be supported by vertical lists like classical Greek columns' (20). The abstract patterning of his scientific categorisation has a parallel in the drawings that Zelda's father does of the power-station being built near her home when she is a child; the book is structured not only on Zelda's gradual discovery of what is being done to her, but on her simultaneous recovery of significant memories from her past: 'Father's drawings were dull. Pale grey lines, very fine and straight, making squares and tubes, and labelled all over with numbers and arrows' (35). Just as the Professor's ideas take an ugly and dangerous physical shape in the induction – while he lectures, 'Zelda's strapped to her bed' (21) – so father's plans take shape in the power-station: 'They were patterns, to be translated, into thick stone blocks, into concrete reality. . . . And poisonous dust dropped, seeping and burning the countryside all round' (117).

So the Professor's ideas and their consequences are part of a larger, destructive, masculine, scientific–technological enterprise, extending beyond the hospital. The murderous reality of the power-station is symbolically emphasised when Zelda's childhood games in the wood come to an end with the discovery of the murdered body of a boy in their 'den'. The children assume the murderer was an eccentric old woman they have labelled as a 'witch', but it turns out to have been a male construction worker from the power-station. The smashed skull of the boy in the den is parallelled with the head of the distressed male foetus, smashing through Zelda's body, unable to get out (Baines 1983 72). The induction, like the power-station, is the source of potentially lethal consequences. The explicit connection is made by Zelda at the end of the novel:

> She hears them [the Professor and his entourage] coming along the corridor, their voices reverent and low, the givers of life according to their own strict patterns. False patterns. Their gods are false: their stiff patterns can fail them. Death can leap up from the depths, gobbling, jump back into the machine; electric grids across the land, sustenance and life meted out in geometric patterns: the lights could go out, the machines fail at any moment, a troll can jump down

from industrial scaffolding, stalk a child in the woods and smash
its skull.

(Baines 1983 118–9)

Once again, we are shown the chaos and brutality lurking in what
claims to be an orderly system.

While Baines presents technological hospital birth as part of
a wider male conspiracy, Weldon mocks this idea in *Puffball*:
the naive and mistaken natural childbirth enthusiasts 'had given
up doctors, who were an essential part of the male conspiracy
against women' (Weldon 1980 91). The primitive woman, Mabs,
is defeated and tamed by modern male medicine. The medical
establishment is life-saving, even though it is presented as largely
male and somewhat misogynist: the specialist Liffey has seen in
advance did not 'particularly like women', being sure that 'all
women were fools, and knaves, and the enemies of their babies'
(201). This fits in with what Rothman sees as characteristic of
the medical model of pregnancy, in which the mother–foetus
relationship is seen 'as a conflicting dyad rather than as an
integral unit' (Rothman 1982 49. See also 38, 48, 135, 184).
But as Liffey's doctor says of the specialist, 'He isn't the most
tactful of men. . . . But on the other hand he won't let you die'
(Weldon 1980 203). The male obstetrician is useful, if irritating.
While implicitly mocking Baines' idea, however, Weldon still goes
along with her division between *male* science and *female* Nature or
instinct, the same division we saw in Bagnold's *The Squire*. Some of
the history of this way of thinking is analysed in Ludmilla Jordanova's
book, *Sexual Visions: Images of Gender in Science and Medicine
between the 18th and 20th Centuries*. In a critique of a feminist
book on radiation, she neatly labels for us the kind of 'gendered
dichotomies' that result, and that seem extremely relevant to the
descriptions of hospital birth we have been looking at:

women	men
creative	destructive
life and inheritance	threats to life and inheritance . . .
plain English	foreign language of science
'you'	'them' (by implication)

She sums up: 'The female side is life-giving and lovely, it is the
realm of nature. By contrast, the male domain of science embodies
a threat to life. . . . The language for women is plain, direct and

' our own; that for men is doubly alien in that it is "scientific" and hence abstruse, and "foreign", that is, of the other' (Jordanova 1989 161).

Appropriation and subversion

What signs, then, are there of women writers reversing or under-mining these 'dichotomies' in their representations of childbirth? Making use of the figure of the primitive woman to oppose technological intervention only, of course, reinforces the polarities, keeping women on the side of Nature and the irrational, even where the 'scientific' side is not definitely identified as 'male'. As we have seen, writers like Bagnold and Weldon see the 'male' side as not necessarily 'destructive' or threatening, though they go along with the other dichotomies, while Vera Brittain also validates the 'scientific' side, but recasts it as 'female'. Some of the most interesting inversions of the pattern occur where medical *language*, the 'foreign', 'abstruse' discourse of science, is appropriated by women writers. This process is most obvious, surprisingly, in a 'natural' childbirth context: Sheila Kitzinger's book of 'real life' stories, *Giving Birth, How It Really Feels*. As we have seen, Kitzinger here is not averse to understanding and negotiating with the medical authorities. While her introduction contains both her lyrical description of birth in terms of water imagery, and a description of 'the usual pattern of labour' in medical terms, in the accounts of birth by the other women in her book, I found that it was the medical account that predominated – there was much use of medical terminology, of books, and especially of written birth-plans, as weapons of power. Rather than letting go and experiencing childbirth 'naturally', these women were using all the resources of culture to gain control over their own experiences. When they did describe bodily sensations or emotions, it was either in medical terminology – 'contractions', 'transition', 'urge to push' – or in the most general or clichéd language, for instance: 'It was such a beautiful and emotional experience' (Kitzinger 1987 90). So, despite the book's title, I did not get any sense of 'how it really feels' – which is something that women writing *fictional* accounts are often very concerned to convey, especially through the use of metaphor; medical terminology is usually banished in order to create an effect of immediacy and authenticity, or it is seen, as in *The Birth Machine*, as an alien, false language to be rejected.

The Kitzinger accounts, however, show women fully aware of the medical version of what is going on in their bodies, *and* of what the medical authorities are up to, and how to combat them. With technical know-how on their side, the women are able to carry on informed arguments with their medical attendants. My favourite example of this is from the account of a woman determined to have twins with as little intervention as possible: 'between contractions I continued the forceps discussion' (Kitzinger 1987 80). Her account is full of an easy and informed use of medical terminology: 'My GP, bless him, mentioned the Mauriceau-Smellie-Veit manoeuvre but even he felt that an episiotomy was probable and pointed out that if the doctor who delivered No. 2 had no experience of this manoeuvre I would have to accept forceps' (78). This woman had also written to her consultant in advance detailing her wishes. By using medical terminology for their own purposes, and especially by the power of written 'plans', these women are able to challenge the authority of the medical establishment's version of events more creatively than could Oakley's informants, one of whom describes the power of writing being used against her: 'When they examine you they write in the file and give a special stamp and I asked her what it was and she said I can't tell you. She said all I can tell you is that you are progressing. She said what is written in the file is strictly confidential' (Oakley 1981 92). In *The Birth Machine* too, we see the 'secret' file being used against the heroine: she begins to free herself by opening and reading it. Kitzinger's women go further: armed with their own written plans, they cause their own versions of events to come into being.

The way in which the medical version of birth has been thoroughly incorporated into these women's personal stories is well illustrated by a particularly idyllic birth described in one of Kitzinger's accounts. The story begins with bread-making and ends with milking the goat. But the actual moment of birth is described like this: 'One more push and my son slid out, with an Apgar level of nine, into the sunshine' (Kitzinger 1987 108). The glossary informs us that the 'Apgar level' is 'a quick and simple way of estimating a baby's health and responsiveness to the challenges of living based on the observation of the baby's reflexes, muscle tone and breathing. It is carried out at one and five minutes after birth. Ten is full marks' (211). Obviously, this woman cannot have known what her son's Apgar level was as he actually emerged from the womb: she must have been told this later by the midwife. But clearly, in retrospect his high score has become part of the whole triumph of his successful birth, and the way the outside technical information is incorporated into her account suggests an effortless appropriation of the official medical description of her son.

Medical terminology is appropriated in rather a different way by Fay Weldon in *Puffball*, which I want to look at now in some detail. One of the most surprising features of the novel is its use of medical terminology, which is usually rigorously avoided by fiction writers in their depictions of birth. In her use of medical terminology, Weldon enacts an extremely subtle take-over and subversion of scientific discourse. The context is not, as for Kitzinger, a questioning of the medical institution, but, seemingly, an endorsement of it, in all its 'maleness'. Scientific discourse, as well as the medical establishment, seems to be endorsed. In Weldon's descriptions of Liffey's pregnancy, scientific discourse is paramount at first, and is used to describe an inescapable moral reality. A number of chapters entitled 'Inside Liffey' describe in technical, medical language what is happening in the heroine's reproductive system – how the cells are dividing, how the placenta is forming in the wrong place. Liffey's unawareness of all this is presented as part of her naive ignorance of the realities of life. Motherhood is to be the climax of her education into reality, an education that begins with her irresponsible and deluded decision to live in the country. Her ignorance of the workings of her reproductive 'inside' is on a par with her ignorance of the wiles and power of the country folk, the perfidy of her city 'friends', the limitations of the London commuter rail timetable, and the rapidly diminishing size of her bank account, as she blithely writes cheques for useless and expensive items. Indeed, at one point there is a very close similarity between the narrator's description of the movement of Liffey's overdrawn cheque through the banking system, and her description of the movement of blood, sperm or ova through Liffey's reproductive system (Weldon 1980 90). Liffey's ignorance is presented as childish, and morally culpable – for instance, after describing the fluid-retaining effect of the contraceptive pill on Liffey's 'inside', the narrator asks:

> Was Liffey's resentment of Richard a matter of pressure on the brain caused by undue retention of fluid, or in fact the result of his behaviour? Liffey naturally assumed it was the latter. It is not pleasant for a young woman to believe that her behaviour is dictated by her chemistry, and that her wrongs lie in herself, and not in others' bad behaviour.

(Weldon 1980 15)

It is not possible to read the medical descriptions as some kind of coldly clinical objectification of the heroine's body – they are part of her 'self', and she should be more aware of them. Medical terminology carries, it seems, the narrator's approval, as when she uses it against the feminist natural childbirthers: when their baby is stillborn 'of placental insufficiency, the baby being six weeks beyond term' (127), the narrator's knowledge of biological facts and figures shows up the ignorant confidence of these believers in 'Nature'. Scientific discourse is set against woolly-minded feminism. There is none of Baines' suspicion of the deceptively bland scientific language of the medical textbook and the Professor's lecture – male language that serves to conceal outrages done to the female body.

Weldon also gives medical terminology value by adopting a tone of wonder, as she describes the intricacy of biological processes: 'The mechanics of her menstrual cycle were indeed ingenious' (23). Despite the technical language, the descriptions are admirably lucid. Weldon is not trying to blind us with science, or repel us with its harsh terms. Anyone of reasonable intelligence could understand and enjoy these little lessons in human biology – she is making the 'inside' accessible. These passages of medical explanation are in fact very close to the wording of the descriptions of the stages of pregnancy in Gordon Bourne's classic *Pregnancy*, a popular manual designed for prospective mothers to read. Either Bourne is Weldon's source, or they both derive from some other common source. If we look at points where Weldon *departs* from Bourne, we can begin to see how her use of medical terminology is not as straightforwardly scientist as it at first appears.

Often, as in the passage above, Weldon can be read as merely providing a précis of Bourne, who is himself lucid and easy to understand (Bourne 1975 45–7. Compare also Weldon 1980 34, 100–1, 105–8, 117, 121, 130, 135–6, 141, 155, 160, 166, 225, 236–7, 255–8 with Bourne 1975 58, 36–9, 59–60, 56–7, 59–61, 66–70, 72, 77, 334, 340, 407, 477, 485, 491, respectively). We might expect that Weldon as a 'literary' writer would be adding metaphorical language to Bourne's matter-of-fact 'scientific' style. However, it mostly turns out that the metaphorical language is already there in Bourne. Emily Martin has pointed out how descriptions in medical textbooks often use 'loaded' language in the most seemingly technical passages – language that implies particular values and purposes inherent in the biological processes they are describing (Martin 1987 13, 45, 48). This tendency can be seen in Weldon's descriptions – she describes the end of the menstrual cycle like this: 'Then the corpus luteum would start to degenerate and on the twenty-eighth day be disposed of in the form of menstrual flow – along, of course, with the lining of Liffey's uterus, hopefully and richly thickened over the previous twenty-eight days to receive a fertilised ovum, but so far, on one hundred-and-twenty occasions, disappointed'. (Weldon 1980 23). The words 'hopefully' and 'disappointed' imply that the conscious purpose of the whole process is conception. Martin points out how this assumption moulds supposedly objective medical descriptions of menstruation, and how analogous processes, such as the shedding of the stomach lining, or the over-production of sperm by the male, are *not* seen in the same terms of failure and waste (Martin 1987 45–50). Interestingly, 'hopefully' is already there in Bourne (1975 47); 'disappointed' is added by Weldon, intensifying Bourne's implication. Similarly, where Weldon *adds* metaphors not in Bourne, they go along with and intensify the 'mechanical' model of the body that Martin discovers in medical textbooks (Martin 1987 54; see also Richards 1975 597). So, when Liffey comes off the pill, 'her body was still recovering from a surfeit of hormones, as might a car engine flooded by the use of too much choke' (Weldon 1980 70). Describing the conception of Liffey's baby, Weldon explains the action of the sperm: 'If it came up against a solid object it would change direction, like a child's mechanical toy' (105). This expands upon Bourne's remark 'When it comes up against a solid object it changes direction' (Bourne 1975 57), adding the idea of mechanism.

So far we can see Weldon as merely reinforcing the 'medical' model, though she does begin to expose a contradiction in it, between the purposeful, personifying language of 'hopefully' and 'disappointed', and the impersonal, technical language of the 'car engine'. Further incongruities appear when Bourne's generalised descriptions are applied to the particularities of Liffey's body and Liffey's situation. This can produce a comic effect, a kind of absurd incongruity between people's feelings and actions, and their biological causes and accompaniments. For instance, a description of Richard's passionate love-making is accompanied by a description of his sperms' genesis and progress into Liffey's reproductive system (Weldon 1980 34), and his ejaculation is described in Bourne's words as 'rhythmic muscular contractions' (58). But the insertion of Bourne's language into a particular situation makes not only the human actions, but also the scientific descriptions seem comic. In other cases, particularisation has the effect of privileging the specificity of Liffey, her history, her feelings, over the impersonal biological events. Thus, Bourne explains the mechanisms of genetics – 'every child has 50 per cent of his genes from one parent and 50 per cent from the other' (Bourne 1975 23) – but Weldon particularises: 'Liffey's brown eyes: Richard's square chin. Her gran's temper: his great grandfather's musical bent' (Weldon 1980 108). Later, at twenty weeks, as Bourne puts it, 'very active movements can easily be observed and felt by the mother' (Bourne 1975 72); while Weldon activates and animates Bourne's clumsy passive construction: 'The baby moved, there could be no doubt of it. A pattering, pittering feeling, like the movement of butterfly wings' (Weldon 1980 182).

Weldon's most noticeable deviations from Bourne occur after the surprising chapter called 'Annunciation', in which Liffey's baby speaks to her from inside the womb, where Weldon validates the 'natural' mother, introducing elements of maternal spirituality and mysticism that seemed to have been banished by her use of medical terminology. The title of the chapter, 'Annunciation', echoes the language of Sheila Kitzinger:

> birth cannot simply be a matter of techniques for getting a baby out of one's body. It involves our relationship to life as a whole, the part we play in the order of things; and as the baby develops and can be felt moving inside, to some women annunciation, incarnation, seem to become facts of their own existence.
>
> (Kitzinger 1984 25)

By making the baby inside Liffey actually speak to her, Weldon pushes the implications of this kind of imagery to their extreme, just as she also pushes the medical model to its extremes. The two accounts, female-spiritual and male-medical, exist, incongruously, side by side. So, at eight weeks, after the 'Annunciation' chapter, a précis of Bourne's description ends, startlingly, like this: 'The spine moved of its own volition, for the first time, although fractionally. The length of the foetus was two point two centimetres. There was no apparent room within for the soul which gave grace to its being' (Weldon 1980 141; compare Bourne 1975 67). 'Apparent' both endorses and undermines the medical version. Later descriptions insist on the baby as a separate person, beyond the impersonality of Bourne's descriptions (Bourne 1975 70; Weldon 1980 166).

The message from the baby, and his increasing humanisation, help to bring together the initially split 'Inside' and outer worlds. By separating the scientific accounts of Liffey's 'Inside' processes into separate chapters, Weldon at first seems to be going along with the 'medical' model of childbirth, treating the woman's body as object, or machine, quite apart from her subjective feelings. The message from 'Inside' bridges the gap, and puts 'outer' Liffey in touch with her 'inner' world. The separation of the technical, inner descriptions from the rest of the plot is also not so absolute as it seems at first. The 'Inside Liffey' chapters do also contain other material, and the 'inside' descriptions begin to appear in other chapters, particularly the descriptions of the development of the embryo. These are sometimes found in chapters that by their title and contents implicitly link 'inner' and 'outer' action; for instance 'Growth', or 'Movement', which label both the embryo's activities, and the development of the 'outside' plot. The narrator also proceeds to make merry with her scientific language and its implications. Thus 'Inside Mabs', who is having difficulty conceiving, 'the ovum dutifully developed the required choriomic [sic] villi with which to embed itself into the waiting uterine wall', but arrived too late, 'and by that time had ignobly perished, for lack of a suitable foothold, or villihold' (Weldon 1985 159). The exaggeration of the language of purpose ('dutifully', 'ignobly'), and the coinage ('villihold') hint at a send-up of the scientific terminology, and a total refusal to be intimidated by it. The 'Inside' chapters also contain meditations by the narrator on the

role of pure chance in the 'cosmic' processes of Nature, at whose
mercy we all are – but these are undercut by a cheerful circularity.
Wondering whether Liffey's life-threatening *placenta praevia* is
caused by chance or by Mabs' curse, she reasons like this:

> One pregnancy in a hundred is a placenta praevia: does every one
> of these foetuses have a Mabs in the background? Surely not;
> such foetuses are merely accident prone, or event prone, as some
> individuals are; at one time or other in their life. Ladders fall on
> them or pigs out of windows, or bombs go off as they approach;
> or, in country terms, their crops fail and their cattle sicken and a
> witch has overlooked them.
>
> (Weldon 1980 220)

So the scientifically objective category 'accident', set up in opposition to Mabs' witchcraft, becomes more and more mystically and
mischievously defined into an 'overlooking' again. Body and mind,
biological and psychic, cannot be so easily separated out.

The chapter called 'Birth', in which Liffey undergoes her emergency Caesarean, is the climax of this intertwining of incongruous,
opposite ways of describing bodily events. Weldon uses precise,
technical language, very similar to Bourne's, to describe the physical realities of the operation: 'He then separated the muscles
of the lower abdominal wall and opened the abdominal cavity'.
(Weldon 1980 255; compare Bourne 1975 407). At the same time,
Weldon includes Liffey's consciousness in the event, by making
the anaesthetic not quite strong enough, and her consciousness
includes an awareness of the spiritual meaning of the event: 'Liffey
sensed the passage of time, and of terrible, powerful, momentous
events. Of struggle, and endeavour, and of the twists and turns of
fate, and of life taking form out of rock' (Weldon 1980 255).

There is a sense in which Weldon has it all ways – she both
makes fun of the absurdities of natural childbirth rhetoric and
medical terminology, while also endorsing both discourses as
inescapably true. But to find fault with her for this would be to
mistake the comic tone of the book – it is a playful exposé of the
inadequacies of our systems of thought, the frames – male-medical
or female-natural – we use to structure our experience.

While Weldon goes along with, exaggerates, and finally subverts
the gendered dichotomies of primitive woman and male medical

establishment, Margaret Atwood in 'Giving Birth' confuses and reverses them from the start. The institution is not particularly 'male', and the heroine, though obviously female, is not particularly 'natural': as we have seen, her 'natural' approach is studiously learnt from books. The 'other woman' who follows her around is only 'natural' in her pain and agony, and so is not in any essential way opposed to the interventions and alleviations provided by the medical institution. Atwood further undermines the dichotomy between 'natural' and 'medical' versions of the birth-story. When it comes to the question of 'pain' versus 'discomfort', neither version turns out to be relevant, simply because the protagonist's subjectivity disappears: 'When there is no pain she feels nothing, when there is pain, she feels nothing because there is no she. This, finally, is the disappearance of language' (Atwood 1984 237). Language is finally inadequate to the experience: in this, birth is like any other extreme bodily experience, 'a car accident or an orgasm', 'events of the body, all of them; why should the mind distress itself trying to find a language for them?' (235). 'Orgasm' is of course one of Sheila Kitzinger's metaphors for giving birth, but its instinctual and celebratory implications are undercut by the parallelism with 'car accident', a metaphor which suggests an extreme medical model of birth as a physical disaster that needs medical help. Atwood does not choose between these metaphors, she just points beyond them to the unrepresentability of bodily experience.

This rejection of both 'natural' and 'medical' accounts is, surprisingly, also present in Anne Oakley's collection of 'real life' accounts of birth. While, for instance, 'Alison Mountjoy' questions and tries to oppose medical interventions like the induction, the breaking of the waters, and later the drips and the epidural, she is not doing so from a convinced natural childbirth point of view, and also disputes the natural childbirth version of events: 'By then these pains were coming quite fast and they were pretty painful. You're not allowed to call them pains, are you? They're contractions. It always makes me laugh when I read that because I *knew* they bloody well hurt. . . . Also the breathing wasn't working – it's a load of old codswallop, that breathing' (Oakley 1981 87). Her whole story is told like this, in opposition to other versions – even the mother's description of first holding the baby is implicitly in terms of having heard or read about this allegedly marvellous

also by an implicit condemnation. Emily Martin shows how the language of medical textbooks presupposes that the *purpose* of the female reproductive system is childbirth: menstruation is described in terms of failure and waste. We have seen Fay Weldon reinforcing this implication from Gordon Bourne's textbook in her novel *Puffball*. Dick Read wastes no time discussing non-mothers, presupposing that motherhood is all women's highest destiny, but his biography reveals his attitude to the single woman, in an impatient, half-humorous outburst: 'Single women of thirty and over should all be pitied, I am told. But my experience is that they are impetuous, imprudent and impertinent. Their impenetrable minds are as impervious as their impassioned bodies and, for the sake of mankind, they should all be either imprisoned or impregnated!' (Thomas 1957 163–4). Kitzinger, too, though less insulting to the single woman, sees motherhood as essential to womanhood, leaving the childless woman with a sense 'that she has missed something, that she is incomplete, in some way, wasted' (Kitzinger 1962 68).

Fiction writers often dramatise attitudes to singleness and motherhood through contrasts between different characters. Several accounts make comparisons between the birthing heroine and her 'virginal' female attendants. Martha, 'engulfed in pain' in Lessing's *A Proper Marriage*, 'most passionately resented that uncommitted virgin with her determination not to be disturbed by suffering', 'the baby-faced nurse' (Lessing 1977 163). Gwen, in Doris Betts's 'Still Life With Fruit', also resents the young novice who administers the shave and enema, imagining her 'sleeping single in her narrow bed, spending her days with women who slept double and who now brought her the ripe fruits of God' (Betts 1974 339). Here, birthing women have a maturity and experience that sets them apart from the immaturity of their single sisters. There is a similar implication in *Puffball*, in the contrast drawn between the immature, powerless Liffey, and the powerful, multiparous Mabs. Only when Liffey becomes pregnant does she begin to have 'powers of her own' (Weldon 1980 142). In both Lessing's and Betts's scenes, however, the birthing woman is shown to be too hasty in her judgement: the 'virgins' have considerable power, and Martha finds herself obeying the 'practical cool little voice' of the nurse, while Gwen is surprised by the novice's knowing comments on the beauty of pubic hair.

In Enid Bagnold's *The Squire*, childless women can gain vicarious satisfaction through devotion to another woman's children: both the midwife and the nurse have given up maternity in order to serve the squire's children. The arrival of the squire's new baby is the 'leap and triumph of her virgin maternity' (Bagnold 1987 7) for the nurse, and the idealised midwife follows a 'profession of repressed maternity' (174). Virgins who do not dedicate themselves to other women's motherhood are seen as destructive, in the person of Mrs Pascoe the cook, with 'her ginger-headed virginity, her malicious prudish anger at the birth' (34), and she confirms her villainy by giving in her notice and throwing the household into confusion at the crucial moment. These contrasts all serve to idealise the squire's role as mother, and this idealisation is further confirmed by the contrasts often drawn between her and her younger friend, Lady Caroline, not a virgin, but also not a mother. Caroline, with her love-affairs, represents the squire's youth: the contrast between them causes the squire to rejoice in her own middle age, in which she has lost her purely decorative femininity, and her involvement in trivial love-affairs; instead, she has become more 'male', and has discovered a new and better sort of 'love' with her children. When she had lovers, the squire thinks, 'she had been female to them then, but now what was left standing at the core was the rock of neutral human stuff, neither male nor female . . . the mysterious foliage of "woman" had died off the rock' (Bagnold 1987 191). Later, she tells Caroline 'Such as *you* ought to be called "women". *We* ought to be called "wumen"; some different word. Wumen are hard-working, faulty, honest, female males – trudging down life, pushing the future before them in a wheelbarrow' (191). Motherhood is thus, surprisingly, not a quintessential function of woman – it is instead accomplished by 'neutral' humans, or 'female males'. Womanhood is associated only with sex-appeal. Motherhood is something that empowers a woman (Caroline is seen as a 'victim'), and paradoxically frees her from her gender, and from the humiliations of love for a man. The squire compares her love relationship with her baby, 'the perfect companion', with Caroline's relationship with her lover, who is 'full of enemy and conspiring thoughts, . . . attacking or in flight' (159). The continuing comparison with Caroline sets out what being a mother means in terms of female identity – interestingly, there are no contrasts between motherhood and career, or motherhood and intellectual life. The squire's task of commanding her household is equivalent to a career, and she also has ample spare time for any other pursuits: after the midwife has gone, charge of the baby will be handed over to the nurse, who already looks after the other children. It is quite clear that class factors play a large part in the way Bagnold formulates the meaning of 'motherhood'.

A. S. Byatt's *Still Life* also pursues a continuing contrast between the birthing woman and another woman whose life takes a different pattern, but in this case the satisfactions of motherhood are brought into question by this contrast. Stephanie, who has a Double First from Cambridge, has chosen marriage and domesticity instead of an academic career, and we are clearly meant to contrast her with her equally brilliant sister, Frederica, who spends most of the novel as an undergraduate at Cambridge. When Frederica visits, Stephanie 'felt a chill, as though she, her house, good and bad, brilliant flowers and warm baby as well as grumbling and responsibility were what Frederica dreaded'. At the end of the novel, Frederica thinks, 'she had perhaps relied on Stephanie to do for both of them things she herself feared doing, perhaps couldn't do' (Byatt 1986 355). But what Stephanie has most recently done is *died*, by a horrible domestic accident. We are shown her undergoing three extreme bodily experiences in the novel, two births and a death. The second birth is more painful and less triumphant than the first. Stephanie's life choice seems to lead downwards into a dead end. We see her trying vainly to keep up her reading and thinking, reading Wordsworth in the antenatal clinic, or in a few brief snatched hours at the library, during which time her mother-in-law and brother fail to look after the baby properly, dropping him on the floor as she comes back in. After her death her husband thinks 'how she had been made dumb, by marrying him, about Wordsworth and Shakespeare' (343). As well as this loss of intellectual life, her marriage is also presented as involving a gradual and irreversible loss of her 'separate self', her 'privacy', as uncongenial relatives come to stay, and her husband's parishioners make demands. The births are part of this pattern, the babies first of all invading her body and then her time. Her death, while trying to rescue a sparrow who has got trapped in the house, is symbolically appropriate to someone whose life is so given up to others.

The darkening pattern of Stephanie's life is contrasted with Frederica's upward trajectory to academic and sexual success. Female life-choices are divided up entirely differently from in *The Squire*, reflecting Stephanie's different class position, and the different assumptions about women's roles that were current in her time: here, the division is between maternity/loss of self/death and sexuality/self-assertion/life. While we can see Bagnold's glorifi-cation of motherhood as reflecting contemporary ideology, Byatt's darker story reflects not so much the beliefs of the 50s when the novel is set, as the beliefs of the 80s when the novel was written. In the 50s, motherhood and domesticity were promoted as ideals for women in reaction to the war years when women were co-opted into industry; from a later perspective these ideals are seen as limiting and destructive. The book's stark contrast between the roles of mother-woman and career-woman is of the 50s; the implied criticism of this polarisation and of its destructive effect derives from a later point of view, perhaps influenced by the intervening rise of the women's movement.

While Lessing, Betts, Bagnold and Byatt all draw contrasts between the birthing woman and the voluntarily childless one, Sylvia Plath and Christine Schutt explore the mother's relation to the barren woman who longs for a child. Plath's poem, 'Three Women' (1962), is set in 'a maternity ward and round about' (Plath 1981). The 'First Voice' is that of a woman giving birth; the 'Second Voice' is a barren woman who has had a miscarriage. The 'Third Voice' brings in the voluntarily childless woman again, in a different context: not a virgin, but a woman who gives birth and then leaves her child for adoption. We see her later in a college setting: perhaps she represents the intellectual life that Frederica exemplifies in *Still Life*. While the willing mother is surrounded with imagery of nature – 'leaves and petals attend me' – the barren woman is surrounded by imagery of 'flatness', mechanical abstraction – 'parts, bits, cogs, the shining multiples' – and dead nature, 'the bare trees'. It seems as if natural motherhood is being endorsed: 'I am found wanting', says the second voice, echoing Kitzinger's idea of the childless woman as 'incomplete', 'wasted'. Plath's poem and Kitzinger's *The Experience of Childbirth* were both published in 1962, and both fit into the 'feminine mystique' of the 50s and early 60s. Yet Plath complicates her position by suggesting later that the second woman's barrenness is as 'natural' as the first one's fertility: 'I lose life after life. The dark earth drinks them. / She is the vampire of us all.' At the same time, 'nature' treats the first woman just as brutally during the birth: 'I am the centre of an atrocity. /What pains, what sorrows must I be mothering?' The third woman, who repudiates her child, and is imaged as an incomplete 'wound' leaving the hospital, nevertheless gets over the experience: 'I had an old wound once, but it is healing. / I had a dream of an island, red with cries. / It was a dream, and did not mean a thing'. The 'island' is an earlier image for her daughter, whose cries try to catch at her mother 'like hooks'; that this 'dream' is now forgotten may mean that the woman is repressing a deep lack, but in that case we must also take seriously the dream that torments the 'successful' mother, the first voice: 'I do not believe in those terrible children / Who injure my sleep with their white eyes, their fingerless hands. / They are not mine. They do not belong to me'. All three women in the poem, willing mother, unwilling mother, and unwilling childless woman, are the victims of terrors visited upon them by 'nature', and the poem does not at the end make judgements as to who is right or wrong, happy or unhappy.

   Christine Schutt's much more recent short story, 'Sisters' (1989), also shows an equal balance of advantages and disadvantages between mothers and childless women, here figured as 'sisters', perhaps indicating their underlying similarity. The 'I' of the story has two sons, but she is divorced; her sister has a very romantically close marriage, but cannot get pregnant; the story takes place in the sister's house, which has 'room to spare for children' (Schutt 1989 139). The narrator compares their plights: 'sometimes she thinks Peter must regret being saddled with her, a useless, *barren* woman. When I hear about their suffering, I feel helpless, probably in the way Mother said she felt when I told her I was getting a divorce. What can you do?' (142). The story, however, ends on a curiously up-beat note, as the two women begin to dance together, and all the tensions and differences between them dissolve: 'Her hand is so warm and familiar, it feels like where we left off. We slow dance, and she flirts with me, sashays around and under my arms'. The children are delighted and astonished: 'They're thinking they've never see[n] this before.

They're wondering who are these women' (143). While Plath's women never actually speak to each other – her poem is a series of interior monologues which are only connected by the imagery – these women make harmonious contact across their differences.

The solidarity between mothers and non-mothers suggested by these fiction writers cuts across the divisions maintained by the 'official' discourses about childbirth. These discourses are totalising in that they assume all women are or should be mothers; but that very totality creates divisions, marginalised 'others' who do not fit the prescription. Even Bagnold and Byatt point towards this underlying solidarity, by making their mothers and non-mothers either *sisters* – Frederica representing a life-choice Stephanie could have made – or different stages in one woman's life – Caroline represents the squire's youth.

Other mothers

While these writers mostly emphasise female solidarity, while also validating motherhood (except for Byatt and perhaps Plath), doubts and questions about motherhood are mostly raised in comparisons with other mothers, other birthing women, where solidarity is often absent. The 'other women' are seen as bad mothers, as suffocatingly 'good' mothers, as enviable upper-class or disgustingly lower-class mothers, as privileged white or deprived Black mothers: differences and divisions proliferate. While, again, the 'official' discourses ignore these differences, they also help to create some of them, and are implicated in others. In the first place, having set up ideals of female behaviour – passivity and obedience in the medical/institutional model, joyful, conscious achievement in the natural childbirth model – they implicitly and sometimes explicitly condemn other kinds of behaviour by 'bad' mothers. We can see this in O'Driscoll and Meagher's extreme disapproval of women who will not fit into their institutional plans, creating 'degrading scenes' with their 'outrageous conduct' (O'Driscoll and Meagher 1980 91). Mostly, however, the medical institution merely ignores dissent, as Oakley's informant found when she objected to intervention: 'I said why, what for? But of course they didn't listen' (Oakley 1981 87).

On the natural childbirth side, Dick Read sets up very firm distinctions between good patients and bad patients. In *Natural Childbirth* he divides the women who come to consult him into the old-fashioned categories of choleric, sanguine, phlegmatic and melancholic. He then tells two exemplary stories, contrasting the choleric and the phlegmatic. Having set up this sort of category, Dick Read can describe the women's characters by means of their outward appearances – but it is plain that an element of sexual appraisal is also going on, the male 'gaze' evaluating their femininity. So the choleric woman, who turns out to be a model patient, despite her initial loudly-expressed fears, is described like this: 'A tall, fair girl, with large blue eyes, a thin, sensitive mouth, slightly tapering chin beneath her oval face, came into my consulting room. She was beautifully dressed in such a way that her excellent proportions were adequately demonstrated to the world' (Read 1933 29). By contrast, the phlegmatic woman, a hopeless patient, is described as sexually unattractive, 'Large, red and plainly dressed' (30). Sexual attractiveness equals true womanhood and results in natural childbirth, via dependence on men. This last point is made clear by the other major difference between the two women: in the first story, the only other character is a dashing, military husband; in the second, it is a dominant and fear-inspiring mother. The first woman responds with a kind of military courage when Dick Read uses the words 'confidence' and 'guts' to her. After the birth, 'Six foot four of magnificent manhood pushed me out of the way. He had just returned from manoeuvres; his field boots were muddy; his spurs clanked across the room; he had a DCO and an MC among other decorations. He had only one thought and one expression on his face – adoration' (31). This adoration is not interpreted as any tribute to his *wife*'s courage – rather it reveals to the doctor that this husband was responsible for his wife's success.

By contrast, the other woman's husband is not in evidence: 'I did not see her husband; he was something in the city' (Read 1933 31). He has, it is implied, left her to the baneful influence of her mother, who accompanies her to the consulting room: 'a large, severe lady with an aquiline nose and a firm mouth above an almost masculine chin brought her daughter in' (30). Notice again that her femininity is being impugned. A similar story is told later in the book, and again the mother's lack of femininity is stressed: 'Her mother was a lady whose experience of life had somewhat destroyed her confidence in men, and not without reason. She herself was suffering from rather pronounced climacteric symptoms' (67). In both cases, the mothers fill the daughters with fears about the pains of childbirth, and by their presence prevent the male obstetrician from exercising his charismatic effect. In the first case, 'the influence of the physician was neither allowed nor expected' (31); in the second, the mother finally yields when 'I pointed out to her that so long as she was in the room I could do nothing' (68), and an easy birth ensues once she has left. In these stories, the mother is clearly set up as the enemy of the male obstetrician, and the husband as his ally. Natural childbirth, for Read, is an essentially male-dominated activity, and women who do not accept this are dismissed as unfeminine.

We have seen that Sheila Kitzinger, too, in her *Experience of Childbirth*, presents an 'adjustment' to conventional heterosexual femininity as essential to a successful natural birth. If a woman's labour does not progress, it is probably to do with problems in her marriage relationship. Kitzinger's psychological model inevitably leads to the language of blaming and prescription. Her hope that a woman 'should long to savour the experience of birth to the full, not wanting to hold back or to give only half of herself' (Kitzinger 1962 103) starts to sound like a prescription which we may fail to live up to. The many exhortations that a woman 'need not feel she has "failed" if . . . ' (136, 147) only increase this reader's sense of anxiety, by introducing the notion of 'failure' in some test of essential womanhood. This prescriptive tone is most strongly felt in a birth-story that Kitzinger tells in the present tense, recounting the experiences of 'the woman' – a character who is both typical and ideal:

> The woman feels as if her whole body is becoming a gateway into the world for her child. . . . [the baby] suddenly turns red and the mother gasps with pleasure at this. . . . She wants to take him into her arms immediately. . . . she realises that this child is exactly what she desired . . . the mother . . . is radiant and transfigured now. . . . [the husband and wife] have experienced together something incomprehensibly wonderful – a peak of joy in their married life. . . .
>
> (Kitzinger 1962 152–5)

The present tense encourages the reader to build up the fantasy along with the writer, to see it as if unfolding before her. At the same time, read differently, the present tense can introduce a prescriptive tone – this *is* how it is, not how some particular birth *was*. But what if the woman does not feel and act as she is meant to? In a more subtle way than Read's portraits of his patients, Kitzinger's birth-story also implies a sheep-and-goats division of women into ideal or unsatisfactory types, on very traditional lines.

Some of the results of this underlying judgementalism can be seen in the real-life accounts by Kitzinger's followers in *Giving Birth*. For most of these women, Kitzinger's ideas have been elevated to the status of religious beliefs. Her introductory chapter in fact ends with 'the atmosphere of a room where birth takes place', according to Kitzinger's teaching, being compared to 'the silence of a Quaker meeting' (Kitzinger 1987 12). This invocation of non-conformist religion seems especially appropriate to the form of the personal accounts which follow. Each recounts a battle with the establishment on behalf of unorthodox ideas, to which the women continuously testify in the face of opposition. They are persecuted and tempted by the medical establishment, but they triumph with renewed faith and often end with an encouraging moral for the believer. There are occasional telling uses of religious terminology in the accounts: for instance, one woman writes of how she 'was sorely tempted to accept Bridget's [the midwife's] offer of pethidine' (72); another tells us how after the birth 'I felt as if "my cup runneth over"' (108). By making this religious analogy, I don't actually want to undermine the credibility or the power of these testaments. Non-conformist Christianity has often given women the opportunity to voice their beliefs and to believe in their own voices (Hobby 1988 26–75). These accounts have an impressive sense of purpose and self-assurance. On the other hand, religious certainty also generates guilt and self-blame in those who cannot live up to its prescriptions – so in an account of a Caesarean birth a woman writes of how 'The experience shattered me and my confidence in myself as a woman and gave me a feeling of failure at not being able to perform the function for which I was intended. ... It hurts terribly to read glowing accounts in magazines about wonderful births' (Kitzinger 1987 113). These feelings are validated by Kitzinger in her introductory note, and not questioned as perhaps *produced* by her system of beliefs and the 'glowing accounts' it inspires, rather than being the 'natural' feelings to have in this situation. Another woman who had a Caesarean writes of how 'I felt an outsider, envious of other mothers. ... I became desperate to be allowed to try' (150). Only by knowing of Kitzinger's promotion of childbirth without painkillers as a profound psycho-sexual experience can we make any sense of this extreme attitude. Kitzinger's prescriptive certainty leads to feelings of failure and abnormality in those women who cannot fit her ideal account of natural childbirth, and must accept the implied definition of themselves as having failed the supreme test of womanhood.

Of course, one can always combat Kitzinger's prescriptions by adhering to the competing medical version of childbirth: the fact that there are *two* dominant, opposing discourses here means there will always be at least two kind of mothers, failing or succeeding according to the two versions. In some of Ann Oakley's accounts in *From Here to Maternity*, we find women casting other mothers as the villainous or pusillanimous adherents of the opposing version, in order to justify themselves as heroines of natural childbirth, or of the medical version. So one woman who had an epidural and 'felt guilty', the expected response in a natural childbirth-story, turns on a representative of natural childbirth in the next bed: 'There was this woman in the bed next to me and she was an intelligent woman and she said if you do the breathing exercises you can cope. I said well, why should I bloody have to cope? She was all for having it naturally. I think that's disgraceful, you know' (Oakley 1981 95), and then becomes a self-righteous convert to the medical version: ' I just said I think it's a disgrace, no other operation in the world does one have to go through so much pain! And they were going yes, but it's not so bad if you learn how to breathe – learn how to breathe!' (96). Conversely, a woman who had an epidural which did not work becomes an equally self-righteous convert to natural childbirth rhetoric:

> Now I am glad the epidural didn't work, at the time I wished it had done. I think I appreciate what I done, I am pleased with myself, that I could do it. I think some people have that just for the sake of having it. Ninety per cent before their pains even start have it, and even a couple of days after I was so pleased to say I had it but it didn't work, that I took the full brunt of it, whereas these people who had had it said that they couldn't

feel a thing. Well to me that isn't having a baby. What's the
point?

(Oakley 1981 93–4)

We find the same sort of natural childbirth self-righteousness in
Toi Derricote's poem: 'i / would not hurt like all those women
who screamed and took drugs' (Derricote 1983 108). But, unlike
Oakley's accounts, which are justifications after the event, this is
a pre-birth ideal, which is shattered by the experience. The poem
takes place in 'a maternity ward set up for/ the care of unmarried
girls and women in Holy Cross Hospital'. Here, her companions
repel her in that they reflect her plight: 'couldn't stand to see these
new young faces, these / children swollen as myself'. She feels
separate from them in their innocent confidence: her roommate
brags about how she 'was going back to her boyfriend and be a
cheerleader in high school. could we ever *"go back"*? / *would our
bodies be the same ? could we hide among the / childless?*' The
narrator is presented as more thoughtful than her companions, yet
the others arouse her fears and worries about her own pregnancy,
its physical and social meanings. She tries to keep separate from
them: 'i tried to get along, be silent, stay in my own corner./ i only
had a month to go – too short to get to know them'. But solidarity
wins out:

> . . . being drawn to the room down the hall, the t.v. room
> where, at night, we sat in our cuddly cotton robes and
> fleece-lined slippers – like college freshmen, joking
> about the nuns and laughing about due dates: jailbirds
> waiting to be sprung . . .

(108)

This leads on into an acute sympathy for a particularly frail girl
whose baby is eventually stillborn. In contrast, the narrator feels
strong and confident in her Lamaze birth-plan: she tries to educate
the others, and becomes a heroine: 'all the girls were cheering when
i went downstairs. i was / the one who told them to be tough, to
stop believing / in their mother's pain, that poison' (110). In a sense
it is the others, and their mothers, who turn out to be right, when
pain overtakes her. The vulnerable, pathetic 'children' are a mirror
of her own state. They represent a collective female fate from which
the heroine cannot escape through her superior knowledge of
natural childbirth ideas. Margaret Atwood, in 'Giving Birth', also

undercuts divisions by suggesting an underlying kinship between her natural childbirth heroine, and the 'other woman' who screams in agony (Atwood 1984).

Atwood's 'other woman' represents all that the heroine fears about the experience of motherhood: she is an unwilling mother, she has a painful birth, and later Jeanie even imagines her having postpartum depression. In a way, she is all that is censored from the cheerful, 'official' accounts. It is this dark 'underside' of motherhood that is explored most often in the comparisons fiction writers make with other pregnant women and mothers. The 'other' women present troubling images of what motherhood can be like, as a physical condition, and as a social role. As Paula Treichler writes, childbirth not only produces a baby, but 'simultaneously transforms the woman into a particular kind of social being, a mother' (Treichler 1990 117). Here, other social categories such as race and class inevitably play a part.

In Bowder's *Birth Rites* (1983) and Drabble's *The Millstone* (1966), we find a fear of motherhood as both a bodily condition and, implicitly, a social role. In Buchi Emecheta's *Second-Class Citizen* (1974, 1987), on the other hand, the heroine comes from a society where motherhood *raises* rather than lowers social status, and her encounter with 'other', white mothers in Britain provides a picture of the privileges they enjoy that she, as a poor Black woman immigrant, does not have. In all three novels, contrasts with other mothers of different classes or race are dramatised by encounters in British National Health Service (NHS) hospitals. The NHS, offering health care to all since 1944, regardless of class or income, theoretically acts as a great equaliser, but also reveals divisions between women assumed by the official discourses about childbirth to be all the same, merely because of their biological predicament. This creates a different situation from that in the USA, where, as Ehrenreich and English (1979) point out, nearly all the male experts' pronouncements and practices concerning childbirth and the 'nature' of women were directed at middle-class women, while lower-class women were left to fend for themselves, or treated as experimental material. There is a similar class division in the pre-NHS Dick Read, though he admires the way lower-class women so efficiently fend for themselves. While Read's description of his 'primitive woman' stresses exotic details like the 'sub-tropical sun' and the attitudes of 'the natives' (Read 1933 40), suggesting an incident taking place in some far-distant tribe, in his official biography it transpires that the description is based on an incident in *Belgium*, during the First World War (Thomas 1957 56). The woman is a Belgian peasant, upon whom Read projects his stereotype of the primitive woman. He only went to Africa much later in his career. His main experiences of seemingly painless childbirths were among working-class women in the East End of London, and he devotes some space in *Natural Childbirth* to arguing that the working classes are more 'primitive' in their mental development than the middle classes (Read 1933 44). It is class, rather than race, that shapes Read's attitude to motherhood. He upholds a very Victorian distinction between healthy, hardy, independent working-class women, and frail, helpless middle-class women who need male help and protection.

Motherhood and class

The paradoxes of the British NHS are summed up by Caroline Bowder's heroine: 'Xenia thanked the National Health for being the great leveller. Then became annoyed at herself for caring whether other people were classier than herself or not' (Bowder 1983 222). She is acutely aware of the class status of all the other mothers on the ward, and of their *maternal* status: the further absorbed in motherhood they are, the more loathsome and threatening they appear. Obviously, Xenia is objectifying her own fears of motherhood as absorption into the body, and into a mindless social role. Her very name, Xenia, suggests her distance, her 'foreignness' to this institution dedicated to the production of mothers. Her fear and loathing centre on a woman called Wendy, who sits in bed knitting 'like a large spider knitting her web and awaiting new prey' (35). Wendy becomes the representative of a certain kind of women: 'they are protected by their fanatical involvement in the material processes of life – eating, being comfortable, nest-building and reproducing'; they have given up 'politics or the arts' as 'too difficult to understand'; instead, they 'stick strictly to the limitations of husband, family and home' (36).

Wendy's absorption in the body paradoxically leads to Xenia seeing her as an automaton, a 'plastic' person, 'programmed to give out only encouraging signals' (Bowder 1983 35). Xenia's horror at

Wendy is expanded into a generalised horror at 'other women' as a category (36, 76). Wendy's all-pervasiveness is underlined when another woman joins the ward, whom Xenia names 'the second Wendy'. These two conduct a mindless conversation, 'so punctuated by well-worn phrases that they seemed almost to be taking each other off' (69), 'confirming each other in their view of life as a series of domestic tasks' (109). This satire of the mindless conversation of 'other' women in the maternity ward repeats closely a scene in Drabble's *The Millstone*, as we will see, where a middle-class heroine holds herself aloof from the meaning of maternity for lower-class women. Wendy is not in fact working class: she seems to come from a stiflingly conformist, comfortable, lower middle-class background. She encapsulates the bourgeois values that the 'artistic' Xenia shuns. The working-class representative on the ward is Mrs Long, who stands for 'real' experience through suffering and hardship. She exemplifies a gritty working-class authenticity, 'like the seams of coal in an opencast mine' (39), telling Xenia 'about her life and hard times: her love for her other children, her lack of money' (40).

Where, then, is Xenia's position in all this? She must in some ways be very close to the Wendies in status, to be so afraid of them: motherhood will turn her into a housewife. But she defends herself from it by clinging to definitions of herself as a glamorous, sexy woman, and as an intellectual, artistic one. The two women she does admire and identify with on the ward, Elise and Lucy, fall into the categories of the glamorous and the artistic. Sexual attractiveness opposes the gross physicality of maternity; artistic pretensions assert her as *mind*, not just body. Lucy is immediately identified as an ally, as she recognises a literary allusion Xenia has made, and notices the volume of poetry Xenia is trying to read. Lucy restores pictures and paints, we discover. Elise is remarkable for her beauty, which she loses after a traumatic Caesarean, but reassuringly regains, leaving the hospital as 'some glamorous woman one would hardly hope to know' (Bowder 1983 214). While the Wendies represent what Xenia fears to become, Elise and Lucy represent what she aspires to. In the same way, as we will see, the women Buchi Emecheta's heroine meets on her maternity ward represent her aspirations, and we find in both books very similar leaving scenes, when friendships begun in hospital cannot be sustained outside. Xenia asks for Lucy's address as she leaves, but Lucy does not ask for hers. Lucy 'unconvincingly' says she wants to meet later, and gives a rather 'high class' address.

As well as identifying with these glamorous and artistic women, Xenia also sets up barriers to protect herself from the Wendies of the ward. Her sexuality is represented by her 'luxuriant auburn' hair, 'her great defense, her great display', behind which she can hide. She affirms her intellectual and artistic pretensions by hiding herself behind a series of books: her French novel is 'a barrier, both physical and intellectual. First, it said, "Don't disturb me, I am reading," then it said, "This is a foreign language which you, O passer-by, are too stupid to be able to penetrate."' It transports her from the physicality of the ward 'into the echoing passages of European abstractions' (Bowder 1983 25). This scene of a pregnant woman defending her identity against the medical institution and/or other pregnant women by reading a book recurs in women's fictional depictions of birth. As all these depictions are themselves literary, and part of a literary tradition, the importance of books here seems very significant. The novel or poetry book (as opposed to the knitting or the woman's magazine) declares the class status of the woman; it represents an assertion of identity in an impersonal institution; and it also represents a clinging to intellect, the mind versus the mindless maternal body.

Bowder's heroine reads a French novel, Keats's poetry (in the loo), and makes literary allusions to Wilfred Owen and Hopkins. Reading is opposed to knitting, which she eschews because 'her mind was engaged on higher things like poetry and modern European literature' (Bowder 1983 132). In Byatt's *Still Life*, Stephanie is deprived by the nurses of the volume of Wordsworth she had brought to read during the early stages of labour; she sees her first baby in terms of Wordsworth's *Immortality Ode*, and her second experience of childbirth in terms of the dark river in Dickens's *Our Mutual Friend*, which she has managed to keep hold of and read during labour. Margaret Drabble's heroine, Rosamund, is interrupted while reading a book in the antenatal clinic, by a child who stands on her foot, and then a mother who asks her to hold her extremely heavy baby: the scene suggests the interruption of Rosamund's academic career by the facts of motherhood. In Doris Betts's story, Gwen protests that she has nothing to read. In a less 'literary' context, Margaret Atwood and Toi Derricote's heroines cling onto their natural childbirth textbooks, and Sheila

Kitzinger's pupils cling onto their written birth-plans, implicitly asserting their intellectual control of the situation, as opposed to their less instructed sisters.

As we can see from some of these scenes, loss of the book implies loss of control, of mind, and a corresponding engulfment in the physicality of maternity. This process happens to Xenia too; while she attempts to distance herself from the Wendies, the very process of becoming a mother is making her like them:

> listening to her own voice, she realised that it sounded like somebody else's, and that she was becoming like Wendy. . . . all the women on the ward, including herself, were to a greater or lesser extent Wendies. . . . On the spectrum she had seen herself at one extreme (the spiritual) and the Wendy [sic] at the other. . . . But it is inevitable, Xenia realised, being female, to find oneself speeding along the spectrum, imperceptibly, away from the spiritual of pure Xenia into the maternal of Wendy.
>
> (Bowder 1983 195)

This insight is involved with a greater sense of solidarity with the other women: 'Having started so detached, she now wanted to be more approachable' (195); 'The women could be seen as allies. She now craved to be accepted by them, though five minutes before she had not seen them as real people' (184). Xenia is having to come to terms with the maternal role, instead of projecting it onto caricatured, unreal 'others'. The fact that the glamorous and independent Elise and Lucy desert her at the end suggests she cannot, and perhaps no longer wants to, escape the physical and social limitations that come with the role of mother.

Acceptance into the community of the ward as an acceptance of maternity also appears in Lessing's *A Proper Marriage*, where 'the woman in the next bed' provides advice and companionship, as well as solidarity against the institutional practices of the nursing-home: 'she disliked the discipline as much as Martha did, and yet could dismiss it all as another of those unaccountable bureaucratic stupidities thought up to plague honest females'. Martha takes this woman as a 'guide', and through her is 'accepted into this community of women'. The other woman provides reassurance, but also arouses misgivings as a role model for the new mother: she is 'frightening', 'because she had three children and was so satisfied to be a maternal housewife', but also 'inexpressibly comforting' (Lessing 1977 170). Martha's doubts and fears are somewhat confirmed when the woman leaves, and while in bed she had seemed 'light and easy', on her feet she is 'heavy and shapeless' (171). We will find this fear of the heavy and shapeless maternal woman repeated in Drabble's *The Millstone*.

Lessing's *Proper Marriage* and Bowder's *Birth Rites* are comparatively open and self-conscious about their heroines' race and class consciousness, and how these affect their very ambivalent feelings about motherhood, through identifications with other mothers. Drabble's *The Millstone* and Emecheta's *Second-Class Citizen*, however, partially conceal anxieties about class, motherhood and race under a cover of maternal solidarity. Drabble's heroine, Rosamund, is the only middle-class woman in a clinic and ward of working-class women; Emecheta's heroine is the only Black woman in a ward of whites. Rosamund's story is presented as one of increasing, educative identification with other, underprivileged mothers, but in the end class identity is more important for her than female solidarity: maternity threatens her with the loss of her middle-class economic independence. For Emecheta's heroine, Adah, female solidarity is valuable, but partly because it seems to offer her a chance to escape racist and sexist oppression through an identification with white middle-class women. This surface solidarity is, however, undercut by racial tensions. While Rosamund shows the same kind of loathing for the maternal female body that we found in Bowder's and Lessing's heroines, and projects it onto women of a different class, as Xenia does, Adah has no such doubts about motherhood as a physical or social role. Instead, she projects fantasies of unattainable economic and marital privilege onto the white 'other women'.

Under cover of a rhetoric of solidarity, Drabble's *The Millstone* enacts a repudiation of the other women encountered through the NHS, in terms of class and of maternity: their disgusting bodies and their lack of social status go together as what the intellectual Rosamund rejects. *The Millstone* is centred on the birth of Rosamund's illegitimate baby. As Rosamund decides to bring up the baby on her own, there is no question of her being stuck in the housewife role that so appalls Lessing and Bowder: she easily escapes the physical and social problems that weigh down the other women. The birth of her baby, in one reading of the novel, is supposed to put the middle-class intellectual Rosamund in touch with both 'womanhood' (Drabble 1966 36) and 'reality'

(172), but the scenes involving the NHS reveal that for her class identity is stronger than female solidarity, which is undercut by a contradictory combination of guilt about her privilege and pride in her difference. This is not, however, how the scenes are overtly presented: they offer themselves as part of Rosamund's education in sympathy with the sufferings of other, working-class, women, in which she now finds herself participating. Nancy S. Hardin reads the scenes in this way, claiming that Rosamund's 'movement is from an intellectual position . . . to a real social awareness which only participation can bring about. . . . The National Health Clinic offers her the first insights of understanding. . . . First comes her heightened awareness of the "others", and second, even more important, her identification with them' (Hardin 1973 31–2). But if we look at the way the 'other' women are described, the narrow terms within which they are constructed, a different message of repudiation emerges – a message in which author colludes with narrator, since we are given no hint of another viewpoint from which to see these women (Spitzer 1978 230). Passive and disgusting victims, they are the creations of a distancing pity which easily switches over into loathing and ridicule.

Rosamund's first visits to an NHS doctor and then to the antenatal clinic are presented as 'an initiation into a new way of life, a way that was thenceforth to be mine forever. An initiation into reality, if you like', as she discovers 'a population whose existence I had hardly noticed' (Drabble 1966 36). But despite the rhetoric of participation, Rosamund keeps herself apart from the others, and quickly escapes again from the constraints of their way of life. The distancing is made easier by the mingled pity and loathing with which the other pregnant women are described:

> I was reduced almost to tears by the variety of human misery that presented itself. Perhaps I was in no mood for finding people cheery, attractive or encouraging, but the truth is that they looked to me an unbelievably depressed and miserable lot. . . . Anaemia and exhaustion were written on most countenances: the clothes were dreadful, the legs swollen, the bodies heavy and unbalanced.
>
> (57)

This view of her fellow patients may be just a product of Rosamund's 'mood', but nowhere are we given any counter to it. Rosamund may be projecting her fear of her own female body onto

these women, but it is significant that they are lower-class women.
By having a baby, not only will Rosamund become 'female', she
could also become declassed – motherhood 'is a disadvantaged
social status' (Oakley 1983 118).

At this point, Rosamund recognises both her distance from and
her inclusion with the other women: 'it struck me that I felt nothing
in common with any of these people, that I disliked the look of
them, that I felt a stranger and a foreigner there, and yet I was
one of them, I was like that too. I was trapped in a human limit
for the first time in my life, and I was going to have to learn to
live inside it' (Drabble 1966 58). But as Colin Butler perceptively
notices, 'at the crucial point the line of thought turns inward and
contemplative', to a rather abstract idea of her own entrapment,
not to solidarity or companionship with the other women (Butler
1978 360). Likeness is again both affirmed and denied in a specific
encounter with another woman at the clinic. The encounter carries
strong symbolic overtones, especially when read in conjunction
with the title of the book, and like the title its meaning becomes
blurred and dissipated when looked at closely (Spitzer 1978 228).
Rosamund is asked by another woman to hold her baby while she
sees the midwife. Rosamund sits 'with this huge and monstrously
heavy child sitting warm and limp upon my knee. . . . I was amazed
by his weight. . . . it was the first time I had ever held a baby'
(Drabble 1966 70). Later, Rosamund sees the woman in the street,
hampered by her children and her six-month pregnancy, and the
weight is again stressed and given symbolic significance:

> She stood there, patiently waiting, like a warning, a portent, like a
> figure from another world. Five months earlier I would have passed
> her without another glance, but now the weight of her child was
> heavy in my arms. . . . I do not know how she could get along that
> road. Nor could I feel that weight till my own arms had tested it.
>
> (71)

Not only is 'no action taken which would lead these encounters
beyond an acknowledgement of "sad necessity"', but the implication that Rosamund will come to share in the oppressions of
motherhood comes to nothing (Butler 1978 360). Rosamund tells
us she did not fully understand the meaning of the incident 'until
after the birth of my own child' (Drabble 1966 71) – we assume
that she is also going to feel this 'weight', and the title, *The*

Millstone, encourages this reading. But her baby turns out to be no kind of impediment: she has a relatively quick, uncomplicated delivery, she immediately regains her figure, and her baby in no way prevents her from finishing her thesis and getting a well-paid academic job. She escapes the conditions that weigh down the other woman. What then is the other woman a 'warning' of? Of the dangers of being lower class, it seems: Rosamund mystifies her into 'a figure from another world', but only too literally she is in another social and economic world, and shared femaleness does not enable Rosamund to make contact.

Rosamund's preference of class identity over female identity is made quite clear in the subsequent scenes in the maternity ward – there is no longer any pretence of participation with other women, all the effort is directed towards marking herself off from them. In the ward, the mothers are presented as in competition with each other, a competition that focuses on comparisons between babies, cards and gifts, and visitors. Rosamund wins on all counts: she is 'fortified by the superior beauty and intelligence of my child', and her friend Lydia arranges an excess of gifts, finally embarrassing Rosamund at the thought of the 'other less gifted mothers' (Drabble 1966 103, 104). One of her visitors is recognised as a television personality: 'I felt my stock would rise through the association' (104). We learn that 'surprisingly enough, my stay in hospital was one of the more cheerful and sociable patches of my life', but not, it transpires, because of any fraternisation with the other mothers. Instead, Rosamund sees herself as holding a salon for her middle-class friends: 'I felt as near to belonging to a Circle as I have ever done. My ways and my acquaintance were defined, made more precious and more themselves, by contrast with those of the other women in the ward' (111). The experience thus only confirms her in her class identity, and the other women are described with the same mixture of pity and revulsion as before, together with a new note of ridicule. Rosamund makes fun of the tedious conversation of her neighbours ('Woman A', 'Woman B' and 'Woman C' – dehumanisation could hardly go further), who talk endlessly and illogically about such trivial subjects as what their families eat, and how to wash clothes, without ever listening to each other. The others are presented as stupid and uneducated, like Bowder's 'Wendies', and are again more disgusting and pitiable in their female physicality than Rosamund:

After the birth, the muscles of my belly snapped back into place
without a mark, but some of the women looked as big as they
had looked before. I am haunted even now by a memory of the
way they walked, large and tied into shapeless dressing gowns,
padding softly and stiffly, careful not to disturb the pain that still
lay between the legs.

(109)

Like the pregnant woman with the two children, these women are
reduced to ghostly symbols in Rosamund's mind, emblems of what
she so easily escapes and distances herself from.

The political assumptions behind Rosamund's repudiation of
other women are made clear in a later hospital scene. Her baby,
Octavia, has had to have heart surgery. After the operation, the
nurses try to prevent Rosamund visiting her baby, but after
uncharacteristically making a scene, Rosamund is allowed to
visit as often as she wants. There is, however, only one other
mother taking advantage of what is supposed to be the hospital's
policy of open visiting for parents, and Rosamund asks her about
the problem of the 'others', 'Those that don't even get in. Those
without money. Those without influence. Those who would not
dare to have hysterics'. The other mother sadly reassures her: 'My
concerns are my concerns, and that's where it ends. I haven't
the energy to go worrying about other people's children. They're
nothing to do with me. I only have enough time to worry about
myself. If I didn't put myself and mine first, they wouldn't survive.
So I put them first, and the others can look after themselves'
(Drabble 1966 140). *This* is the 'reality' that Rosamund is being
educated in. She can do nothing for these 'other' women, and
the possibility has never even arisen that, when they were all in the
same female predicament, they could have done anything for her. The
NHS scenes pinpoint this victory of class over maternal solidarity.

Drabble is putting forward an early version of Thatcherite
individualism, or perhaps the 'I'm alright, Jack' attitude of the
Macmillan years. An equally political, but diametrically opposed,
attitude to the 'others' is taken by Vera Brittain in her pre-NHS
novel, *Honourable Estate*, from the left rather than the right.
Ruth's birth experience, when her life is saved by the hospital,
arouses in her feelings of solidarity with other birthing women,
across history and across class. As she struggles to get to the
hospital (there is no transport because of the General Strike,

which she supports), she remembers Agnes, her grandmother's maid, turned from the house when her pregnancy was discovered: 'This is how Agnes must have felt' (Brittain 1936 540). She feels it is 'damned good for a lady socialist, a Staffordshire bourgeoise', 'to know what life's like without any conveniences' (540–1). After she recovers, she wonders 'suppose I'd been a working man's wife, with no salary to help me pay my doctor's bills, and no private income to meet the expense of staying in this nursing-home till the twins are safely over their first weeks and I've had all the rest I need?' (546). All this leads to a political aim: to stand for Parliament and to 'do what I can for women in small houses for whom the process of birth has no mitigations of comfort or decency' (547). This ideal could be seen as what led to the NHS.

As well as a socialist aim, Ruth has a feminist one: the birth makes her sympathise with her frustrated mother-in-law, Janet, the woman who had the painful home birth and who had the 'sinful' attitude to motherhood. Comparing their lives, Ruth reasons to her husband, 'Don't you see that it is just because I *am* better qualified than your mother and still able to go on with my work, that I care for the twins so much? Naturally a woman with strong political interests resented a child when public opinion insisted that he ought to monopolise her whole time to the exclusion of everything else!' (Brittain 1936 550). What is interesting in *The Millstone* is the way in which, by the 60s, the feminist aim has separated out from the socialist one: Rosamund is well able to combine career and motherhood, but this separates her from other, less privileged mothers; her feminism is entirely individualistic:

> 'My mother, you know, was a great feminist. She brought me up to be equal. She made there be no questions, no difference. I was equal. I am equal. You know what her creed was? That thing that Queen Elizabeth said about thanking God that she had such qualities that if she were turned out in her petticoat in any part of Christendom, she would whatever it was that she would do.'
> (Drabble 1966 12)

'Feminism' means equality with men, not solidarity with women; it means independent individualism, not community. The ideals of female solidarity of earlier and later women's movements are not available in England in 1966. Again, the example of Queen Elizabeth provides an uncanny premonition of the imagery

surrounding Mrs Thatcher. Mrs Thatcher, like Rosamund, is a
mother who allowed no feelings of solidarity for other women
to stand in the way of her career. Rosamund, like Mrs Thatcher,
could be seen as the male-identified career woman, which would
go a long way towards explaining her loathing for other women's
maternal bodies.

Race, class and motherhood

Buchi Emecheta's novel, *Second-Class Citizen* (1974, 1987), high-
lights a different complex of assumptions about class, gender
and race in an episode in an NHS hospital. Though Emecheta's
heroine, Adah, is, like Rosamund, ambivalent in her attitude to the
other inmates of her maternity ward, unlike Rosamund she does
experience there a sense of female community which sustains her in
her subsequent life, giving her a more confident sense of her rights
as a woman. By the time of her encounter with the NHS maternity
services, Adah's position in regard to class is complicated and
confused by issues both of gender and race. Her job in a library,
and her education, qualify her for the middle class. But, as a woman
looking after several children and a husband, who neither earns nor
helps with childcare, she is economically declassed. The patriarchal
attitudes her husband, Francis, brings from their Nigerian culture
also serve to demote her socially and economically: he takes her
money and controls her actions. Racism chiefly seems to affect her
in regard not to employment, but to housing. Crowded, substandard
housing contributes to her feeling of being declassed, of being classed
as a 'poor nigger woman', not a member of Nigeria's elite, as she
once was.

How then does the birth of children fit into Adah's world? In
Nigeria it does not confer 'womanhood' in any abstract sense,
rather it confers a precise social status: 'in her society she could
only be sure of the love of her husband and the loyalty of her
parents-in-law by having and keeping alive as many children
as possible'. Boys are worth more than girls, and can give the
mother 'the status of a man in the tribe' (Emecheta 1987 68).
Having many children is no problem for Adah in Nigeria, where
she has servants to look after them, but in England she greets each
pregnancy with dismay, fearing she will lose her job. On the other

hand, pregnancy and child-rearing are not presented as the totally crippling burden that they are for poor women in *The Millstone*. Rosamund, we are told, only escapes this burden because of her class and her money, but Adah battles on and manages to keep both her job and her children. After her fourth child, she does give up work, but easily organises her time in order to write a book. Alice Walker comments on this refreshing lack of the 'traditional Western' conflict between artistic creativity and childcare, and links it to Adah's African background: 'Just as the African mother has traditionally planted crops, pounded maize, and done her washing with the baby strapped to her back, so Adah can write a novel with her children playing in the same room' (Walker 1984 69). Is Lessing's Martha perhaps right about the easier attitude to maternity of her African native woman? Walker's explanation finds some confirmation in Emecheta's book, when English and Nigerian attitudes to child-rearing are contrasted:

> At home in Nigeria, all a mother had to do for her baby was wash and feed him and, if he was fidgety, strap him on to her back and carry on with her work while that baby slept. But in England she had to wash piles and piles of nappies, wheel the child round for sunshine during the day, attend to his feeds as regularly as if one were serving a master, talk to the child, even if he were only a day old!
>
> (Emecheta 1987 50)

Though she is now in England, Adah clearly retains some of this matter-of-fact Nigerian attitude. Motherhood is not charged with such high positive or negative implications as it is in *The Millstone* or *Birth Rites*. There is no need for Adah to separate herself off from other mothers, or to despise her own female body: motherhood does not threaten to engulf her whole identity as it does Rosamund's or Xenia's.

Adah is not so much worried about motherhood as about poverty. At first, she is planning to have this baby at home, because she will not have to buy the equipment needed for a hospital stay – nightdresses, housecoat, etc. Instead, the NHS will pay her six pounds, which she plans to use to feed her family for a week. But Adah has to have a Caesarean, and ends up in hospital anyway, where the lack of a nightdress acts as a focus for her anxieties, as she compares herself to the other women, and also as a catalyst in her realisation that Francis is her enemy. Interestingly, the importance of the nightdress as a marker of status also features in *The Millstone*, where Rosamund, of course, has a superior 'garment covered in Mexican embroidery', which 'drew screams of admiration' from the nurses (Drabble 1966 102). And as in *The Millstone*, cards, gifts, flowers, visitors and babies are all compared to establish the status of the women in the ward. But while Rosamund sees the situation as a competition she is winning, Adah's anxious comparisons are presented as an effect of her deprivation, a paranoid reading of the situation.

Throughout the account of Adah's stay in the maternity ward, there is a tension between her fears about the other women's prejudiced reactions to her as a poor Black woman, and the narrator's sometimes intrusive insistence that these fears are only paranoid imaginings. The narrator's version is backed up by Adah sometimes also feeling a sense of community with the other women, especially so when she looks back on the experience, and sees it as something of a missed opportunity, spoiled by her groundless suspicions. Yet where did these suspicions come from, if society is largely composed of women like those on the ward? Are only men racist, or is it only the working class who are? These issues are not faced up to – the suspicions are explained away as caused by Adah's personal experiences within her own culture. Adah at this point has more to gain from a gender and class identification with the other women than from a racial identification, but her unexplained suspicions of racism suggest the contradictions in her position that cannot be fully suppressed.

Adah finds herself on a 'big open' hospital ward. The other women are first seen as mostly 'young mothers like herself', not as a quite different species. There is a communal spirit present, and Adah only feels 'singled out' because of her pain, and the tubes and drips that hamper her movement and speech: 'These women were all happy and free. They seemed to have known each other for years and years' (Emecheta 1987 120). It is the other women who give her the will to live: 'They were kind, those women in the ward. For the first few days, when Adah was deciding whether it was worth struggling to hold on to this life, those women kept showing her many things' (121). In particular, there is one woman who has had a child after waiting seventeen years. She keeps showing the baby around, and Adah at first resents this, seeing it as competitive. But then she is told the truth, and annoyance changes to sympathy, as she 'imagined herself in the woman's position' (122). Similarly, the 'sleek woman' in the bed next to her has endless gifts and visits from a handsome, attentive husband, but Adah's envy and resentment is undercut by sympathy when she learns that the woman was an adopted child:

> Why was it she could never be loved as an individual, the way the sleek woman was being loved, for what she was and not just because she could work and hand over her money like a docile child? . . . All Adah could see at the moment was the sleek girl being kissed and loved. . . . She did not think of what life was like for a little girl who was aware that she was adopted; that the little girl might sometimes wonder whether her parents ever wanted her?
>
> (126)

Here we are presented with the kind of rhetoric of 'unfairness' that Rosamund uses in *The Millstone*, but from the other side. As Rosamund puts it, 'Life is not fair. . . . It is unfair on every score and every count and in every particular, and those who . . . attempt to level it out are doomed to failure' (Drabble 1966 84). But this reading of the situation is undercut by the narrator's sympathy for the other women, the implication of shared suffering. Moreover, if we look closely at what Adah is envying in the other two, it is nothing innate or irreversible, but rather the way they are treated by their husbands. These comparisons lead her into further realisation and resentment of Francis's oppression of her, a realisation produced by her identification with the other women.

But there are still times when Adah does feel cut off from the other women by her race and class – she imagines the others and their visitors saying:

> *Look at that nigger woman with no flowers, no cards, no visitors, except her husband who usually comes in five minutes before the closing time, looking as if he hates it all. Look at her, she doesn't even have a nightdress of her own. Is she from Holloway, from a prison? Only patients from prison wear hospital dresses in the ward.*
>
> (Emecheta 1987 130)

But we are reassured by the italics that these are only Adah's imaginings, and again we see her focusing on Francis's behaviour. She determines to make him buy her some nightdresses, as 'Coming into hospital had opened her eyes a good deal. Why, many English men took home their wives' nightdresses to wash them. She was determined to try it all on Francis' (131). But Francis, when he arrives, finally reveals his true colours, proposing to spend some extra money Adah has been given on another course for himself. This precipitates a row, and she declares, '"I hate you now, Francis, and one day I shall leave you"'(133). She lacks energy to demand the several beautiful nightdresses that she had wanted, and gets one ugly one: 'She did not bother to show it round as she had planned, because she was not proud of it. . . . So for the rest of her stay she learnt another rule. She should keep to herself' (134). But this is again seen as a consequence of her treatment by Francis – it is he who is keeping her from the other women: 'If she got herself involved in any kind of gossip or conversation, she might be lured to talk about herself, about her children and also her husband. She did not want to do that any more. There was nothing to talk about' (134).

From this point on, Adah becomes more and more separate from the other women, refusing opportunities to make contact. But there are continual hints that she is mistaken in her attitude, and after she has left she suddenly regrets these missed opportunities, and sees the experience in retrospect as uniquely valuable. The first opportunity comes when the 'sleek woman' with the attractive husband leaves the ward. She is only going to another ward, but the question comes up of whether contacts made in the hospital can be continued outside. Adah is checked in her friendship by her sense of class differences:

> she was tempted to act just as she would have in Nigeria. She wanted to ask the lady for her address, but something in the lady's politeness stopped her. It was the type of politeness one usually associated with high intelligence. She could talk to Adah in the hospital ward, she could joke with her, she could tell her the story of her life, because she knew they would never meet again . . .
>
> (Emecheta 1987 135)

This is very odd, as we know Adah herself is intelligent, and prides herself on her education: Adah seems to be falsely undervaluing herself here. This suggestion that friendships made on the ward *could* be continued outside is reversed in Bowder's *Birth Rites*, where Xenia is given the brush-off by the superior Lucy, and reflects, 'of friendship, and that close relationship with other women, what remained? Elise? Lucy? They had sped on into their own lives, like actresses leaving after a show' (Bowder 1983 230). Adah again misses opportunities for connection when she herself leaves. She sees it as an 'ordeal': 'You dressed yourself and your new baby in its brand new clothes and new shawl. Then the baby would be shown round in his first civilian clothes, and everybody would coo and remark on how smart he looked' (Emecheta 1987 135). Shame at her poverty intrudes: the shawl has been much used and is off-white. The narrator sympathises, but also suggests Adah is over-reacting: 'to twenty-year-old Adah, a new shawl was the end of the world' (136). Adah hides in the corridor, while a nurse shows round the baby. Adah imagines the women are 'all laughing at her and saying "poor nigger!", while in fact the nurse is 'showing them all . . . that this was their special baby, born miraculously'. Adah wonders, 'Did these women in the ward really admire her baby or were they just curious to see what a new African baby looked like?' (137). Again, it is suggested that these fears are only her imaginings when she starts to regret the lost opportunity of saying goodbye to 'these women who were doing their best to be friendly', but now it is too late: 'She could never get that very same group of people, in the same ward having their babies, again' (138).

The hospital stay is seen in retrospect as a uniquely valuable · female communal experience. It has taught Adah to respond to friendliness, a 'new code of conduct', learned 'from staying together with other women for thirteen days', which 'was to be with her for a long time'. The fears and suspicions that kept her from fully participating in the female community are explained not as her internalisation of racial prejudice but as the effect, again, of her 'betrayal' by Francis and his family, their lack of love for her: 'Was it this betrayal of Francis and his people that made her so suspicious of the women in the ward?' (Emecheta 1987 138). She has more to gain from identifying herself as an oppressed woman, and making common cause with other women, than from a racial identification.

The hospital scenes might give the impression that it is only with white or professional women that Adah wants to identify herself, to escape her 'second-class' label. But soon after we have a scene in the Family Planning Clinic, where Adah deliberately sits down next to a young West Indian mother, so as to feel 'on home ground', and so she can hold the other woman's baby when she goes in to be equipped, and vice versa (Emecheta 1987 157). Racial and maternal identification operates here, and we have a neat comparison with the scene in *The Millstone* in which Rosamund holds the other woman's baby. This idea of being 'on home ground' with another Black woman is in interesting contradiction with Adah's earlier attempts to distance herself from the uneducated, lower-class Nigerians she was forced to live with. Questions of the woman's class or education do not enter her mind here. Obviously, in contrast to the fears and suspicions aroused by her encounter with white women in the ward, she need fear no racism from this woman. In addition, by this point in the novel it is Black *men* like Francis from whom she is distancing herself, and the patriarchal culture he represents. An identification with other women, through the shared experience of reproduction, has helped her to attain this distance.

Despite her visit to the clinic, Adah does get pregnant again (Francis disapproves of birth control, and finds out where she has been). This time she is determined not to be humiliated: 'she was not going to that hospital as a poor nigger woman. . . . She addressed twenty greeting-cards to herself. . . . Two big bunches of flowers were to be sent to her, one on her arrival, with Francis's name attached to it with sentimental words' (Emecheta 1987 175). She goes home in a taxi, 'in style', not telling the others that 'Francis had refused to come for her' (177). Again, it is Francis's shortcomings that she is covering up. This is all we learn about her second hospital stay – all this pretence in order to gain an appearance of equality may make it easier for her to relate to the other women on the ward, to seem the same, but also must surely cut her off from any real reciprocity.

In Adah's hospital experiences, a sense of identity with other women both undercuts and intertwines with class and race identifications. Adah rejects the 'second-class' status that comes with her race in England, and identifies herself as an oppressed woman, who aspires to become one of the (comparatively) liberated women she is brought into contact with. But she is not able to transcend her consciousness of the economic differentials between herself as a poor Black woman and the others as (comparatively) rich white women, and the class connotations that go with these differences. A combination of shame and pride conspires to cut her off from the other women, while she struggles to *appear* as economically privileged as they are. The shame and pride are intensified by her sense of once having been part of an economically privileged elite herself. She is also ashamed of and conceals what she sees as her poverty *as a woman* – that is, her oppression by Francis: this again cuts her off from real participation in the female community, unless the price of participation is that all the women should indeed appear the 'same' in terms of their lives outside the hospital. It is interesting that in both *The Millstone* and *Second-Class Citizen*, markers of outside status – nightdresses, cards, gifts, flowers, visitors – are obsessively focused on, and it is these seemingly trivial markers of difference that the experience is *about*, not the shared sufferings or triumphs of the motherhood which is what brings these women together in the first place.

The kind of female solidarity in childbirth between Black and white women that is both longed for and questioned in *Second-Class Citizen* appears with similar ambiguities in Toni Morrison's *Beloved* (1987). Here, the birth takes place in the open, with no medical attendance, in nineteenth-century America, rather than in the British NHS hospital. The Black woman, Sethe, gives birth; the white woman, Amy, is not another mother, but an impromptu birth attendant. What brings them together is not the socialist state, but a shared (though not equal) oppression. Both are runaways, Sethe from slavery, Amy from a life as an indentured servant. Both are marginalised figures: 'A patroller passing would have sniggered to see two throw-away people, two lawless outlaws – a slave and a barefoot whitewoman with unpinned hair – wrapping a ten-minute-old baby in the rags they wore' (Morrison 1987 85). The scene allows that class can be a similar oppression to race, though the degrees of oppression are also made clear. Looking at Sethe's wounded back, Amy says, '"I had me some whippings, but I don't remember nothing like this"' (79).

The co-operation of the two women in birthing Sethe's baby sets up an ideal of female friendship across the racial divide. Denver, the baby concerned, later sees the story in this hopeful way: she sees a ghostly white dress embracing her mother, and thinks 'The dress and her mother together looked like two friendly grown-up women – one (the dress) helping out the other. And the magic of her birth, its miracle in fact, testified to that friendship as did her own name' (29). Denver's name commemorates Amy: '"She's never gonna know who I am. You gonna tell her? Who brought her

into this here world? . . . You better tell her. You hear? Say Miss
Amy Denver. Of Boston"' (85). Denver, miraculous child named
for the helpful white woman, is going to be the one to save her
mother, and to go on to a better future, helped by another white
woman, Miss Bodwin. Her birth can be read as a symbol of a
new co-operation between Black and white women, at the end of
slavery.

And yet this hopeful construction is also undercut. There are
ways in which the half-crazed Amy's help seems almost haphazard:
she is not that interested in Sethe, but is fixated on the idea of
getting on to Boston to buy velvet. And the trustworthiness of
white people is continually questioned in the novel. 'Good' white
people are scrupulously presented: Mr and Mrs Garner, Amy, Mr
and Miss Bodwin. But Sethe comes to question her belief that 'she
could discriminate among them. That for every schoolteacher there
would be an Amy; that for every pupil there was a Garner, or
Bodwin' (Morrison 1987 188). The Garners' model of enlightened
slavery is nevertheless an exploitation, and fails with their deaths.
The non-racism of the Bodwins is questioned when Denver notices,
without comment, in their kitchen 'sitting on the shelf by the back
door, a blackboy's mouth full of money. His head was thrown
back. . . . And he was on his knees. . . . His mouth, wide as a
cup, held the coins needed to pay for a delivery or some other
small service. . . . Painted across the pedestal he knelt on were the
words "At Yo Service"' (255). Amy's helpfulness is not undercut in
such an obvious way – unlike the Garners and the Bodwins, she has
no power, though as a white person she would have had the power
to betray Sethe to the authorities as a runaway slave. Is it her
wandering wits, or her sense of solidarity that prevents this? It is
not clear. The co-operation of Black and white over Denver's birth
is allowed to remain as a *possibility* of female solidarity between
the races, brought about by the extremity of birth.

Remarkably, Sherley Anne Williams' *Dessa Rose* (1988) uses
childbirth in a similar way to bring Black and white women
together, in a story about slavery and freedom. The heroine, Dessa,
flees from prison while pregnant, after taking part in a slave revolt.
She gives birth on the flight, helped by one of the male ex-slaves:
the birth itself is minimally described. She regains consciousness at
the house of the white woman, Ruth, and one of the first things
she sees is Ruth suckling her (Dessa's) newborn baby. Given the

oppressive meanings of a Black woman suckling a white woman's child, to reverse the situation in this way has deep implications of equality and reciprocity. The incident foreshadows the hard-won friendship that eventually flowers between the two women: Dessa is at first very suspicious of the white woman suckling her baby; and Ruth has only done it in an absent-minded way. Through other shared experiences, such as Dessa helping Ruth to fend off a rape by a drunken white man, the women eventually come to trust and like each other. The implication is that the shared female experience of birth (Ruth is also suckling one of her own children) is part of what brings them together. Class is also a factor, as in *Beloved* – though Ruth is from a wealthy middle-class family, and her husband from the aristocracy, she has been declassed by loss of money and husband, and her isolation among Black people. Given an economic levelling, Morrison and Williams both suggest childbirth can operate as a cause and a sign of commonality and (eventual) friendship between women of different races.

Old wives

The totalising effect of the official discourse about childbirth is undercut in a whole number of ways: women writers show up differences of class and race where there is meant to be a uniform state of motherhood; they reveal highly ambivalent feelings about maternity, which is meant to be every woman's natural destiny; they assert solidarity between mothers and childless women, where there is meant to be a sharp division; they highlight the clash between the two dominant official versions of the birth-story, where there is only meant to be one 'true' version. In articulating the unacceptable, they are nearer to a third, marginalised, discourse about childbirth, the 'old wives' tale'. That is, the oral stories women tell each other about birth, especially those told by mothers to daughters. Not surprisingly, both 'official' discourses about birth fiercely repudiate the old wives' tales, yet it is surprising that the one type of story that comes from personal experience should be so rigorously suppressed. Partly it reflects the misogyny of the official versions: men have always tried to appropriate the birth experience, its management and its representation, from women. Partly, experts are jealously guarding the status and value of their expertise from encroachments by lay-people. The campaign against old wives' tales by experts has been so virulent and so effective, that we will find suspicion and repudiation of the old wives' tale even in women's accounts of birth that would seem to be a continuation of that tradition.

Medical experts' hostility to the old wives' tale can be represented by Gordon Bourne, who claims in his authoritative book on *Pregnancy* that 'the majority of old wives' tales are essentially destructive or demoralising. . . . Probably more is done by wicked women with their malicious lying tongues to harm the confidence and happiness of pregnant women than by any other single factor' (Bourne 1975 6, 7). O'Driscoll and Meagher are also concerned to protect their first-time mothers from other women who have actually experienced birth: they urge that primigravida should be kept apart from multigravida, since 'Parous women tend to have closed minds on the subject and are wont to extrapolate from what is a unique occasion in terms of personal experience'. These women have to undergo 'an exercise in rehabilitation' (O'Driscoll and Meagher 1980 67).

Interestingly, natural childbirth discourse shares this prejudice against the authority of the experience of women who have actually given birth. As we have seen, Dick Read is very concerned to establish the authority of the male obstetrician in childbirth. The primitive woman does not get to tell her own tale: she is observed and interpreted by the male expert. When it comes to putting his ideas into practice on British middle-class women, he finds a powerful adversary in the women's *mothers*, who also want to control the process, and pass on their own advice, their own version of the birth-story. As we saw, Read's 'bad' patients are unfeminine and dependent on dominant mothers; his 'good' patients are sexually attractive and dependent on strong husbands. The mothers are particularly censured for the *stories* they have told their daughters about their own experiences of childbirth: 'She had told her of the trials of childbirth . . . this girl had been introduced to all that was terrifying in parturition' (Read 1933 30).

Sheila Kitzinger, of course, has the authority of the experience of having given birth herself, yet she too is hostile to the gloomy stories of the old wives, preferring her cheerful, painless natural childbirth version. In *The Experience of Childbirth*, like Dick Read, she is suspicious and dismissive of the female oral tradition

of birth-stories and advice: 'the dread and horror that is associated
with most "old wives' tales", and the gory accounts of labour
which many women are able to produce for the benefit of expectant
mothers' (Kitzinger 1962 18). It is significant that the context
of this is Kitzinger's promotion of the *husband* as the ideal
birth-partner, who is to 'stand between his wife and the sceptics,
the bearers of old wives' tales and those who see birth as a sort
of major surgical operation' (100). He is to protect his wife not
just from soulless medical 'experts', but also from old wives and
their stories. As in Read, the elevation of the husband goes along
with a denigration of mothers: the later editions of *The Experience
of Childbirth* include a searing attack on dominant mothers as a
pernicious influence on daughters who cannot fully separate and
take on their own mothering role (Kitzinger 1984). In novels, too,
we often find that repudiation of old wives' tales goes along with
a repudiation of the heroine's mother, who is made to stand for
all the unacceptable meanings of motherhood.

Kitzinger's collection of real-life stories, *Giving Birth*, is more
ambivalent about old wives' tales; in a way, of course, the stories
are such tales. They exist in a context of inter-female intimacy
– Kitzinger's pupils are reporting back to their female mentor. It
is interesting, however, that actual mothers very rarely feature in
these accounts – Kitzinger has to some extent taken on the function
of the mother for these women: several accounts tell of a phone call
to her to seek advice and support at crucial moments of decision.
The traditional function of the oral birth-story is thus reversed in
these accounts: instead of the mother giving her story as advice
to the daughter, the daughter tells her story as a tribute to the
mother. Kitzinger's motherly advice, and her own story, appear in
the introduction, where she displays an ambiguous attitude to the
female oral tradition, and its relation to the purposes of her book.
She derides the insulting dictionary definition of 'old wives' tales',
and an obstetrician who advised patients 'never to talk to other
women at all about childbirth'. She insists that it is the medical
care system, and not other women, 'who instil and fuel anxiety in
most pregnant women' (Kitzinger 1987 16), and seems to be aligning
her book with the female oral tradition as a useful way for women
to share their experiences. But at the same time she deplores both
women's *reticence* in telling each other about childbirth, and certain
'other women who describe with apparent relish each ache and pain

and who flaunt obstetric difficulties as if they were rosettes, prizes for
having suffered in labour, to be exhibited proudly in front of those
who have not yet been put on trial' (15).

In emphasising women's reticence, and in reviving the stereotype
of the horrific old wives' tale, Kitzinger creates a place for her book
– if women were communicating usefully, there would be no need for
it. Moreover, as a self-appointed 'expert' herself, she must necessarily
be suspicious of folk-wisdom – when she does appeal to it, it is in the
reassuringly remote context of the 'Third World', where women still
have access to a culture of 'emotional support and sharing between
women' during childbirth (Kitzinger 1987 10). Her contradictory
attitude to the female oral tradition reflects the contradictory nature
of her book itself – women's first-hand accounts of birth, carefully
contained within several introductory and concluding chapters that
expand Kitzinger's own beliefs about birth. Thus the women's words
are being used in the service of an expert's advice book.

Ann Oakley's collection of oral birth-stories, *From Here To
Maternity*, on the other hand, has a different axe to grind. Oakley is
not posing as a birth-expert, and her book is dedicated to showing
up the differences between theory and her informants' experiences.
Oakley's book is much more favourable to the female oral tradition
as a source of both truth and support. The book itself is relying on
oral testimony, and the stories told by women to each other are
set against the 'official' versions adhered to by doctors and natural
childbirth educators. Several women recount their mothers' stories of
their own births, which often have the ring of folk-tales, celebrating
powerful women and extraordinary events. For instance:

> My mother had eleven; she nearly had me in a drill of potatoes. . . .
> she was digging potatoes and she felt all wet down one of her legs
> – that was the water breaking. She had her little case packed, my
> mother always had her little case packed, which a lot of women in
> Ireland didn't, they were very backward. She used to take her little
> case and run down the lane about half a mile and thumb a lift from
> anything that was going along the road to take her to hospital; it
> was 22 miles away.
>
> (Oakley 1981 78)

and

> She told me not to worry. She told me not to listen to anybody that
> only had one baby because she had seven and she lost two – one

set of twins after she had us. I came out bottom first, I was the second twin, I was the heaviest. . . . There was two midwives and two doctors – there was about twelve people all lining up in the passage – the blood unit, the flying squad, everybody. They were just worried in case anything happened because we was premature; we went to the hospital because my brother just fitted in the palm of my Mum's hand – he was that tiny.

(78)

Oakley does, however, include one woman who takes the official line on the female oral tradition: 'I'm not going to listen to my mother or my mother-in-law because they do go on. . . . They just describe how awful it was for them. . . . My mother said oh it was terrible; I had such a rotten time, of course it was because I've got a contracted pelvis: that was the trouble. I didn't listen. They rather *enjoy* telling you about it' (Oakley 1981 79). But it is interesting that Oakley later makes a point of telling us that this particular informant, 'who when pregnant refused to listen to her mother's tales about birth, is now beginning to wonder whether her mother might not be right after all' (193). The high value placed on mothers' verbal accounts contrasts with the continual repudiation of books and experts throughout the book. Oakley seems to be claiming the authenticity of the female oral tradition for her accounts. As responses to interviewers' questions they do not really qualify as mothers' birth-stories, which are traditionally occasioned as advice to other pregnant women, but a high degree of woman-to-woman intimacy seems to have been generated in the interviews, and one of the informants confesses that 'I could never speak to my own doctor about it. You see I feel like this, but I can talk to you about it and I can talk to my sister about it' (282).

On the other hand, inter-female intimacy about birth is presented as abhorrent and disgusting in several fictional accounts. In Margaret Drabble's *The Millstone*, the heroine tells us with distaste of the birth-stories told in the antenatal clinic: 'I hated most of all the chat about birth that went on so continually around me in the queue: everyone recounted their own past experiences, and those of their sisters and mothers and friends and grandmothers, and everyone else listened, spellbound, including me. . . . Birth, pain, fear and hope, these were the subjects that drew us together in gloomy awe' (Drabble 1966 60). The other women's birth-stories are part of their disgusting and degrading world of lower-class maternity, that the heroine so neatly avoids. She herself has an easy birth, with no complications: *The Millstone* is not itself an old wives' tale, it does not dwell on the physical details, or the pain and drama of the birth process. Caroline Bowder's *Birth Rites*, on the other hand, does: it goes into great detail not only on the routine of the hospital, but on the bodily experiences of the heroine and some of the other women on the ward. Mrs Long's particularly painful delivery is described at length, as is Xenia's nightmarish Caesarean. Part of the nightmare of maternal physicality that Xenia is subjected to is, as for Rosamund, the telling of gruesome old wives' tales by the other women: 'Mrs Long was their superior, the experienced, the thrice mother, and Xenia could not help listening as she told of the horrors . . . the details fascinating and repelling her at the same time' (Bowder 1983 16).

Mrs Long's experience, as we have seen, is accorded a certain gritty authenticity: not so the two 'Wendies', the maternal stereotypes, whose favourite topics of conversation are 'perinatal complications and obstetric histories. Points were scored for knowledge of multisyllabic words, pseudo-medical jargon and most extreme personal experience. . . . Xenia was to hear versions of the same conversation many times before she was released from the maternity ward' (Bowder 1983 73–4). Though Xenia distances herself here from the stories of the other women, the whole book *Birth Rites* is, in effect, one long old wives' tale. By caricaturing the form in the conversation of the two Wendies, it attempts to escape the bad reputation of women's talk about birth: accusations of triviality, melodramatic exaggeration, and trespass on the territory of the medical experts (those 'multisyllabic words'). A similar move is executed in A. S. Byatt's novel *Still Life*. Here, the birth-stories are not told as part of the communal life of the ward, but by a fearsome mother-in-law. Whether attributed to peers or to mothers, the old wives' tales seem to attach themselves to the threat of a suffocating maternal physicality. In Byatt's novel, the pregnant heroine is told several times by her obnoxious mother-in-law the story of her son's birth, 'a monodrama with its single character, brave and persecuted by men, authorities and inadequate nurses' (Byatt 1986 86). Though this account is mocked here, the heroine's own birth experiences could be summarised very much in this way – but the book seems unaware of the irony.

Doris Lessing's *A Proper Marriage* also attaches the old wives'
tale to a threatening mother-figure, Martha's mother, Mrs Quest.
Martha is trying to get her mother to reveal her feelings about
being pregnant with Martha, but all she gets is a standardised
account of 'the difficulties of the birth itself – a painful business,
this, as she had so often been told' (Lessing 1977 111). As we
have seen, Martha is terrified of repeating again the suffocating
emotional effect her mother has had on her. It is in order to
avoid her mother that she books herself into the nursing-home,
when Mrs Quest suggests a home birth supervised by herself.
Martha flees to the medical experts to escape the old wives. Yet the
nursing-home and its ideology do not save her from the painfulness
of birth, though the African cleaning woman does perhaps suggest
a different approach to maternal physicality that would make it
less painful.

Though perhaps a peasant crone, the native woman here is
no old wife dispensing gloom and doom. There is a division of
stereotypes here: none of these accounts attribute old wives' tales to
the *midwife*, though there would seem to be a connection between
old wives, peasant crones, and midwives. This is perhaps because
of the increasing training and professionalisation of midwifery in
Britain, and its virtual extinction in North America. In so far as
midwifery has been revived by the home birth movement, it is
seen as an adjunct of the natural childbirth-story, which, as we
have seen, frowns upon the gloominess of the old wives' tale.
There is an odd sense in which the medical experts' account
of childbirth is more in harmony with the old wives' tale than
the natural childbirth movement is. Both medical experts and old
wives admit the painfulness of the experience, and the need for
drugs and/or interventions, though the medical experts are more
interested in stressing that these will *work*, while the old wives
are interested in the drama that ensues when it all goes wrong,
and 'there was about twelve people all lining up in the passage
– the blood unit, the flying squad, everybody' (Oakley 1981 78).
Vera Brittain in *Honourable Estate*, a novel which goes along
with medicalised childbirth, allows her ignorant patriarch to be
bored by an old wife's birth-stories, whose 'gruesome' implications
turn out to be only too true: just before his wife's confinement,
he visits Mrs Pedler, 'whose maternal history, as she was never
tired of telling him, consisted of nine births and three miscarriages'

(Brittain 1936 37). But Mrs Pedler's bad experiences can, we are
to assume, become a thing of the past, once 'Dr Geraldine Vane'
and her medical training are allowed to take over the conduct of
childbirth.

What all the old wives share is the sense of birth as a disaster
story, full of drama, struggle and agony, centred on a female
heroine. Some of Oakley's informants, finding no correspondence
to their experience in the official versions, turn instead to fictional
– in this case cinematic – representations. 'Kate Prince' explains
her disillusion like this:

> I felt I'd been *tricked*, actually *tricked*, by the health visitor, by the
> books I'd read – by the Gordon Bourne book, because he said that
> the word pain should *not* be applied to labour contractions. And
> somebody had said well it's not like it is in the films or something.
> And I thought well it's exactly like 'Gone With the Wind' – it's
> *exactly* like those old movies when they're all writhing about in
> agony: that's *exactly* what I was doing.
>
> (Oakley 1981 109)

'Pauline Diggory' uses the same analogy: 'I think women ought
to be told that it's painful. I suppose if I recall all those films of
women in labour. . . . holding onto the bedstead and all this sort
of thing – I suppose if I'd recalled that . . .' (97). The old films
provide an image of struggle and agony to set against both modern
accounts, the 'medical' and the 'natural'. And, as I have been
suggesting, nearly all the fictional accounts do this too (Bagnold's
The Squire is a notable exception here). However committed they
may be to natural childbirth or medical versions of the birth-story,
by dramatising it from the point of view of the female heroine, they
inject her doubts and fears into the homogenous official versions,
and break them up into stories of conflict, struggle, disaster and
drama.

4
Subjectivities: two in one, one becomes two

In this chapter, I want to investigate the representation of women's subjectivities – their sense of 'self' – during pregnancy, birth and immediately afterwards. Of course, everything I have written so far has touched on this question: the 'primitive woman' is one identity that is offered to women in childbirth; the medical institution, with its definitions of the maternal body as machine or meat, impinges on their sense of identity; and 'other women' are often used as projections of identities birthing women fear or admire. I have deliberately kept this exploration of interiority until the last chapter, in order to make clear how much that interior sense of self is impinged upon and even created by external factors: dominant discourses, social institutions and beliefs, divisions of class and race. As we will see, the same bodily predicament can have quite opposite effects on different women's sense of self: a mother can feel in harmony with the foetus inside her, or she can feel it as a hostile antagonist; she can experience birth as a splitting apart of her body, and of her mind from her body, or as a flowing process that integrates body and mind in harmonious co-operation; childbirth can create a new, more solid self for the mother, or it can disperse her sense of identity. These different constructions are nearly always conditioned by the social dimension: how the mother's role is valued and defined by her society; what her economic status is; how she is treated by the institutions that control childbirth.

The bodily experience of giving birth throws these questions into focus: it almost inevitably raises questions of self and other, role and status. Being pregnant, harbouring another inside the self, challenges our usual notions of identity and individuality: two

people are in one body. Birth then further disrupts our categories
as one 'individual' literally 'divides' into two. As Julia Kristeva
puts it, 'there is this abyss that opens up between the body and
what had been its inside. . . . Trying to think through that abyss;
staggering vertigo. No identity holds up' (Kristeva 1986 178–9).
As a process in time, motherhood puts into question a woman's
sense of identity, as her body changes shape and splits apart, and a
new social role is thrust upon her. Discontinuities between her self
before and after birth, and in her relationship to the foetus/baby
inside and then outside her, force reformulations of her sense of
who she is. The identity of the foetus is also at issue here: is she/he
a person or not? And when? And if not a person, is she/he just
a part of the body, an animal, or a god? All these unanswerable
questions and unresolvable paradoxes, which are sidestepped or
smoothed over by the official discourses on childbirth, are opened
up by women writing about the experience of childbirth. The
maternal body, though always culturally mediated, creates its own
particular problems for the male-centred discourses of our culture.
While I have been concerned to see what happens when childbirth
is written about from the point of view of the woman giving birth,
it turns out this is not a single or simple 'point'. It is only 'audience'
point of view narratives that are able to give single and simple
accounts of childbirth: experienced from the centre, that 'centre'
becomes diffuse, multiple, fractured.

The problems of making clear divisions have extended from the
definitions of the maternal self, to the actual structure of this
chapter. I have found that my material does not divide into four
or five neatly separate sections as in previous chapters. Instead, it
is arranged under three large headings, each of which is split into
a number of much shorter, interconnected, parts.

Two in one: the relation of mother and foetus/baby

For Julia Kristeva, the maternal condition, the other inside the
self, provides a radical challenge to concepts of identity and
difference that underlie our whole signifying system. As Mary
Ann Doane explains:

> The maternal space is 'a place both double and foreign.' In
> its internalisation of heterogeneity, an otherness within the self,

motherhood deconstructs certain conceptual boundaries. Kristeva delineates the maternal through the assertion, 'In a body there is grafted, unmasterable, an other.' The confusion of identities threatens to collapse a signifying system based on the paternal law of differentiation. It would seem that the concept of motherhood automatically throws into question ideas concerning the self, boundaries between self and other, and hence identity.

(Doane 1990 170; quotations from Kristeva 1977 409)

These questions are, however, easily evaded by the two dominant discourses about childbirth, by assimilating an anomalous situation to one or other extreme of definition. As Barbara Katz Rothman explains, while the 'medical model' sees mother and foetus (and later mother and infant) as 'a conflicting dyad' in which 'the needs and interests of the mother-host are pitted against those of the fetus-parasite', the 'midwifery model' (what I have been calling the natural childbirth model) sees the two as 'one organic unit', with needs in harmony (Rothman 1982 48, 135). While women's accounts of birth give expression to one or other of these extreme positions, many accounts confuse the issue by articulating *both*. Once again, ambivalence and variety are introduced into the totalising world of the 'official' discourses.

In this section, I am going to look at representations of the mother/baby relationship in pregnancy, birth and the period immediately after birth, since similar ambiguities operate in all three stages, and different writers divide them up differently. Some see an absolute division between foetus inside and baby outside, while others see a continuum; breast-feeding of course continues the sense of the baby as parasitic on/an extension of the mother. These varying points of differentiation again defy normal definitions, challenging conventional ideas of where and when an individual begins and ends.

Paradoxes

Alicia Ostriker's 'Propaganda Poem: Maybe for Some Young Mamas' presents us with all sides of the paradoxical mother/baby relationship. The poem is addressed to a group of young 'feminist' students who have no sympathy with the poet's delight in pregnancy; they want 'our freedom', 'to live our lives' (Ostriker 1980 26). For them, babies are an antagonistic 'burden' that would deflect them from themselves. Here we see that the presentation of the interests of mother and baby as opposed is not just a feature of the 'medical model' of childbirth, but of a certain kind of feminist discourse as well. But while in the medical model the baby is usually seen as the important individual, this feminist model reverses the hierarchy, and sees the woman as the important individual. The poet, however, openly making 'propaganda', emphasises the *harmony* of the mother-baby bond. In pregnancy, you are 'one animal', 'both gently just slightly / separated from each other / swaying, swinging / like a vine, like an oriole nest' (25). The metaphors refuse to distinguish *which* of the two is the vine, the nest. Is the mother the vine holding up the nest? But the baby clings to her like a vine, and she is a nest for the baby. The category 'slightly separated' refuses to go to either extreme of definition, while the whole description emphasises reciprocity and harmony. After the birth, both parties are separate 'wholes' – 'there is no / good time like the good time a whole mama / has with a whole little baby' – but again related in an interdependence that challenges conventional definitions: 'the dazzling circuit of contact without dominance' (27). Here I am reminded of Hélène Cixous' suggestion that women can attain a more fluid sense of self, outside the hierarchical divisions of patriarchal law, because of their capacity for the 'other': 'all women do all virtually or in fact have an experience of the inside, an experience of the capacity for other, an experience of non-negative change brought about by the other, of positive receptivity' (Cixous 1981 18).

On the other hand, the students Ostriker is preaching to do not have this sense. The poem makes clear this is not an inborn, 'natural' trait of women, but 'propaganda'. And in its second section, 'Postscript to Propaganda', Ostriker gives the other side of the picture, the limitations children impose, the mess and chaos they create, while 'your life' is 'peeling away / from you like layers of cellophane' (Ostriker 1980 27), and the reciprocal relationship is undone: 'you disentwine yourself from them, lock the pores of your love / set them at a distance'. In this section, the mother's life is merely of use to the children's lives: 'you are wheels to them . . . you are grease. / An iron doorway they kick open'. This image of the woman's self being *used*, by the baby, by Nature, by the human race, is one that recurs in women's accounts of birth. She is a pipe, a channel, a seed pod: a passive container or transmitter, not an active self. Birth reminds a woman of dispensability, mortality; but this is the human condition, as Ostriker reminds her audience in a final rallying cry, 'Come on, you daughters of bitches, do you want to live forever?'(28).

The double attitude to maternity that is dramatised in Ostriker's poem, where the relationship to the baby is both a life-enhancing harmony and a life-destroying antagonism, can also be found in Fay Weldon's *Puffball*. While the mother-foetus relationship is presented as harmonious and interdependent, the novel also hints that a price is to be paid in autonomy and independence by the mother once the child is born. The mother is pushed from centre stage by the new actor, she is used by forces beyond her control. The harmony and unity with the foetus is created in the 'Annunciation' chapter, where the baby speaks to Liffey from inside the womb. Both are presented as separate persons, but they are in perfect communication, and the baby gives Liffey extra power and insight. The doctor tries to puncture Liffey's self-satisfaction, by suggesting that, in accordance with the medical model, the baby is a parasite which is using her: '"Anyone would think it was your doing. All you have to do is just exist. The baby uses you to grow. You don't grow it."' But 'Liffey knew better. She hugged her baby in her heart. Ah, *we*, we have done it. We are doing it' (Weldon 1980 180). The anatagonistic 'you' and 'it' becomes the unified 'we'. Lillian Robinson comments on a similar transformation in some poems by Kathleen Fraser: in 'Poem Wondering if I am Pregnant', the foetus is using up the mother:

> Are you there,
> thief I can't see,
>   drinking,
>   leaving me at the edge
>   of breathing?

But in 'Poem for the New', 'a union and a transformation occur':

> My belly has tracks on it –
>   hands and feet
> are moving
> under this taut skin.
> In snow, in light,
> we are about to become!

Robinson comments, 'Childbirth itself can be transformed into
something the woman does, rather than something that happens
to her' (Robinson 1986 282, quoting from Konek and Walters
1976 94–6). In the same way, Liffey insists that 'We are doing
it', despite the doctor's claim that 'You don't grow it'.

Nevertheless, as we have seen, Weldon is expert at subverting all
fixed definitions, and at the end, when the baby is born, he claims
precedence:

> She sensed its triumph. None of that was important, the baby
> reproved her: they were peripheral events, leading towards the
> main event of your life, which was to produce me. You were
> always the bit-part player: that you played the lead was your
> delusion, your folly. Only by giving away your life do you save
> it.
>
> (Weldon 1980 264)

And the book ends with the baby claiming 'everyone, as bit-part
players in his drama, dancers in his dance, singers to his tune'.
This is clearly not, however, a negative ending – Liffey has 'saved'
her life through her recognition of her own unimportance, her
vulnerability to forces – natural, economic, medical, emotional –
beyond her own control. Liffey is the baby's victim, but this is a
fact of life. This somewhat harsh moral lesson is emphasised by
the symbolism of the puffballs, round, white and swelling, that
obviously parallel the pregnant Liffey, and she feels appropriate
pains and fears when Mabs or Tucker kick the puffballs to bits,
or when her predatory city friends cook them and slice them up.
Pregnancy makes her vulnerable. At the end, however, it turns
out the puffballs make good firelighters – 'They burned slowly,
patiently and brightly, and she thought there was some good in
them after all' (272); similarly, Liffey's body has been put to some
good use as fuel for the baby's life.

Continuities and repetitions

Ostriker and Weldon dramatise both sides of the paradoxical
mother/baby relationship, harmony and antagonism, though both
imply a final acceptance of maternal sacrifice. We find this acceptance also in Bagnold's *The Squire*, where it finds compensation
in an expanded sense of identity as part of a larger process of

continuity and repetition. But as we will see, other writers find this no compensation, simply another threat to the independent self. For the squire, her foetus is ancient and god-like: 'It acted like a god, as her master, directing her. She had no control over it' (Bagnold 1987 30). As in *Puffball*, the baby has spiritual power: the Christian and pre-Christian myth of the woman pregnant with a god is again invoked. Interestingly, Sheila Kitzinger also makes use of this imagery in *The Experience of Childbirth*, when she writes

> I would not suggest that one should approach childbirth borne on the wings of a pseudomysticism which might collapse at the crucial moment; nevertheless, to anyone who thinks about it long enough, birth cannot simply be a matter of techniques for getting a baby out of one's body. It involves our relationship to life as a whole, the part we play in the order of things; and as the baby develops and can be felt moving inside, to some women annunciation, incarnation, seem to become facts of their own existence.
>
> (Kitzinger 1962 25)

It is this religious sense of an 'order of things' that Liffey shares with the squire and Kitzinger, and all three imply the 'individual' self can be expanded and transcended by submitting to this larger order: Liffey longs 'to feel herself part of nature's processes; to subdue the individual spirit to some greater whole' (Weldon 1980 156). The squire too feels herself part of a larger process: '"To give birth, to bring up the young, to die," thought the squire, and for the first time saw her own end as endurable. "I was solid and I was myself. But now I am a pipe through which the generations pass"' (Bagnold 1987 154–5). These images of continuity focus especially on her relationship and identification with her daughter, Lucy, rather than with the new baby, who is a boy: 'She took her place then in a line of women like a figure on a roll of film, her mother before her, her children behind. . . . "Lucy," whispered the squire, and had an odd sense that Lucy was herself, that she herself was her own mother, that these three women were one' (263–4; see also 67).

That the squire focuses on the matriarchal line here, merging her own identity with that of her mother and her daughter, is very significant in view of Nancy Chodorow's theories of female identity. Chodorow (1978) argues that female identity is more fluid than male identity, since a boy defines himself in opposition to his mother, while a girl identifies herself in similarity. So, for a girl, the pre-Oedipal period of attachment to and merging with the mother lasts longer and remains a part of her personality. This may be so, though women's attitudes to this maternal identification can vary greatly, according to social pressures. The squire feels a kind of pleasure in the continuation of the matriarchal line: her experience of the mother's role is pleasurable, something she wants to see continued. In *A Proper Marriage*, however, as we have seen, Martha is horrified at the idea of a 'repetition', in which rebellious daughters are converted into repressive mothers, and she will sit 'where her mother now sat' (Lessing 1977 109). The horror of matrilineal repetition also appears in a short story by Joyce Carol Oates, 'A Touch of the Flu'. A young single mother is totally wrapped up in a harmonious dyad with her baby daughter: 'She sang to her little girl, talked to her almost continuously, for there was no one in the world except the two of them, and by way of the two of them, their delicious union, the world became new, newly created' (Oates 1988 176). Pre-Oedipal oneness is celebrated. But one day, she hands the baby over to her mother, and goes to bed for ten days: 'Her mother brought her little girl to nurse, and she pushed her away, in revulsion, and could not explain, for it was herself she saw, in her mother's arms, as it had been, so suddenly, herself she'd seen, in her little girl, that morning on the beach; and she thought, I cannot bear it. Not again'. It is not just circularity, but regression that is the horror here: the woman is lying 'in her old girlhood bed' (176).

A feminist consciousness, however, can once again introduce celebration into the idea of matrilineal repetition, seeing it also as progress: in Erica Jong's poem 'On the First Night', the speaker is

> The second daughter
> of a second daughter
> of a second daughter,
> but you shall be the first.
> You shall see the phrase
> 'second sex'
> only in puzzlement,
> wondering how anyone,
> except a madman,

could call you 'second'
when you are so splendidly
first,
conferring even on your mother
firstness, vastness, fullness . . .

(Jong 1989 124)

The daughter's progress confers a retrospective importance on the mother.

Daughters in particular bring out the concepts of repetition and identification across the generations, but the mother's feeling of being a vehicle for the foetus applies to babies of both genders. While the squire feels a certain pleasure in being 'a pipe through which the generations pass', other mothers do not accept this identity so cheerfully. Xenia, in *Birth Rites*, at first sees her new baby as quite separate from her: 'He was a phenomenon, and not linked to her by any continuing thread. He lay in his bed, she in hers, and both were neutral and unjoined' (Bowder 1983 168). But breast-feeding re-establishes the connection, and provides a revelation about the nature of motherhood: 'I see that I am not a separate person, she thought, I am a channel of life. I simply give all that I have in order that he may grow. I didn't understand this at first. She saw the bulge of her breast becoming his pink face: where she stopped, where he began, was not clear' (201). This could be a celebration of a fluid, dual identity, but the implication of inequality and exploitation in her *giving* and his *growing* is disquieting. The baby, it is implied, devours the mother: as we will see, other women writers explicitly use the image of being eaten by their baby, as their bodies, lives, selves are given up to its growth. It becomes clear that Xenia is not accepting this situation when she uses similar images in a tirade against the hospital as institution. She complains about the unsympathetic routine, which makes the mothers feel 'as though we were in the way, cluttering up the place, interfering with routine'; this leads to a loss of identity: 'I've more or less forgotten who I am. We're in limbo, we're just part of a process, we're just the pod that encloses the bean, or the shell you crack to get the nut out' (196). It is clear here that being a 'pod' or a 'shell' is not a 'natural' consequence of being a mother: it is to do with the way the medical insitution has treated and defined these women.

While such images of being used as part of a larger process are deployed both by writers who take on the natural childbirth model, and those who have the medical model thrust upon them, the difference seems to be that the advocates of the 'natural' (Kitzinger, Bagnold, Weldon in places) can joyfully accept this as a dignified and important condition, part of an 'organic whole', while the victims of the medical institution see themselves defined as waste, impediment, 'in the way' of an antagonistic force. On the other hand, Xenia's protest also arises from her strong feminist sense that she *has* a separate, non-maternal self, while Kitzinger, Liffey, and the squire find complete fulfilment in motherhood; as we have seen, it is this sense of an independent self that produces Xenia's horror of the 'Wendies' and their submergence in the housewife role, and now also produces a rebellion at being a mere 'shell' or 'pod'. Like the feminist students that Ostriker addresses, she also wants to live her own life.

Mother/baby antagonism

Conflict between a woman's independent life and motherhood is the keynote of Stephanie's story in *Still Life*. This socially conditioned conflict affects the way her relationship with her unborn baby is described. The baby inside intrudes on her privacy, its movements preventing Stephanie and her husband from making love: 'even in bed there was no privacy' (Byatt 1986 29). As the baby grows, 'what had been swimming . . . was now tightly packed and bone grinding . . . she was not sailing, she was weighted . . . She had lost her autonomy. Something was living her life; she was not living' (84). Only one life is available to the two of them, and the baby has got it. This sense of antagonism between the two of them persists into the description of the birth itself, where the labour is seen as a contest between female body and foetus, as Stephanie is battered by 'a furious blunt block', a 'bursting thing' (92). Like Xenia in *Birth Rites*, Byatt has a vision of Stephanie being used by larger processes. In this case, the idea is not caused by her treatment in the medical institution, but it is put in the alienating language of science, after her second child is conceived:

> There is a theory current now that the sexual function is an aberration from parthenogenetic hermaphroditism, the product of 'parasitic DNA' which puts out a pilus, a 'genetic syringe' to

impart, cuckoo-like, a factor of its own into the nucleic acid of another organism. Whilst they slept with their heads together on the pillow, the cells pullulated and divided, boiled and extruded, arranged genes, chromosomes, proteins, plans, patterns, another life, the same life in another form. And as the immortal life of the genotype is transmitted, some say, so the phenotype, the individual body, becomes redundant, dispensable: it is economic for it to age, cease to function, die.

(236–7)

While this may be scientifically 'true', it also coincides neatly with the social structures that mean Stephanie has to sacrifice her independent life to her babies.

Sylvia Plath's poetry, written around the time *Still Life* is set, also implies a conflict between the mother's life and the baby's. Her poem 'Morning Song' (1961) presents the mother as 'effaced' by the baby: 'I'm no more your mother/ Than the cloud that distils a mirror to reflect its own slow/ Effacement at the wind's hand' (Plath 1981 156). The baby's life results from and reflects the disappearance of the mother's life. In 'Three Women' (1962), the Third Voice, who rejects her baby, openly wishes, 'I should have murdered this, that murders me', and even the First Voice, giving birth, protests, 'Can such innocence kill and kill? It milks my life'. Like the squire or Xenia, she is being used as part of a larger process: she is 'a seed about to break', she is 'drummed into use' by her labour. Afterwards, she is still to act as container for her baby, as a reassuring environment: 'I shall be a wall and a roof, protecting./ I shall be a sky and a hill of good'. This sounds like a joyful acceptance of her 'natural' role, but the strain of the role is also revealed: 'How long can I be a wall, around my green property?/ How long can my hands/ be a bandage to his hurt . . .?' The baby too is described in natural images – 'green property', 'little, blind, bright plant' – but his cry is also 'a hook'. Here, the hook gives support to the woman in her maternal role – 'It is the hook I hang on' – though the negative implications of infant 'hooks' are suggested by the Third Voice: 'Her cries are hooks that catch and grate like cats' (Plath 1981 179–85).

Plath's suggestion in 'Morning Song' that the baby grows at the mother's expense reappears in several more recent writers. Gwen, in Doris Betts's 'Still Life with Fruit', feels devoured by the baby even before birth: 'she had been shrinking. The baby ate her.

Now the baby's container was huge but Gwen, invisible, had no body to live in' (Betts 1983 341). Similarly, Mary Gordon in 'The Unwanted' writes, 'Your growth kills mine./ So tinily you eat me all/ To shreds' (in Konek and Walters 1976 102). Susan Macdonald's speaker feels the same after birth – now it is her time the children eat: 'Yes, they are here, and firm/ eating my days' (108). Two writers in Laura Chester's collection, *Cradle and All*, elaborate this image of being eaten by their babies, placing it, as Macdonald does, after birth, and contrasting it with the 'oneness' of pregnancy. Joyce Thompson describes dreams of antagonism and devourment:

> The baby bites your nipple off and spits it out in the dusty corner behind your rocking chair. Blood pours from the wound, and you are paralyzed by the hurt. The baby howls in rage at the red milk that flows so fast and tastes so salty strange until, infinitely adaptable, she rallies and learns to drink your blood.
>
> (Thompson 1987 201)

The antagonism comes from the baby's 'imperfect separation'. The harmony of pregnancy, its 'communication, reassurance' are gone. The mother and baby have different rhythms, as in Lessing's *A Proper Marriage* – 'She sleeps and you do not' – yet bodily interdependence is still there: 'She was born holding your heart in her hands, clutching your nerves like reins in her tiny fists' (200). Another dream picks up the woman's role in the matrilineal scheme:

> Your mother is not dead. If you can find her and apologize for the misapprehension of death, she will not die to you again. Your baby lives, and needs your milk to go on living. It is long and dangerously past her feeding time and she screams with hunger, somewhere out of sight. Two lives to save, and you must answer for two deaths, rooted here in sensuous memory, trapped between generations, unable to move.
>
> (Thompson 1987 201)

This is not the smooth progress from grandmother to mother to daughter that Bagnold describes, but an immobilising division between the competing identities of daughter and mother.

Jane Lazarre, in *The Mother Knot*, is similarly divided between 'that girlwoman who had once been all I needed to know of myself', and her role as mother. This 'inner self' has to be 'banished' during breast-feeding: 'For if she was present when the baby needed me, she was of necessity pushed aside, sent to go hungry' (Lazarre 1976 210). Again, there is a competition for nourishment between mother and baby, and again it is the combination of separation and dependence that creates tension: she tries to imagine 'that we were still one person', but he 'was at once separate and a part of me'. Lazarre is quite clear about what has happened: 'If anyone had told me what it would be like, I might have saved my life in time' (209). She tries hard to resign herself to being 'used', to accept the baby as 'My Life': 'Suck, darling, take me, use me to grow. Live, My Life, and love me, love me, while I try desperately to love you' (210).

Margaret Atwood, in 'Giving Birth', on the other hand, gives a comic version of devourment by the baby. The story begins with a description of the present life of the narrator. We hear about her everyday, happy interactions with her baby daughter, a way of life that is 'realistic in detail and slightly sentimental', like 'Dutch genre painting'. The self-conscious comment here on her own descriptive style alerts us to the constructed nature of her idyllic world; and one small, descriptive detail imples another reading of what is going on: in the playpen is 'a small naked woman', made of soft plastic, and 'the other day I noticed that the baby had managed to make a tear in the body with her new teeth'. Today, the baby has eaten her feet, and the mother imagines finding successive parts of the woman in her daughter's diapers, 'like the relics of some gruesome and demented murder' (Atwood 1984 227). In this both comic and disquieting vision of the baby devouring the mother, we find the recognition that the mother is the baby's victim, while at the same time the 'solidity' and realism of the world that the baby creates for its mother is also celebrated.

The paradoxes of the mother/baby relationship, and imagery of *mutual* devourment, are taken to fiercer extremes in Toni Morrison's *Beloved*. Sethe's 'thick', protective, maternal love leads her to murder her baby to save her from re-enslavement. This action is based on her complete identification with her children as the best, the 'magical', part of herself: 'The best thing she was, was her children. Whites might dirty her all right, but not *her* best thing, her beautiful, magical best thing – the part of her that was clean' (Morrison 1987 251). When the ghost of the murdered baby reappears as a young woman, it seems at first that a beautiful, valuable interrelationship has been restored. Like a baby, Beloved

is fixated on her mother's *face*, and identifies completely with her:
'I am Beloved and she is mine. . . . I am not separate from her
   there is no place where I stop   her face is my own' (210).
This chapter of monologue by the returned Beloved moves into an
interchange blending the three voices of Sethe, Denver and Beloved
– the mother and her two daughters – with a twice-repeated refrain
of 'You are mine / You are mine / You are mine' (216, 217). All
three women are linked in a Chodorowian identification.

But warning notes have already been sounded: soon after Beloved first arrives, we are told that she 'could not take her eyes
off Sethe. . . . Sethe was licked, tasted, eaten by Beloved's eyes'
(Morrison 1987 58). Beloved's only two dreams are 'exploding and
being swallowed': appropriate both for a ghost and a new-born
baby, with uncertain relations to their physical forms. Beloved's
later monologue includes imagery of her mother 'chewing and
swallowing' her. After the three-voiced harmony between Sethe,
Denver and Beloved, Denver finds herself excluded from a destructive, long-drawn-out love-fight between Sethe and Beloved. Child-
like, Beloved imitates Sethe, so that 'it was difficult for Denver
to tell who was who' (241). The identification is becoming more
and more complete. Beloved has a hold over Sethe, because of
Sethe's guilt at having murdered her, and Beloved's rage at the
separation. The symbiosis is both that of mother and baby, and
murderer and victim. Beloved gradually gains the upper hand,
and begins to devour her mother: 'the bigger Beloved got, the
smaller Sethe became. . . . Beloved ate up her life, took it, swelled
up with it, grew taller on it' (250). This is the familiar imagery
of the baby growing at the mother's expense, intensified by the
context of guilt and victimhood, which has in turn been produced
by slavery's distortions of motherhood. Beloved devouring Sethe is
the counterpart and the consequence of Sethe murdering Beloved
through her excessive love and identification.

The destructive circle of identification is broken by several
means: by Denver, and her seeking help from the rest of the
community; by Sethe turning her rage on the white man ap-
proaching her house; by Paul D's final comment that Sethe herself
is her own 'best thing', not Beloved, as Sethe thinks. The intrusion
of other people into the closed circle is vital to the mother's
salvation, as is her directing her violence away from her baby to
those responsible for her oppression, and her valuation of her own

subjectivity. Beloved is destroyed in this process – but the second daughter, Denver, survives, by separating herself from her mother and sister and their destructive identification. Beloved, re-living her lost babyhood as an adult, figures as unhealthy intensification of the mother/baby symbiosis, as does Sethe in her original murder of Beloved, and her later obsession with the ghost. This is no kind of comment on mother-love in itself, but on the ways slavery can distort it, turn it into a destructive over-compensation for what has been lost. Unlike the other narratives I have looked at, that end with joyful or despairing acquiescence to the demands of the mother/baby relationship, *Beloved* instead ends with the beginning of the discovery of the mother's independent selfhood – '"Me? Me?"' asks Sethe in reply to Paul D's '"You your best thing, Sethe, You are"' (Morrison 1987 273; see also Hirsch 1989 198).

The baby as expansion of the mother's identity

While most of these writers either celebrate or lament the 'using up' of the mother by the baby, a few present the baby as an unproblematic extension of the maternal self. Rosamund, in *The Millstone*, rejoices in 'this small living extension of myself' (Drabble 1966 145). The baby, Octavia, has just torn up the manuscript of a novel written by Rosamund's friend Lydia, in which there was a very critical, unflattering portrait of Rosamund. The baby, in tearing up the manuscript, has clearly done just what Rosamund herself wanted to do. Rosamund also finds herself being more selfish and self-assertive, for Octavia's sake: their interests are not in conflict. At the end of the book, Rosamund does realise that her love for Octavia is 'a bad investment' for the future, presumably because Octavia will grow up and leave her, but for the moment it contains no conflicts. In Marianne Gingher's 'Camouflage', also about an illegitimate birth, the baby is also imagined as increasing the mother's sense of self-importance and self-worth:

> She supposed she should hate the baby now, hate how it had changed her life. But she didn't hate it, had never hated it. The truth was that having the baby had made her feel bolder and expansive. She was not just herself anymore. From now on she was herself and a baby, filling up two places in the world, not one.
>
> (Gingher 1988 161–2)

It is surprising how very rare this kind of happy self-expansion is in women's writing about birth; even here, it is partly fantasy, as Mary, the mother, is going to give the baby up for adoption: 'they would always be absent from each other but never alone' (162).

Elizabeth Baines' *The Birth Machine* also involves an element of fantasy in presenting the baby as an unproblematic extension of the mother. He is made to stand for her recovery of her buried self. The medical institution at first persuades her their interests are in conflict, and she should sacrifice hers to the baby: Roland insists that '"We must do whatever is advised to ensure the baby's safety." Oh, yes, he was right. He was so right. Baby first. Oh, God, she must call on her dried-up selfish soul' (Baines 1983 65). Her freedom and self-discovery come after the birth, when she first looks properly at the baby and lifts it from its cot: 'here it is in her hands . . . the thing that was sown and immediately buried. Buried too deep and never acknowledged. She stares. The baby waits, its eyes wide open, receptive' (119). Zelda then escapes from the hospital, clutching this very accommodating baby. As in *The Millstone*, it sounds as if the heroine is going to make her own life, with the baby, apart from men. The baby here, however, is so over-loaded with symbolism that it is hard to imagine it as part of a reciprocal relationship: it is rather like the baby fantasised by the heroine at the end of Margaret Atwood's *Surfacing* – another symbol of a woman's recovered self. These symbolic babies contribute to a reading of childbirth as the birth of the *mother*, as well as the child – an interpretation I shall be looking at later in this chapter.

The divided maternal self

In this section, I want to look at the relationship of mothers to their own bodies, particularly during labour and the moment of birth itself. What sense of self persists or comes into being during this process? Where is subjectivity located and how is it represented? Two opposed images dominate these descriptions: flowing and splitting. Either the self becomes a flowing process, or it is fractured and destroyed. These two extremes obviously bear some relation to the harmonious and antagonistic models of the woman's relationship to her baby, the 'other' inside her. In the 'splitting' model, not only is the woman split between herself and her baby, but often between her mind and her body, and between outside and interior perspectives on what is happening. Her body itself is also split open by the baby, and seems to split into component parts, related to each other in absurd, abnormal ways as the tremendous bodily changes of labour take place. It is hard to locate a consistent sense of self, mental or physical, during this process, and the self often disappears altogether. This loss of subjectivity is of course increased by a medical institution that treats the woman as an assemblage of bodily parts, a mindless object: the 'split' model of subjectivity is partly caused by the medical model of childbirth.

Similarly, the 'flowing' model is the ideal of the natural childbirth movement – but it is not as simple or as unified as it seems. It is often conditional on an initial *splitting* of the self, in which one half keeps an intellectual eye on the medical procedures, while the other 'flows' with the body, or one half consciously practises techniques to induce a self-forgetful flowing in the other. Images of harmony or co-operation are often used, as in the relationship between mother and foetus, implying a relationship between *two* selves, a mind and a body, or a 'civilised' and a 'primitive' woman inhabiting the same body. While the aim of this book has been to look at what happens when the story of childbirth is told from the woman's point of view, that 'point' turns out not to be stable and unified – not a single 'point' at all. Not only do dominant discourses, institutional and social structures condition subjectivity, but the bodily processes of pregnancy and childbirth in particular challenge notions of individuality, as Kristeva has pointed out.

'Subjective' and 'objective' viewpoints

There are, of course, obvious physical limitations to a woman's 'view' of the event of birth. Not only may she be occasionally semi-conscious, but also, as one of Ann Oakley's informants in *From Here To Maternity* puts it, 'you've got your legs on the table and you have a foot on each nurse's shoulder, so you have to rick your neck to look down and you can't do it, because you are trying to breathe at the same time. Alan see it. . . . He saw the head . . . and then he said they cut you and I said to him, how did you know, and he said, well I see it didn't I?' (Oakley 1981 93). This reliance on the husband to report back on what is happening 'at the other end' recurs in the accounts: 'he kept running down the other end and looking and coming back and telling me what was happening' (207). This disabling division of the woman into two 'ends' is partly bridged in some of Kitzinger's accounts, when the women ask for *mirrors* so they can have a view of the head emerging, or of their stitches. Mirrors appear in some of the more recent fictional accounts, but interestingly they are not always of help: 'And there's the mirror where i can see, except he's standing/ in the way' (Marlatt 1980 98); or 'Then they held a mirror down for Julia to see how her perineum was changing, but she only saw a mess of blood' (Chester 1989a 128). Barbara Katz Rothman, an American home-birth advocate, in fact opposes the use of mirrors:

> Encouraging a woman to watch herself in a mirror giving birth moves her from being a participant to an observer of the birth. The emphasis on 'seeing' the birth comes out of the context of prepared, in-hospital, doctor-directed births. . . . If the mother wants to be awake, 'be there' for the birth, then the only role they have to offer her is that of observer.
>
> (Rothman 1982 177–8)

Instead, birth should be seen as 'an activity that woman *do*', not something they watch. If mirrors are used, the woman merely crosses over into the 'audience' point of view from which birth has traditionally been described, instead of giving us the 'inside', participant point of view.

This inability of the merely visual to portray birth explains the unsatisfactory (to me) nature of attempts to photograph women giving birth; for instance, I find the photographs in Kitzinger's book *Giving Birth* very disturbing. They are mostly full frontal black and white pictures of women giving birth. The grainy black and white photography contributes to an effect of realism. Kitzinger's photographs affront the usual conventions that govern visual images of women – the women are unkempt, unattractive, gory. Here we are supposed to be seeing birth as it 'really feels', as the book's title claims. And yet what we are being shown is what no birthing woman herself actually experiences, unless she uses a full-length mirror. The point of view is that of the audience at 'the other end' – the woman herself is unaware of the gory picture she presents. As one of Kitzinger's writers in *Giving*

Birth puts it, after the birth 'I then noticed all the blood and shit on the bed and was surprised that I hadn't been aware of this before' (Kitzinger 1987 59). The photographs do not in fact tell us anything about the subjective experience of giving birth, and hence they do not contribute to Kitzinger's often stated aim to put women themselves in charge of the birth process. They put the viewer in a voyeuristic position, and disturbingly mix the conventions of pornography (naked women with legs apart) and war photography (blood and gore). The women portrayed seem cruelly objectified, divorced from any subjective viewpoint.

On the other hand, without help from mirrors, pictures, or the viewpoints of outside observers, the woman's 'inside' point of view on what is happening can be limited and even wrong. Rothman celebrates all the stories in which the woman is *right*, and the medical institution wrong:

> I have heard countless stories of hospital births in which the staff discounted the mother's reports, went with the 'objective' criteria, and then found that the mother had been right. Most common is the story, often told in the first person, of staff's ignoring the mother's pronouncements that she is ready to give birth *now*.
>
> (Rothman 1982 101)

We can find such a story in *The Millstone*, where stupid nurses will not believe Rosamund is about to give birth, and are almost immediately proved wrong. In 'Giving Birth', Margaret Atwood also dramatises such a moment of triumph: 'The baby is being born when Jeanie said it would, though just three days ago the doctor said it would be at least another week, and this makes Jeanie feel jubilant and smug' (Atwood 1984 238). But Atwood also dramatises moments when Jeanie is wrong and the hospital is right: 'Only *four*?' she exclaims, feeling cheated, and 'they must be wrong', when the doctor says she is four centimetres dilated; 'This is absurd', she thinks, when asked not to push yet (237, 238). This kind of discrepancy between the 'objective' version and what the woman thinks and feels is happening is especially marked when the woman is well informed of the medical version of events. As we have seen, this is particularly true of Kitzinger's natural childbirth followers, armed with their written birth-plans. For instance, in one story in *Giving Birth* the woman's husband refers to the plan, while she is 'getting on with what I was doing': 'I noticed that he was reading the labour plan again and that he was devouring the page about transition. It struck me as ridiculous and although I said nothing to him I thought he was being incredibly hopeful, if not downright panicky' (Kitzinger 1987 174). It turns out, however, that he, and the plan, are 'right' – she is in the transition stage already. Laura Chester dramatises such a moment of discrepancy: 'Then she began to think that they were lying. They were simply being nice, at her expense. Encouragement was a useless token. The head *wasn't* descending. She couldn't believe it when Dr Chou said that the head was through the cervix, and the body was entering the birth canal. It didn't feel that way at all' (Chester 1989a 127).

As well as these discrepancies, we find in many of Kitzinger and Oakley's accounts that there is a kind of dual point of view, as 'objective' information from outsiders is incorporated with the woman's own story of what is going on. Kitzinger's women are, as you might expect, more aware that there is an 'objective' version of what is going on: for instance, 'At some point the lip must have gone, but I was not aware of having been told that it had' (Kitzinger 1987 72); or, from the same account, 'At 1.45 the baby's head was visible. I didn't take in the fact that crowning had occurred' (73). Here the woman is giving us both the 'objective', technical acount of what was happening, and her own subjective unawareness of it. But the technical terms 'lip' and 'crowning' are also part of her own version of events, reconstructed afterwards from the medical knowledge acquired beforehand. Oakley's accounts are less technical, and more reliant on the attendants' reports, but these are also incorporated as part of the story: for instance, 'He was stuck in the neck of the womb, he got stuck coming round the corner. They told me that' (Oakley 1981 98). Kitzinger's women do also need help from attendants to reconstruct their stories: 'I didn't remember the sequence of things so I asked her [the midwife] to review what had happened' (Kitzinger 1987 147). As well as incorporating outside sources of information, the women also use their imaginations to picture what is going on inside them: 'I could feel her head coming out, then her arms and legs and I could envisage the shape of her body as she came out' (122); or, 'I was very conscious of the muscles pushing down and had a good image of the baby and what was happening to it' (174). Obviously these pictures can only be imagined because the women have 'objective' information about what is supposed to be happening inside them at this point – in one account, imagination is assisted by the midwife with a pelvic girdle model, 'trying to show me what was going on inside' (176). Imagination incorporates this knowledge into the woman's subjective experience. In contrast, most of the fictional accounts stick scrupulously to their heroines' points of view – that is, they tell us only what she could have felt and known at the time.

Mind/body/body splits

While sticking to an 'inside' point of view, fiction writers often dramatise an internal split between body and mind, in which the mind is the watchful observer, bent on remaining in conscious control of the uncontrollable, independent body. In the previous chapter we have seen how pregnancy induces in some women an extreme revulsion from the maternal bodies of other women: the body is projected as the grotesque representation of a maternal self that threatens to engulf the protagonist. The woman's identity as 'mind' is sometimes propped up by the books she reads, which differentiate her from the other, merely 'bodily' women. Distance between mind and body is often increased by the way the medical institution treats the woman as merely body, especially when she is anaesthetised or even operated on during the birth.

In *The Millstone*, Rosamund holds herself at an intellectual distance from her body during labour by the very way she describes her 'sensations that did not seem quite reasonable or endurable'. After the painkilling drug takes effect, 'the pain did not diminish but my resistance to it disappeared, and every two minutes regularly it flowed through me as though I were some other person, as though I myself, what was left of me, was watching this swell and ebb from many miles away' (Drabble 1966 99). Similarly, in Doris Betts's 'Still Life with Fruit', the anaesthetised heroine is divorced from her bodily actions: 'So when they said bear down, Gwen thought about that, and somebody else bore down somewhere to suit them. . . . She might even rise up . . . and float loose . . . like a dust mote' (Betts 1974 352). This sense of mental detachment from the body is strongest in scenes portraying Caesarean births: it is interesting that the three novels which portray Caesareans, *Puffball*, *Birth Rites* and *The Birth Machine*, all include their heroine's consciousness in the experience. There have been several

recent cases of inadequate anaesthetic during Caesareans: but what
is important here is not at all a protest against incompetence, but
an insistence on the *presence* of the woman's self in some way at
this momentous occasion. This seems to be a carry-over from the
natural childbirth attitude that a Caesarean is the ultimate failure,
in that the woman is not aware or active during birth. In *Birth
Rites* and *The Birth Machine*, not only is the heroine mentally
aware (though also hallucinating), she undergoes an out-of-body
experience, as mind splits completely from body: 'She sits up.
Unhinges her head and shoulders from the rest of her body, unclips
them easily. Green underwater light fills the room. As she floats,
swims up, she sees that light is coming off the gowns, and from the
sheet that covers this side of the belly she's left behind on the table'
(Baines 1983 74). In this novel, detachment of head from body is an
image of a false splitting encouraged by the medical institution (it
also happens during the breathing exercises). In *Birth Rites*, on the
other hand, the heroine desperately tries to hang onto her role as
'mind', while the institution of motherhood tries to overwhelm her
with 'body'. Prepared for her Caesarean, 'hovering above herself,
she sees the trolley wheeled, with her inert body on it . . .' (Bowder
1983 155). During the operation, she tries desperately to cling to a
sense of 'self': 'I will not go under, I will go on!' – but this controlling
'self' is eventually blotted out: 'She, being space, clings to her parting
limits as they break away. She hangs on into the void. The pain cracks
her open. In horror, she is gone. . . . There is nothing' (156).

But this sense of separation between mind and body, and even
a complete loss of 'self' during birth, appears also in accounts of
unanaesthetised births. Alice Hoffman, in 'Fortune's Daughter',
describes an out-of-body experience during a painful home birth:
'It's only your body, she told herself. . . . Lila left her body behind.
Her spirit leapt up into the pure white air. . . . Below her, she
could see her body propped up on two pillows' (Hoffman 1985
121). The experience is presented as a brief ecstatic escape from
bodily suffering for a downtrodden, uneducated heroine, rather
than a painful split for an intellectual heroine. Less extreme, and
less ecstatic, splits are created for book-reading heroines. In *Still
Life*, Stephanie experiences birth like this: 'The spine, Stephanie's
shrinking mind stated, is a plane, *flat* on the bed, as though by
butchery the belly is severed and the flanks fall' (Byatt 1986 92).
This image of a separate, 'shrinking', mind reflects the social

constraints on Stephanie, as her intellectual life is split off from and diminished by her role as mother.

A similar split is elaborated in *A Proper Marriage*. During pregnancy, Martha is 'essentially divided. One part of herself was sunk in the development of the creature . . . a process . . . which dragged her back into the impersonal blind urges of creation; with the other part she watched it; her mind was like a lighthouse, anxious and watchful that she, the free spirit, should not be implicated' (Lessing 1977 44–5). During labour, these two parts are in contest, as Martha tries to keep her brain 'alive and watchful' against the asssaults of a pain that dims the 'small lit place' (163). Martha is now divided between the state of pain, during contractions, when her self disappears, and the state between contractions, when she cannot remember or imagine what the other state was like: 'there were two Marthas, and there was nothing to bridge them' (164). The 'free spirit' is defeated by this contradiction. In particular, during the state of pain she is delivered over to bodily processes which link her to her mother and destroy her separate individuality: 'And behold, Martha, that free spirit, understood from the exquisite shore of complete, empty non-sensation that she had been groaning out "Mother, Mother, Mother!"' When eventually the native cleaning woman comes to the rescue, with her hint of a more 'natural' motherhood, Martha attains relief by letting go of her mind: 'Martha let the cold knot of determination loosen, she let herself go, she let her mind go dark into the pain' (165). Here it is hinted that Martha's mind/body split is partly the fault of the institution: the institution of motherhood in her society and the medical institution's 'unnatural' methods of childbirth. Similarly, in *Still Life*, Stephanie's mind/body split is caused by social structures, and by the hospital's unsympathetic attitude to her bodily instincts: left to herself, mind and body co-operate rhythmically.

The complete loss of self that Martha experiences during the pain of childbirth is also described by Margaret Atwood in 'Giving Birth': 'When there is pain she feels nothing because there is no *she*. This, finally, is the disappearance of language' (1984 237). The disappearance of self is not presented as the fault of the institution here, nor as the solution offered by a natural childbirth approach: it is to do with the unrepresentability of *any* extreme bodily experiences: 'Why should the mind distress itself trying to find a language for them?' (235). For Atwood, without language there is no self. The metaphors that Atwood uses to describe the actual moment of birth refer only to the rather absurd physical mechanics of the process: the baby is 'a stone, a boulder', and 'she opens like a birdcage turning slowly inside out' (238). The idea that the body itself becomes unrecognisable during childbirth, performing absurd feats, displacing inside and outside, and, most often, splitting into component parts, recurs in many descriptions. Xenia, after her operation in *Birth Rites*, feels 'She has come through something terrible, she is not herself. . . . Dear God, she feels, I am all in pieces. Her head is elsewhere' (Bowder 1983 158). Stephanie, in *Still Life*, imagines that 'the belly is severed and the flanks fall', as 'the body split in half'. Her pain is imaged as another separate component in the struggle going on: it is 'a suffocating net', it 'gripped like a claw' (Byatt 1986 91–3). Lessing uses a similar image, as Martha feels 'wrung out . . . by a pair of enormous steel hands' (Lessing 1977 162–3). This image of something metallic and mechanical mangling or cutting the body recurs in other descriptions: for Gwen, in 'Still Life with Fruit', 'something thudded in her middle like a pile driver' (Betts 1974 350); Ruth, in *Honourable Estate*, feels 'harsh torturing pangs, grinding round inside her like a blunt circular saw', 'clawing iron fingers' (very similar to Lessing's 'steel hands' and Byatt's 'claw'), and finally 'a red-hot sword seared the lower half of her body, and tore it apart' (Brittain 1936 541–2). While in descriptions of medical intervention in birth, machines and instruments threaten the body from the outside, here they are within the body, produced by it. Interestingly, none of these women are describing a 'natural' childbirth: Brittain, because she does not believe in it, and profoundly distrusts 'Nature' as the enemy of women's individuality; Byatt and Lessing because their heroines are prevented from, or have not yet been shown, a 'natural' relation to their bodies; and Betts, because her heroine had 'decided not to try natural childbirth, mainly because the doctor who advocated it was male' (Betts 1974 338).

Flowing and dispersal

Descriptions of natural childbirth, on the other hand, predictably use organic, not mechanical imagery for the activities of the body. Sylvia Plath uses organic images of 'splitting': 'I am a seed about to break', 'I am breaking apart like the world' ('Three Women',

Plath 1981). The pain is inflicted by 'horses', not machines, though significantly they do have 'iron hooves'. As we have seen, Plath, though depicting all three of her women through natural imagery, does not gloss over the cruelty of Nature. But even a committed natural childbirth enthusiast like Sheila Kitzinger finds it hard to eliminate 'mechanical' images from her description of birth 'in terms of water and its movement' in *Giving Birth*: 'The uterus works mechanically like the heart, without my willing or dictating what it shall do. Its muscle fibres contract and constrict – feel as if they must grind and pulp, like a ripe peach pressed till all its juice pours out, and everything in the deep well of the pelvis is squeezed and trodden as if in a wine press' (Kitzinger 1987 23). The simile of the 'ripe peach' attempts to reintroduce the organic, but it is totally unclear to what it refers: is the uterus simultaneously press and peach? Kitzinger then changes the image to the familiar one of female body as container for the baby/life: 'My body has become a vessel from which life is poured' (24), but baby and mother are also part of the same flower: 'The child's head, like the hard bud in the middle of the peony, pushes forward between all the uncurled, spreading petals. Wait, as the flower opens' (24). The organic images of seed and flower deal with the opening-out of the body more harmoniously than the metallic splitting images of other writers. But here too there is a sense of complete displacement and dispersal of identity: where and who is the actor, the acted upon? Kitzinger, however, revels in this process, instead of finding it terrifying.

In spite of her willing engulfment, her attempt to turn herself into part of Nature – 'My cliffs and beaches are relentlessly eroded' – there is also a strong sense of a self-conscious *mind* hovering above, or willingly co-operating in, these bodily processes: 'Soar above the raging waters, the swelling wonder of creation', she admonishes herself, 'The waves come faster, and I must go towards each with measured pace, keeping above them with my breathing. If I try to turn and run away, they will engulf me' (Kitzinger 1987 24). Just as much as for Xenia, or Martha, there is a clinging to the conscious 'me' who must not be 'engulfed'; beyond that, there is also the voice that admonishes the self, that orchestrates the whole process.

We find a similar effect in Bagnold's descriptions of a 'flowing' natural birth in *The Squire*. The squire is supposed to unify body and mind during labour: 'her mind went down and lived in her body, ran out of her brain and lived in her flesh' (Bagnold 1987 144). But she also addresses and exhorts herself, divides herself into two, and cannot avoid some 'mechanical' imagery:

> Swim then, swim with it for your life. If you resist, horror, and impediment! If you swim, not pain, but sensation! Who knows the heart of pain, the silver, whistling hub of pain, the central bellows of childbirth which expels one being from another? . . . Keep abreast of it, rush together, you and the violence which is also you!
>
> (145)

Other descriptions of natural childbirth also imply a co-operation between two actors: mind and body, woman and pain, civilised and primitive woman. So Stephanie, in *Still Life*, before the nurses prevent her, finds a way of co-operating with her contractions, turning pain into rhythm. Similarly, in Toi Derricote's 'Natural Birth', though the heroine does not attain the painless Lamaze birth she wanted, she does learn how to co-operate with the 'other woman' inside her body:

> i felt something pulling me inside, a soft call, but i
> could feel her power. something inside me i could go
> with, wide and deep and wonderful. The more i gave
> to her, the more she answered me. i held this conversation
> in myself like a love that never stops.
>
> (Derricote 1983 115)

This harmonious, loving co-operation between mind and body, or different parts of the self, is reminiscent of the loving harmony Ostriker sees between mother and baby, 'the dazzling circuit of contact without dominance' (Ostriker 1989 27). Once again, I am reminded of the more flowing, dispersed sense of self some writers (Chodorow 1978; Cixous 1981; Waugh 1989) have seen as possible to women, because of their experience of reproduction. The fragmentation of identity involved in the birth process may be horrifying; it may also be enlarging.

New selves

It is nearly always the social dimension that shapes how these processes are felt. In this section I want to look at the social identities created for both mother and baby after the birth, as the baby is 'recognised' as a person, and the mother takes on a new role. As Paula Treichler points out, childbirth both 'establishes the offspring's independent existence and simultaneously transforms the woman into a particular kind of social being, a mother' (Treichler 1990 117). This separation into two identities is, of course, fraught with paradox and contradiction, as the mother and baby are interdependent, and the point where the foetus/baby attains personhood is different for different writers. Paradox and mystery are often represented as the supernatural, and the baby is recognised not as a social being, but as a divine, mysterious other. The bodily conditions of maternity throw the social and the supernatural, the cultural and the natural, into disturbing proximities and contradictions.

The new person

Lillian Robinson, discussing the poem by Kathleen Fraser in which the poet addresses the foetus inside her as 'you', remarks that the poem gives 'a feeling that a relationship suffused with living, that is, with social as well as physical aspects, has already begun' (Robinson 1986 282). The opposite effect is created by a short piece by Anne Waldman, called 'Enceinte', which consists of a long list of miscellaneous metaphors describing the foetus: ' . . . sponge, rising loaf, butterfly, trapped bird, wax, mold, flame, a small man writing, small woman eating & lifting elbow, a bat, succulent plant, something in the oven, a potato doll, a doll of seashells, sandbag, large fish swimming in circles, a clock, something silent, a silent toy car, a memory . . .' etc. (Waldman 1983 68). As Kristeva suggests, the situation of pregnancy challenges our usual ideas of personhood and conventions of representation: the foetus is both all and none of these things – the endless list is an attempt to name the unnameable. But some writers *combine* the two ways of representing the foetus, encapsulating the paradoxes involved. For instance, Plath has a poem to her foetus called 'You're' (1961), which consists again of a list of metaphors and similes:

> Wrapped up in yourself like a spool,
> Trawling your dark as owls do.
> Mute as a turnip . . .
> O high-riser, my little loaf.

> (Plath 1981 141)

Erica Jong, in 'The Birth of the Water Baby', similarly addresses her foetus as a person, and describes it with different animal and plant images: 'little egg', 'little rose', 'Oh avocado pit/ almost ready to sprout,/ tiny fruit tree', 'little swimming fish'. The paradoxes of oneness and separation are explored:

> Here, under my heart
> you'll keep
> till it's time
> for us to meet,
> & we come apart
> that we may come
> together . . .

> (Jong 1983 72)

Sethe, in *Beloved*, imagines her kicking foetus as an 'antelope'. This is not the simple animal image it appears at first: it comes from Sethe's dim memories of her own mother, and of the (perhaps African) dances she took part in: 'And oh but when they danced and sometimes they danced the antelope. The men as well as the ma'ams, one of whom was certainly her own. They shifted shapes and became something other. Some unchained, demanding other whose feet knew her pulse better than she did. Just like this one in her stomach' (Morrison 1987 31). The image links the foetus back to her ancestry, and to an image of freedom, the 'unchained, demanding other' who is within all the slaves. While not addressed as 'you', the foetus is recognised as an 'other', who is also the self, and also a manifestation of the society of her ancestors.

In these passages, the 'you', the 'other', both is and is not a person. Writers who imagine the foetus as an unequivocal person tend to produce a rather grotesque effect. This is especially true of two writers in Laura Chester's collection *Cradle and All*, who imagine the foetus present as a person while the woman makes love with her partner. Barbara Rosenthal describes how

> The baby moves inside my body and Bill reaches for me with his palm open. I think the baby is a boy – two males inside and outside pushing their bodies into mine, moving around me inside and out.
> The baby is a girl and Bill reaches for us both, fucks us, loves us both. He kisses my sex, laps at the lips of my vulva where the baby will squeeze through soon, head first, lips first.

> (Rosenthal 1984 71)

The boy/girl uncertainty keeps the baby's identity unfixed, but imagining it as definitely either produces, for me, unsettling suggestions of incest, gang-rape and child abuse. The 'social' intrudes with a vengeance. Gladys Hindmarch's 'A Birth Account' is less direct:

> When he kissed my belly I felt he was kissing both me and you, little one, inside, his love to you direct. That instant I thought you moved to him and I felt you there for the first time, he more with you than I am, how can that be, now I feel you are here, there, I was more afraid of love than he. All three of us are tied in this heart, this belly.
>
> (Hindmarsh 1989 63)

The repetition of the pronouns – you, I, he, me, him – produces an effect of confusion and merging of identities, including the male lover too in the merging of mother and foetus.

These women address the baby as 'you' while it is still in the womb, whereas Enid Bagnold and A. S. Byatt reserve this direct address until the first moment of recognition of the new-born by the mother, in strikingly similar scenes. '"So it was you!"' says the squire to her new baby, 'thinking of her nine months companion, of her hardness towards him, now melted . . . and thinking with wonderment "So it was *you*"' (Bagnold 1987 182). Stephanie too 'recognised' her baby: '"You", she said to him, skin for the first time on skin in the outside air, which was warm and shining, "you"' (Byatt 1986 94). Both mothers attribute a unique personhood to the new baby, as opposed to the impersonal foetus – a 'god' for the squire, a 'thing' for Stephanie – but the implications of the scenes are rather different. For the squire, birth is the moment when the divine, ancient foetus gives up its divinity and becomes part of humanity, vulnerable and in need of care. The foetus 'had nothing to do with the born baby that . . . once born, would throw up its mastery and lie, shocked and naked, just within the gates of the world' (Bagnold 1987 30). The transition from one state to another is presented as a mystery, a paradox – while she is in labour, she catches sight of the cot, and watches 'the things laid out with which to wash what WAS NOT THERE, to warm the feet of what DID NOT BREATHE, the settling of the pillows and the blankets for what COULD NOT BE TOUCHED' (144). The parallel paradoxes, and the impersonal 'what', turn this sentence into a riddle, whose answer is the baby. The embryo, before the birth, both is and is not there, both is and is not a person. But, once born, the new baby gradually loses his special mystery: 'He was unpacked now from his mystery and put into his family life' (218).

For Stephanie, on the other hand, suggestions of mystery and divinity only appear once the child is born: the 'you' she recognises is a semi-divine new being, not part of a human social relationship. After her negative experiences of pregnancy and childbirth, during which the foetus is a very physical antagonist, Stephanie experiences 'ecstasy' at the sight of her new-born. She and the child have a Wordsworthian experience of 'light': 'the light poured through the window, brighter and brighter, and his eyes saw it, and hers, and she was aware of bliss' (Byatt 1986 94). As in the 'Immortality Ode', the child is born 'trailing clouds of glory' (Wordsworth 1971 460–2 v. 5). But Wordsworth's birth-myth completely excludes any mention of woman's physical role in giving birth – his child arrives on earth direct from heaven, with no female intermediary. When a woman uses his myth to describe her own experience of giving birth, the reintroduction of the physical aspect must challenge or revise Wordsworth's account: as Anne Stevenson puts it in 'The Victory', 'The stains/of your cloud of glory/bled from my veins' (Couzyn 1985 191). Byatt does not challenge Wordsworth directly like this, but Wordsworth's myth is implicitly revised. Thus, while for Wordsworth the 'prisonhouse' closed its shades on 'the growing boy', during Stephanie's labour, 'the thing launched itself again against its prison walls' (Byatt 1986 92). Here, the child comes from a prison, not from heaven, and enjoys a brief moment of light, before other shades of everyday life close in. The woman who has to carry the child in her womb, and physically to give birth, cannot subscribe to Wordsworth's male myth of transcendent origins. The 'light' that momentarily bathes Stephanie's child is left as an anomalous and sourceless phenomenon.

The moment of 'light' is a private recognition between mother and baby; when the social dimension intrudes, 'mystery' is lost again. Society exerts its pressures on Stephanie and her baby almost immediately, as she is 'ground between two communities, the ward and the family, both it seemed intent on forming her and William to their own rites and classifications' (Byatt 1986 99). The presence of the other women in the ward, listening to her conversation with her husband, prevents her from telling him about her ecstatic experience with the new-born baby. The nurses, with their routines, 'dehumanise' the babies: 'There was no mystery in the eyes of William in the hands of a cross nurse at two in the morning' (100). Stephanie names the baby William, after Wordsworth, but the family immediately asserts its influence, as she remembers it is also her father's name. Her desire to keep the baby '*separate*' is undermined: "'He's getting tied into the community and he's only been here a few hours"' (97). As successive family visitors hold the baby, he takes on different appearances. His heredity takes possession of him. These transformations are seen as a contamination: 'After a day's visiting William's heat was wrong – he was sweaty with other people's sweat, damp in nappies other people had touched. . . . His smell was obscured by others' (106). Assimilation into the family is seen as a negative process: he is 'pounced' on by Stephanie's father, he 'vanishes' into Daniel's mother's gross body. There is an antithesis between the baby's bright new separate self, and the weight of inheritance he cannot avoid: this antithesis of course fits in to the Wordsworthian model that structures Stephanie's thoughts about the birth.

The comparison between Bagnold and Byatt suggests that recognising the baby as 'you' can either imply recognising a new social being, *or* recognising a divine other. We have already seen how several writers use myths of incarnation to attribute divinity to the foetus/baby. In *Puffball*, Liffey, like Stephanie, also has a totally private 'spiritual' relationship with her baby, though this occurs while he is still in the womb. Implications of the divine and mysterious point to the unrepresentability of the relationship, its paranormal quality. In Laura Chester's 'The Stone Baby', immediately after the birth Julia, the mother, is totally wrapped up in 'this wonderful baby, fresh from another world' (Chester 1989a 129), echoing the Wordsworthian myth again. Naomi Shihab Nye feels her newborn is 'an Angel, a Miracle', not just 'a boy' (Chester 1989b 194). Sylvia Plath's 'First Voice' imagines new-born babies 'showering like stars on to the world – / On India, Africa, America, these miraculous ones . . .' (Plath 1981 183).

The miraculous moment of first greeting is the traditional high point of natural childbirth accounts: 'beautiful and emotional', 'fantastic', 'words can't describe', write Kitzinger's pupils in *Giving Birth* (Kitzinger 1987: 75, 90, 152). And yet these descriptions contain very little reference to the *baby* – they are mostly celebrations of the woman's triumph: 'I did it!' (152). Quite often the

baby as it is born is referred to by its name – 'Andrew', 'Emma' –
or as 'my son' or 'my daughter': these are clearly projections back
from a later recognition of distinct, social, personhood. Kitzinger's
own prototypical description in *The Experience of Childbirth*
suggests not so much the miraculous nature of the baby, but his
very human 'indignation' at being born: 'The child's legs slither out
and his screams get louder and louder, and all the muscles of his
little body seem to be clenched in protest, in indignation at being
born. His mother laughs; he looks so annoyed, so helpless, his rage
is so futile, and she wants to protect him from himself and his own
violent emotions' (Kitzinger 1962 152).

Ann Oakley's book of 'real life' accounts explicitly sets out
to debunk the marvellous moment of recognition: seventy per
cent of her informants were 'not interested' on first holding
their new baby. While Kitzinger dramatises the baby's rage and
bewilderment, but presents the mother as totally delighted,
Oakley's informants report bewilderment on both sides: 'They
said oh its a little girl – like in the films. They gave her to me:
I felt bewildered. She was looking at me: I was looking at her. She
looked very bewildered herself really' (Oakley 1981 97). Seen as a
social relationship, not an instinctual or a divine one, it is distinctly
awkward, as Xenia notices in *Birth Rites*: 'Mothers who'd done it
before talked naturally to their new babies, but the others were too
afraid, too shy, to converse with their firstborns. They had hardly
been introduced, after all' (Bowder 1983 202). Joyce Thompson
and Jane Lazarre, as we have seen, describe how later on the babies'
separate personhood asserts itself as habits and needs that conflict
with the mothers' own. Doris Lessing describes a similar process
in *A Proper Marriage*: Martha's relationship with her daughter
develops from pre-birth harmony to post-birth antagonism: 'before
Caroline was born she had seen her as "a baby" merely, something
felt in the deep, driving egotism of maternity as an extension of
herself and dependent upon her. Yet here she was, not at all a
baby, but a creature who became every day more independent,
strong-willed, determined. . . . The rhythm of Caroline's needs was
in sharp discord with her own' (Lessing 1977 279).

The baby's separate selfhood is perhaps most clearly stressed in
those few accounts which, rather than address it as 'you', imagine
it speaking as 'I'. Again, this can be a semi-divine 'I', as in the baby
who speaks to Liffey from the womb in *Puffball*, or a thoroughly

human and social 'I', disgruntled and indignant. Laura Chester's
'Song of Being Born' imagines the sensations of birth from the
baby's point of view:

> My head hurts in circles get heavier
> squeezed through a tightness
> Can't look now
> I've lost it
> Just cold and noise and light down the suck hole
> Won't give either way
> crammed inside
> outside it's confusing
> Something gripped over my ears hurts metal sounds silver
> Like a screech my blood begs
> A suction snarl pulling my head off it's
> no here come my shoulders
> dragged into harshlight . . .
>
> (Chester 1975 77–8)

Bowder also imagines the consciousness of Mrs Long's baby
as he is born, though as a 'he', not an 'I': 'These attacks of
unknown, mighty forces . . . all terrified him in a united, a
continuous aggression' (Bowder 1983 43). For both babies, birth
is a disappointment, an expulsion from Paradise: 'To get back to
the perfect harmony of his first resting place was all he wanted,
and the only thing he could never have again. His struggle . . . was
rewarded with this, this disappointment, this aloneness' (Bowder
1983 43):

> never again
> that best sleep
> that very far back
> smooth
> snug one
>
> (Chester 1975 78–9)

Both accounts repeat the Wordsworthian myth of happy pre-
existence, though locating it in the womb, not in heaven. The
mother is reduced to 'unknown . . . forces', an aggressor, or a
breast: 'It's soft too and round too and part of it juts/ parts of
me and my lips fit' (Chester 1975 78). Again we have the two
models, organic whole or antagonistic opponents, though both
blot out the mother as a person. These accounts of the baby's
consciousness seem too easily to repeat myths and models that

discount the mother's existence as a consciousness, as any more than an environment for the *real* person, the baby.

The new mother

In Doris Betts's 'Still Life with Fruit', a nurse asks the heroine if she has thought of a name for the baby yet. '"No." Gwen lied. *She* needed the new name. *She* was the one who would never be the same' (Betts 1974 353). Surprisingly, the naming of the new baby is not a particularly important scene in women's fictional accounts of birth, while the re-naming of the woman appears in several, and the implication that she has a new identity after the birth is all-pervasive. At the end of *The Birth Machine*, as Zelda escapes from the hospital with her baby, 'She names herself: Teacher, Scientist. . . . At last, to acknowledge her own insights, to be her own author' (Baines 1983 119). She is performing 'Metamorphosis' (120). This all implies that it is not just the baby, but her new self who is born, 'authored', and as we have seen the baby itself is very much a symbol of her recovered self. This image of childbirth as the birth of the *mother* is made explicit in Ostriker's poem: 'no matter what your age is you/ are born when you give birth/ to a baby you start over' (Ostriker 1980 25).

Re-naming and rebirth of the mother are both part of Atwood's short story 'Giving Birth'. At the beginning, the narrator claims 'This story about birth is not about me' (Atwood 1984 226), and yet we discover at the end what we may have suspected all along, that Jeanie, the protagonist, is a name for the narrator's earlier self. Jeanie is presented to us first as a *fictional* character – 'Jeanie isn't real in the same way that I am real' (228). A little later, however, the narrator plays with the reader's suspicion that Jeanie may be her earlier self: 'you may be thinking I've invented Jeanie in order to distance myself from these experiences', while in fact, she is 'trying to bring myself closer to something that time has already made distant. As for Jeanie, my intention is simple: I am bringing her back to life' (229). In a story about 'giving birth', this claim raises the possibility that it may be Jeanie, the narrator's former self, who is being 'reborn' in and by the story. At the end of the story, this expectation is reversed, or perhaps just added to, by the narrator's climactic insight: 'It was to me, after all, that the birth was given, Jeanie gave it, I am the result' (239). The opening description of the narrator's happy, solid existence with her baby shows us this 'result'. The narrator contrasts her 'solid' world with the insubstantiality and vagueness of Jeanie's existence – 'washes of light, shifts, nebulous effects of cloud, Turner sunsets, vague fears' (227–8). A vague and insubstantial heroine attains definition through the birth of a baby. In Drabble's *The Millstone* too, a new, more solid personality is acquired by the mother. George, the baby's unwitting father, is contrasted in his vagueness and indifference to the baby with Rosamund's love and commitment: 'he was myself, the self that but for accident, but for fate, but for chance, but for womanhood, I would still have been' (172). In a different way, Ruth in Brittain's *Honourable Estate* (1936) discovers a new, political self through the birth of her babies: she is educated in sympathy with less fortunate women, and plans a political career to help them.

These re-namings and rebirths of the heroine suggest a discontinuity of subjectivity over time, while the 'splittings' of the actual birth-process suggest a dispersal of subjectivity through space. While the writers I have looked at so far see this rebirth as positive, giving birth to a more definite, purposeful self, others experience bewilderment and even loss, as a former sense of self is dissipated. In Marianne Gingher's 'Camouflage', the heroine looks back to 'the cavelike void of who she'd been once' (1988 158). The baby gives her a brief sense of importance in the world, but gradually, after she has given up the baby for adoption, the sense of meaning fades: 'First you are in one place, then another, misfortune simply part of the landscape of travel. That simple. Having a baby had been like stopping off for a minute in a ghost town. You certainly couldn't get off the bus and stay. There was nothing for you there, so you just rode on and you didn't ask where' (164). Has she just reverted to her former self: 'Had she really gone backwards to this: such girlish safety and goodness?' Yet her friends are curious: '*Who was she now*? She was different and remote and her knowledge was forbidding' (168).

Toi Derricote also ponders the question of whether you can go back afterwards to your old self:

> my roommate, snotty,
> bragging about how she didn't give a damn about the
> kid and was going back to her boyfriend and be a
> cheerleader in high school.   *could we ever 'go back'?*

*would our bodies be the same?   could we hide among the
childless?*

(1983 108)

Sylvia Plath's Second Voice, who has the miscarriage, does, un-
happily, put on her old identity again: 'The nurses give back my
clothes, and an identity'. But the Third Voice, who has abandoned
her baby, gladly escapes from the maternal self: 'There are the
clothes of a fat woman I do not know' ('Three Women', Plath 1981
183, 184). Martha in Lessing's *A Proper Marriage* also attempts to
discard her pregnant identity by relentless dieting: 'she had refound
that slimness which had been hers before she had married. Looking
incredulously in the mirror . . . she confronted a slight, firm young
woman with high breasts. . . . She was herself, though a new
self' (Lessing 1977 178). Other mothers find this 'girlhood' self
impossible to recover:

> I turned to that self inside of me, that girlwoman who had once
> been all I needed to know of myself, whom I had fought to
> understand, to love, to free – I turned to her now and I banished
> her. Into a protective shell tied in a knot, she retreated, four,
> five, six times a day, whenever Benjamin wanted to nurse. Soon,
> even when I sought her, she would not come, but began to stay
> out of reach longer and longer, sometimes not reappearing for
> whole days.
>
> (Lazarre 1976 209–10)

The old self is lost, and no new self has been born to take its place:
childbirth is more a death than a birth of the mother's self. Other
mothers who feel in competition with their babies produce images
of dispersed, hazy new selves: Plath's 'cloud' in 'Morning Song', or
this image from Carole Itter's 'Cry Baby': 'To collect whatever is
myself at the end of the day is about as interesting or possible as
collecting raindrops from the windowpane' (Chester 1989b 217).

Childbirth as the death of the mother, rather than her rebirth,
is perhaps most clearly expressed by Byatt in *Still Life*. Stephanie's
births seem to lead inevitably to her death in a horrible domestic
accident. Byatt uses the language of Wordsworth to describe the
gradual darkening of Stephanie's life, the loss of her separate self.
Wordsworth's 'Immortality Ode' is used not only to describe the
new baby, but the progress of Stephanie's life. When she has a few
hours off from looking after her baby, she studies the 'Immortality

Ode' in the library. First, she cannot concentrate, and thinks instead of the University Library at Cambridge, and 'of "my life", of the desired shape of "my life" as it had seemed so clear and so bright in that earlier library' (Byatt 1986 153) – and then she realises she *is* thinking about the 'Immortality Ode': the gradual darkening of the light in that poem is happening to her. This is confirmed later, when she is pregnant with her second child, and this time 'cycled more slowly to the hospital, her mind dense with times, weights, measures, precautions, vitamins, blood sample, Will's diet, yeast, little cakes for the Mothers' Union. Custom and frost, frost and custom' (242–3. See v. 8 of the 'Ode'). But notice that the imagery of the 'Immortality Ode' functions somewhat differently when it is applied to a *woman's* life – Stephanie's moment of 'light' was when she was a young woman at Cambridge, full of bright prospects; Wordsworth's was when he was an infant, or at most a young boy. It is not the coming of adulthood as such that dims Stephanie's light, but specifically marriage and motherhood.

We can contrast this British gloom with the American confidence of Sharon Olds' rewriting of Walt Whitman in 'The Language of the Brag'. Here, maternal self-creation and physical accomplishment is celebrated:

> slowly alone in the center of a circle I have
> passed the new person out . . .
>
> I have done what you wanted to do, Walt Whitman,
> Allen Ginsberg. I have done this thing.
> I and the other women this exceptional
> act with the exceptional heroic body . . .
>
> (Olds 1980 134–5)

The language here reminds me of Bagnold's and Karmel's images of birthing woman as heroic achiever: soldier, boxer, athlete. But here the heroic female body is not an equivalent to the heroic male body, but better than, more truly heroic than the male poets who have only 'wanted' to do this heroic act of birth. While some women, as we have seen, find their identities dispersed by the experience of childbirth, in this poem the woman's identity is confirmed, gathered together 'in the centre of a circle'. 'The new person' is, ambiguously, the baby, the mother's new self, and the poem.

These two examples, Byatt and Olds, from different cultures, suggest once again how far cultural context can determine the meaning of childbirth for different women. Whether figured as a death or a heroic rebirth, childbirth is, however, always a turning-point, a narrative crisis that destroys, confirms or creates a woman's sense of identity. What women writers on childbirth have been doing is giving that turning-point shape, voice, representation, whether they speak from the centre of a circle (Olds 1980 134–5), or from a point somewhere up on the ceiling (Baines 1983; Bowder 1983; Hoffman 1985), or from several dispersed centres: mind/body, mother/foetus/baby.

Conclusion

I wouldn't have written this book if I hadn't myself given birth. I might not have been so critical of the natural childbirth movement if I hadn't given birth by emergency Caesarean. The autobiographical investment of the critic in the criticism is a topic that needs further research (Stanley 1992; Tompkins 1991; Jouve 1991). This seems to be the moment to tell my own birth-story: but I want to come at it rather obliquely, through a dialogue with other women and different stories. In the summer of 1992, I was engaged in a project that involved recording women's oral birth narratives. The idea was to discover what contemporary 'old wives' tales' were really like. While the forms of oral narrative are quite different from written accounts, involving great use of repetition, stategic pauses, and re-tellings of the same story with different emphases, these stories too revealed women in negotiation with the 'official' discourses of childbirth, finding ways to cast themselves as central, significant characters in their own birth-stories.

Obviously, the presence of the tape recorder meant that the characteristic situation for the telling of old wives' tales (inter-female intimacy) couldn't be exactly reproduced, but I chose women I knew well, from a variety of cultural backgrounds, and as the interviews proceeded I found myself becoming more and more involved, telling more of my own story. The form of the old wives' tale – women telling each other birth-stories – was claiming me. I was pleased to discover that this inclusion of the interviewer in the interview is now seen as good feminist practice (Nielsen 1990; Roberts 1981; Stanley 1990). What was interesting from the point of view of my story was the way it came out differently, with different emphases, when told to different women, in the context of their stories. Oral narrative can give this sense of stories in process, different versions being tried out: some of the other women found their stories changed in the telling of them. What I want to do now is to investigate some versions of my own story, in the context of other women's stories: to present my story like this, from a context of spontaneous conversation, means I have more chance of catching myself unawares, revealing my own cultural assumptions. In writing down these oral narratives, I am also contributing to writing the childbirth-story.

The three women to whom I told most of my story all told what could be regarded as 'horror stories', true to the literary stereotype of the old wives' tale. Mine too can be read like this. We all, thus, have to negotiate our way around the prevailing optimistic childbirth-stories. Interestingly, all of us expressed extreme tact and hesitation about the idea of telling our stories to pregnant women: unlike the stereotype, it seemed these old wives' tales were more likely to be told to other mothers than to the uninitiated. The three women were Beth Brown, a married teacher of autistic children; Keiko Ishimaru, a single mother and student; and Janice Mitchell, a married childminder and cleaner. Some of these are assumed names, at the women's requests. My words or interjections appear in round brackets in the text, as in (Laughs); interjections by the interviewees in square brackets, as in [Laughs]. [Laughter], however, indicates that both of us laugh. When I am telling my own story to the other women, I change my transcription conventions, so that mine becomes the main voice, and the interviewees' interjections are in square brackets.

Beth Brown teaches at a special school. She is white, born in 1958, married, and has two children, aged six and four at the time of the interview. Beth's story was from the point of view of someone who had been prepared by a very accommodating hospital and by her reading to enjoy an easy, natural birth, and who was horribly disappointed when the whole experience turned out to be 'horrendous', a tale of unhealthiness and loss of control. Before the interview, Beth had told me that she had found this experience impossible to talk about for a long time, though she had made an attempt at writing about it. Her telling it to me was especially full of pauses and hesitations, and sympathetic noises from me. There was a lot of laughter, which could have been a defence against the unpleasant feelings aroused, and also a way of making the story socially acceptable. Beth apologised at one point for sounding 'dramatic', but at the same time emphasised words like 'ghastly' and 'horrendous'. She contrasted her experience several times with the 'wonderful stories' told by other women about birth, and complained about the silence about experiences like hers. There was clearly a tension going on between her need to tell her story and the feeling that it was not an acceptable one. Some of the laughter was ironic, at the contrast between the wonderful stories, her wonderful expectations, and the reality of what happened to her.

Her story had two 'afterwords': in one, she emphasised the loss of control which was a main theme in her story. While in the main story it was her usually healthy body that had let her down, here some complaints about her treatment by the (seemingly enlightened) medical institution emerged. In the second afterword, she began to complain of the silence about experiences like hers: far from having been exposed to horrific 'old wives' tales', she had heard and read only 'romantic' natural childbirth-stories. This developed into a conversation between us about the problems of telling this sort of experience to other women, and then, logically, into me telling her about my experiences, in so far as parts of her story had resembled or suggested mine.

Beth's story starts quite hopefully: the hospital classes turn out to be unusually 'progressive': 'I was just very impressed with how, um, they were promoting their new birth room, and also they were actually talking about birth-plans, and different ways of going about it'. The beautiful 'birth room' becomes a focus of ironic humour later in the account, as hopeful expectations are defeated:

> I was all ready for, you know, to be shown in, 'cause at the hospital they were *nice* rooms for ordinary births (Mm, mm), you know, they were all very pleasantly done up, really very nice, and then there were a couple of, er, complications rooms (Yes, yes), but we'd assumed we'd be one of these nice ones with the lovely curtains [Laughter], that's right, and we, we were all planned, you know our little case being put in there, and I was just being checked over, and, um, the next, they suddenly discovered well, she was until that moment an undetected breech, so everything suddenly changed from that minute.

Like the classes, the books Beth had read also created false expectations:

> I sort of was very keen to have sort of as natural a birth as possible
> (Yes), and sort of read all the books . . . so I felt I was fairly genned
> up on, on a lot of those things, and I'd always assumed, wrongly as
> it happened, that it was going to be, you know, a fairly OK time
> (Yes), you know, we were going to do things properly, so, we'd
> got all the, er, the nice beautiful tapes to listen to, for sort of the
> birth, and we'd got it all sorted out, you know, it was going to be a
> really nice experience, and, um, yes, and nothing, nothing worked
> out according to plan.

Beth's irony at the naive young couple's expectations is apparent
here.

While here Beth creates the clash between innocence and experience, in her story as told to me after the event premonitions of
disaster are evident from the beginning, even before the birth. The
whole story is a series of 'trials' and defeats by her body: fertility
problems, worrying test results, varicose veins: 'I mean, right from
the word go it just seems to have been difficult, and I think having
been what I felt a really quite healthy person, having a very healthy
lifestyle, it came as, it was very hard (Yes, yes) for the first time
in my life suddenly to feel, feel unwell'. Beth's body is letting her
down, her identity as 'healthy person' is threatened: 'there's this
sort of vegetarian, sort of tall slim, I thought this is not the right
person for this child'.

The complication that caused all the problems with Beth's labour
and delivery of her first baby was the 'undetected breech' (the baby
was coming out feet first). In her descriptions of the actual birth the
medical personnel come over as incompetent and confused:

> There was a lot of panic around that room, which, I don't know,
> I wasn't, I wasn't aware of things particularly, but I can remember
> when she was born that there were, there were just doctors flying
> into the room, quickly putting their coat on, you know, so when
> she was born there must have been, I mean, half a dozen people
> there, it was really, um, it was really quite horrifying.

Her characterisation of the whole situation is that it 'was falling
apart', as they are taken to 'the complications room'. She herself
feels 'badly prepared' and 'floundering': she allows an epidural,
but her inappropriate training in non-intervention, and the hospital
staff's lack of explanation, mean she refuses to have it topped up,
and consequently is in agony. Her story does not characterise the
staff as a hostile 'they', acting upon her: both staff and patient

are incompetent and confused, neither are actors, nor in control. The only 'actor' appears to be the labour itself, taking everyone by surprise.

Apart from telling me about the epidural, Beth finds details difficult to remember:

> I mean I, well, I suppose it's difficult to try and actually talk, think it all through, because I think I must have blocked off or, it's funny isn't it, looking back (Yes), I mean you, I mean, I just find it so horrendous, that you almost feel it didn't happen (Yes), and I can't remember the whole, the whole pattern of events you know, um, when forceps arrived, or when the stirrups came up [Laughter], I mean it just merges (Yes) into this one ghastly experience where I didn't feel in control.

The overriding theme of loss of control is stressed again.

Beth was very conscious that her story wasn't the usual or acceptable birth-story among the women she knew. She introduced it by saying, 'when people talk about, er, wonderful pregnancies, wonderful births, I feel I just can't share those experiences', and she concluded her brief description of the birth of her second daughter (also a breech, detected this time): 'you hear some people talk fondly of the birth (Mm), and, you know, the baby coming out, and isn't it wonderful, and I've never been able to share that experience'. Her second afterword is about the way unpleasant birth experiences are 'swept under the carpet':

> But I think I would have appreciated someone telling me, 'Well, it was absolute hell as far as I was concerned' (Yes, yes), I mean I, I do feel it's [Pause] it's, you know, swept under the carpet a little bit (Mm), and OK, all right, I accept that a lot of people didn't have such an unpleasant experience as I did, but, you know, I mean to most people, I mean, whether it's sort of five minutes or five hours of, of a hell of a lot of pain (Mm, mm) the like of which they've never known before, whereas I never got (You never got, mm, yes), no, I never got that, that impression from people particularly (Because I had, I had people telling me horror stories, and I was terribly upset, I thought, how can they tell me this?) Mm (but actually then I found myself, sort of, telling other women) Right (and when I was telling it wasn't a horror story, it was just telling them what it was like) (Laughs), Right, right, yes (but when you don't know, it just seems, you know, when you're pregnant, and people are telling you these awful stories, so I actually did get

a couple of –) Did you? Right (and I thought, how tactless, how can they be doing this to me) [Laughter] That's right (they could be just trying to warn me).

I interject here and bring up the problems of 'warning' people: one can slip into frightening 'old wives' tales'. Beth ends by affirming again the extremity of her experience: 'I was absolutely out of my mind with pain and agony (Mm, mm), and I really sort of felt I, you know, I would never survive this (Mm), you know? (Yes, yes) I mean, does that happen to other people?' Her question here set me off telling her about my experience, and an interchange of experiences developed.

I teach English at a university, and do research on women writers. I am white, born in 1947, and I have one daughter, aged six at the time of the interview. In telling my story to Beth, I picked up on her wish for more 'horror' stories like hers, and her question, 'does that happen to other people?':

> That experience you had of the, the topping up of the epidural, they gave me an epidural at first because they were inducing, [Right] but no-one had ever told me that inductions don't work, sometimes [Right], so, so I didn't expect that, and then they said, 'You have to have a Caesarean', so when they'd said that, they didn't bother to top up the epidural, and then it was, there was a *queue* in theatre, someone had a retained placenta and so on, so it was *two* hours, according to Greg, I was just having these sort of, um, these awful induced pains [Laughter] [Oh no] to no purpose, because I was going to have a Caesarean [Gosh], so that was my, my horrible bit, but it was, it was just like you say, it was just blur in the middle of the night [Mm], and I have no sense of how long it was, nor what [Mm, is the, is the –], I just knew that I had some contractions and I didn't like them. [Right, right, mm, it's a very unreal experience, isn't it? I find it very difficult to, to be accurate about] Yes, [you know, all that sort of, middle bit, um, yeh, I mean sort of Richard who's obviously overlooking things, I mean he couldn't] Mm, [he couldn't really be very involved because there was just so many] Yes [medical people around, I mean he was sort of very much pushed to the, um, outside . . .] Yes, poor old Greg had Alice thrust into his arms while they were still sewing me up, so there was Alice sort of going like this, [Laughter] and he was thinking 'What can I do?' [Laughter] So he must have a different story, obviously he has a

different story [Yes, that's right], but he, um, was awake and I was, um [Yes, yeh] (Pause), [one of them was put in my arms ... and I just, you know, was not in a position to] to react [to react, I think], Yes, yes [which goes against all these wonderful romantic stories] The wonderful stories [you're told, because I mean, you know, I was] Yes, [I can remember being genuinely sort of *delighted* about having a baby] Yes, yes, [but you know just was, was probably still in that sort of state of shock probably, not, not being able to respond as one, one feels you ought to really; I can't really remember an awful lot about that] Yes, I'd been told about the wonderful moment of looking into their eyes, [Oh] and Alice had her eyes screwed tightly shut [Laughter] [Yes, yes], and looked really cross. [Yes, I mean, I mean, I'm sure, you know, you can do all those sorts of things] Yes [if you've if you've gone through] if you're feeling really good.

Here we share the telling of 'horrible bits' and the repudiation of the 'wonderful romantic stories'. I start by responding to her story of the epidural; then she sympathises with my loss of the sense of time. I then respond to her talking about Richard with my story of Greg: both of us briefly imagine the story from the different point of view of the husband. This moves into our both countering the 'wonderful moment' of first recognition with our own experiences. We recognise features of each other's stories, both in terms of content (the epidural, the 'blur'), and form (the husband's version; the 'wonderful first moment'). We give each other permission to reveal 'horrible bits' and to laugh at the perfect natural childbirth-stories.

Keiko Ishimaru is an undergraduate student of Women's Studies at a British university. She is Japanese, born in Japan in 1952. She comes from a middle-class family, and did various 'alternative' activities for a while. She was married to an Englishman, but is now a divorced single parent. She has two children, aged eight and seven at the time of the interview. Keiko's was my first interview with a woman from a non-Western culture. Her children had been born in Japan, but in what she considered a very 'Westernised' way, due to the influence of her British expatriate husband. In an 'afterword', she drew very explicit contrasts between Japanese and British attitudes to birth. She had also been influenced by the Western feminist health and natural childbirth movements, through translations of Western books by herself and her friends: her resulting belief in non-interventionist birth was not seen as contrasting with Japanese beliefs. The main cultural contrasts she drew were between the woman's *mother* as opposed to her *husband* as main partner in the birth-story; and between Japanese family intimacy and British embarrassment.

In her two birth-stories themselves, however, cultural contrasts are less important than an overriding and (to me) unexpected moral that she finds in the experience: childbirth taught her to accept her own vulnerability and helplessness, and tempered her previous individualism; she was able to sympathise with other 'losers' whom she had previously despised, and to appreciate interdependence through her relationship to her babies. So she emphasised the same experience of loss of control that other women had told me about, but instead of interpreting it as the fault of the medical institution, or her female body, or her own failure of will, she sees it as a beneficial learning experience. This learning experience is perhaps parallelled by the trajectory of her life story so far, from middle-class childhood, through an irresponsible 'holiday' period doing 'funny alternative things', through childbirth, to divorce, homelessness and single parenthood.

Keiko begins by telling me she wanted a 'natural birth' at home, not the 'white walls' of a hospital. The idea of this came from a feminist consciousness-raising group she was in, who were translating *Our Bodies Ourselves*. Later she told me of another friend who had been translating a book called *Natural Birth*. Her ideas came from both the feminist and ecological movements, which made her and her friends 'quite aware of what doctors have done to us'. On the other hand, despite setting the births in this wider ideological context, she stressed three times in her account that books conveyed no sense at all of what the experience was like:

> I had no idea what actually, you know, I have to, I have to go through. (Yes, you mean) I read lots of books (Yes) and breathing, yoga, whatever (Yes, yes), but I think how the whole, it's another, like a [Inaudible] concerning with this so primitive, but at the same time so strong ex, experience (Yes, yes) I had.

Later she includes books about mothering in her criticism, and I agree with her: 'All this textbooks (Yes, yes) makes me feel like I'm worst student in the world kind of [Laughs] (Yes). I felt everybody else was doing very well. Did it feel in that way? kind of (You mean other mothers or) Mm (Oh yes, yes, that they knew how to do it somehow) Mm'. Here she recurs to a metaphor she uses several times in her account: birth as a kind of academic test. She both criticises the practices and ideologies that make it seem so, and shows how the experience, being beyond the 'books', can suggest there is another set of values or way of seeing that can liberate a woman from this competitive attitude.

Keiko's original 'dream' of a home birth has to be given up because of opposition from her husband. This ex-husband appears several times as an obstructive and jealous figure: here he is afraid of being 'excluded' by a midwife who can't speak English. Keiko's story of her first birth experience has two sides: on the one hand she emphasises its difficulty, painfulness, and difference from all the books; on the other, she emphasises it as a 'good' experience, teaching her valuable lessons:

> A painful story was (Yes), but I didn't kind of, I think I couldn't imagine this, this sort of 16 hours, or 20 hours, or whatever (Yes) laying there. . . . I was just so (Mm), so vulnerable, mm, pain, you know, having a pain and vomiting and sort of not easy to move around (Yes), so yes, I, I think maybe it's the first time in my life I feel so uncontrollable, kind of. [Pause] Yes, as I suddenly remember, I talked about this to my friend. Usually if you work, study, or do something (Mm) somehow we think kind of like nothing is impossible, like we, we try, we put effort (Yes), and we get certain kind of result, according to (Yes, yes) effort you have put (Yes), but I think starting with this sort of contraction (Yes), everything, and also dealing with children, was the first time I felt, you know, it's not just only my willingness or my (Yes) attitude. I've been really good [Laughter] and still punished. But this sort of, kind of, there's something else. (Yes, yes) This sort of baby has got her wishes (Yes), her own plans, so it's not me sort of delaying, lazy or anything. (Yes) Mm, it was I think one of the best experience I think I, I ha- (One of the best?), sort of to realise (Oh, to realise that).

'A painful story' is also 'one of the best experience'. The useful lesson is not just her own vulnerability, and the failure of her 'self-help' ideology, but an appreciation of the 'other': she is the only mother I interviewed who thought of the birth as the *baby's* story as well, the baby with her own 'willingness' and 'plans': 'Children has got their own sort of ability or sense, the wish to survive (Mm). It's not me (Mm), I was just helping (Yes), but this little thing has got, you know, her own sort of (Yes) willingness or whatever'. She returns to this point when she describes the birth of her second child, a much more difficult delivery involving a suction machine and a very weak and possibly brain-damaged child: 'he wanted to come out, I felt really, kind of, it's part of myself, it's not me just only myself (Yes) pushing a baby out, (Yes) baby has to come out by herself or by himself (Yes, has to do something) also, so, so we're kind of like working together'.

After Keiko finishes telling me about the birth of her son, I tell her about my Caesarean. I tell it much more as a self-contained story than with Beth, with Keiko interjecting sympathetic agreement and laughter. In telling my story to Keiko, I emphasised the loss of control theme:

> I think part of it was just I'd never been in hospital before, so it was that completely losing control [Yes], and that the general anaesthetic was the extreme of that [Yes]. I mean, up till then, you know, I'd been doing all the right things, arguing with them, saying couldn't I do something else [Yes], but they won all the way down the line [Yes] [Laughter], and in the end they knocked me out completely [Yes], so I was completely, um, you know, made helpless [Yes it is] [Inaudible] [like you are kind of big thing] Yes, [like a big baby, you are very useless] Yes, yes, yes. [It's really interesting, I think it is strongest experience in my life to feel weak] Yes. I felt so kind of violated afterwards [Mm], it really took me a long time.

It's interesting, however, that my story is still about the medical authorities doing something to me that I'm not able to withstand; I don't see it as a 'primitive' experience overwhelming me (obviously this is hard with a Caesarean!). Though we can agree on the 'loss of control' theme, I don't draw a moral lesson from my experience, and I remain feeling 'violated', not just vulnerable. Keiko's emphasis on the value of feeling vulnerable, of realising one's relationality to others, fits in with the psychological theories of feminist writers like Jean Baker Miller and Nancy Chodorow; though interestingly, contrary to Chodorow's theory, Keiko is not herself equipped with a 'relational' sense of self from her own upbringing as a girl. Her birth-story becomes part of the story of this discovery; while this discovery would be part of any account I would give of my subsequent career as a mother, my birth-story follows a different model, in which my right to be in control is violated by technical intervention.

Janice Mitchell is a cleaner and childminder. Her husband is an electrician. She is white, born in 1955, and has two children, aged twelve and thirteen at the time of the interview. Janice's was one of the longest interviews I did: we know each other well, and often spend time together talking about our children. After she had told me her stories, she turned to me and asked, 'What was your experience like?' and I told the fullest version of my story in these interviews, while she took on the role of the interviewer/listener. Janice told me two stories, one a 'straightforward' birth, but frightening because it was the first; the other a complicated and painful double breech, which resulted in her twice-repeated decision never to have another baby. It is in the vehemence of this reaction rather than the description itself that the nature of this experience is conveyed. In her recounting of these births, Janice shows a very clear grasp of medical terminology, and the medical version of what is going on, though she also sometimes stresses that she didn't know this at the time.

Her stories also show a mixture of contradictory attitudes towards the hospital staff: she feels you have to 'trust' them, they know best, they are probably doing things for your own good, but on the other hand she criticises them a lot for their impersonal, unhelpful attitudes, and even incompetence. In her telling of her birth experience, there is a sense of acceptance and realism: these things happen, and have to be put up with; but at the same time she decides never to do it again. Janice's story of Russell's birth is similar in events to Beth's horrendous story, but much more calmly narrated. She also did not have any expectations that this *was* going to be an easy or wonderful event, though she is clearly aware of women who do experience birth in this way. Similarly, she is aware of the contemporary custom of having husbands present at the birth, but defends her decision not to.

Janice's story about Victoria's birth begins with the superior knowledge of the hospital as to what is going on:

I went to the hospital in the afternoon, and they just, I thought they were telling me to come back the following week (Mm), and they, they gave me an internal examination, said, 'Oh, could you come back about six o'clock tonight?' very calm. They obviously knew (Yes, oh) that labour was on its way, and I, I just had backache, presumed it was the way (Yes) I'd been sitting or (Mm) . . .

But when she gets to the hospital, the juxtaposition of their knowledge and her innocence turns into a story of misinformation:

The nurse came about midnight, and said, 'Oh yes, you're well on your way', and I always remember thinking, 'Well, if this is as bad as it gets (Uhuh) it's, it's OK, I can cope with this' (Yes, yes), but then about five o'clock the next morning I kept thinking, 'Why did they tell me I was well on the way?' because they, kind of, they mixed me up a bit with all the stages. I kept thinking when (Oh), when she said that to me (That it was about to happen), that it was nearer the, you know, third stage (Yes, yes), and I was, I was well on my way (Yes), but it obviously was only the very early stages of the first, kind of, stage.

Interestingly, Janice now knows the correct order of stages and can tell this story from a position of knowledge. Later, in answer to a question of mine about the hospital staff, Janice recurred to the story about Victoria's birth, and revealed more resentment about her treatment:

(Do you remember any of the staff particularly, any of the midwives or doctors and what they were like?) Um, yuh, I had, I had the Irish midwife that when I went in with Victoria (Mm) the first time. I think I really needed then, the first one, a really friendly kind of nurse, and I didn't get one. The midwife, because she was Irish, very, very fiery (Oh), very efficient (Yes, but not sympathetic), but I remember ringing and calling for her, say at half past eight or something. I didn't feel very well (Yes). 'You, you won't feel well, you won't feel on top form, and you're about to have a baby' (Yes). Then, when she went away, I'm thinking, 'Well, there's something not right' (Yes, yes), and being too frightened really to ring her again (Yes) and say, and then a young nurse came and, not, not a midwife, just a nurse (Mm), and she was so kind and friendly, but I felt at ease then (Mm, mm). But she was the mid-, Miss McMann was the midwife that was (In charge) in charge of me . . . and I just wished, well, I don't know, perhaps if I'd have had a softer midwife I probably wouldn't have gone on with it as easy as I did do with one that was a bit assertive and (Yes) could (Yes), you know, get me through it (Inaudible), rather than one that was fussing over you (Mm, mm), you know.

Here her attitude to Miss McMann is balanced between resentment and a possible acceptance that this was what she needed: two interpretations are possible and Janice hesitates between them.

The same mixed attitude is present when she relates the story of Russell's birth. This is a horrific story, but told calmly and with a knowledge of the technical details:

> (So what happened with Russell?) Um, it was because it was a double breech, which meant he was bottom first (Oh), and then, um, the bottom comes out first, and then they got his legs (Yes), so his head's the last thing to come out, and he was like a face presentation, which dragged on for about, it was about 25 hours . . .

I asked whether the breech presentation had been detected beforehand:

> (Did they know that he was breech beforehand?) He'd been breech, and they kept doing this thing of (Turning him) turning him round (Yes, yes), and then when I went into labour, he just turned himself again anyway, but they hadn't reali-, there is a special name for this double breech (Yes). I can't, can't remember what it is but, um, apparently this happens: they're actually breech, and then something makes them jerk, and they bring their legs up and then (Oh, yes) they trap themselves (Yes), so, yuh, and there's really nothing they can do then, they've just (Yes) got to. If they'd have known soon enough, they would have done a section (A section), but because it had been so long (Yeh, yeh), and he finally got trapped in (Yes), and was way down (Yes), it was, I was thinking, 'Well, why why did they put me through that, why didn't they – ' but there again, they really, there was nothing really they could do.

Here 'there's really nothing they can do', contrasts with 'why did they put me through that?' Later Janice sums it up philosophically as 'just one of those things that happens, I suppose'.

While Janice's attitude to the medical authorities was mixed in this way, she was quite definite about her decision never to have any more babies, at the end of Victoria's story, where she mentions Russell's birth: 'I always swore, and managed to keep to it, that I would never have another baby'; and at the end of

Russell's story: ' I always said I, I don't know if I would do it
or not, if I ever got pregnant again I would have contemplated
having an abortion, because I'd have been so frightened to, to
go through it again'. This decision is part of the story of her
childbirth experiences, and conveys her strength of feeling about
Russell's birth.

Janice is conscious that her stories do not fit the fashionable
positive birth-story:

> The only way I could look at it was the pain was there for a
> reason, and I had to get on with that pain (Yes, yes), but I
> couldn't say it was, you know, fulfilling, and I really felt like a
> woman (Yes), I felt like hell (Yes), you know, just wanted (Yes),
> but there, there're other people that it's the best thing they've ever
> done (Yes) isn't it?

But she puts this down to the differences between women, not
to the falsity of the prevailing birth-story. Janice had not heard
only good stories beforehand: 'You always got one or two that
had been through horrendous births and wanted to tell you every
detail'. These stories did not affect her, because 'I was wise enough
to know that each birth's different anyway (Yes), so I just had to
think positively (Yes, yes), think, "Well, there's no real reason
(Yes) that that's going to happen to me"'. However, she did also
say that not enough of her kind of 'horrible in-between stories'
were current: only one extreme or the other, Caesareans or easy
births.

It was clear that she did not think in natural childbirth terms
at all about her births: there was no opposition to intervention
as such. When I asked about 'natural' birth, she interpreted
it in terms of the unavailability of epidurals at the time: '(I
mean, had you thought beforehand that it was going to be,
kind of, natural, you know?) Um, yeh, because I then, because
then . . . you weren't able to go in and say, "Well, I want an
epidural" (Anyway, yes, yes), which you can now'. Her attitude
when Victoria is born shows some of the natural childbirth sense
of pride in achievement: 'the actual feeling of having a baby handed
to you, you know, you've done it on your own (Yes), that kind of
feeling'; but her descriptions of the first sight of her babies are in
no way romanticised: 'I looked down at her, and all I could see
was Jack's dad lying in the, you know, she looked so like him,

wrinkled ... and I remember looking at Russell and thinking, "God, he's ugly, he really is ugly, people will come and look and think (Laughs), you know, and they'll just be polite"'.

In telling my story again to Janice, a lot of emphasis falls on feeling awful afterwards: both of us had had the experience of having both an epidural and a general anaesthetic, and both of us suffered postnatal depression. Another way in which the telling of my story is like hers (partly induced by her questions) is the double attitude to the medical institution: on the one hand you have to believe them; on the other, they might be wrong. Janice questions my middle-class faith in rational argument with them. We also both believe, like Beth, that stories like our own are not current: while Janice thinks Caesarean stories *are* told, but not 'in-between' stories like hers, I found that I had not heard Caesarean stories, or been prepared for that eventuality.

I begin by summing up my experience as 'pretty awful'; 'everything went wrong as far as I'm concerned'. The shape of my story is a series of defeats, as I'm pushed from natural childbirth to induction, to epidural, to Caesarean with general anaesthetic. As I pointed out to Keiko, this involves increasing loss of control. I complain to Janice that my NCT classes did not prepare me for this outcome: 'but we went to these, you know, the NCT classes [Yuh], where they tell you all about how it's going to be natural [Yuh], and, um, I mean they didn't say anything about Caesarians [Yuh] or inductions or anything'. What puts me at the mercy of the medical institution is my high blood-pressure: an indisputable fact, one would think, but then:

> They took me down to the labour room, whatever, delivery room, or whatever it's called, and, um, at that point my blood pressure actually dropped [Yuh] [Laughter], you know, I think it was something to do with 'At last they're doing something'. I was in this state [Yuh] of tension [And then you're not] (Inaudible) [Yuh] quite, quite normal it went by then.

Janice has also earlier remarked that the antenatal clinic (where the high blood pressure was first detected) was enough to raise anyone's blood pressure. So we introduce this note of doubt about the medical 'facts'. Similarly, when the decision is taken for a Caesarean, 'I don't know, there was all this ambiguity about whether the baby was getting distressed or not'.

The medical personnel also do not come over as sure of what they are doing:

> They were, um, so many different doctors [Yuh], and coming in with different ideas [Yuh], so one of them was going to try this induction, so at first they tried one of those pessaries [Yuh], that they put in [Yuh], so they tried that, and didn't think that would, and then he said, 'Oh, we're going to leave you', you know, we won't do anything now, and this other doctor, the Indian I think it was, the Indian lady [Yuh], rang up and said, 'No, no, I will do an induction tonight', so all of a sudden just after he'd come in and said, 'Right' . . .

In arguing against whatever intervention they propose, Greg and I follow an NCT line, but it doesn't work, we are defeated: 'We were, kind of, arguing with them all the time, saying do, do they really have to do this [Yuh], do they have to do that, and of course they always, they'd have to (Laughs)'. Janice, however, questions this interpretation of defeat, and introduces another interpretation, 'all for the best':

> It was like we'd been arguing with them, and and we'd lost (Laughs) [Yuh, yuh] all the way through, that I wasn't going to be allowed to do [Yuh] anything myself. [But did you realise it was for the best, or did you still think you could have done it on your own?] Oo, I don't know, you just have to believe what they say [What they say, yuh].

I follow this with a positive story about the medical staff, in which a retrospective certainty is conferred on what at the time seemed an ambiguous event:

> What was nice, was, the next day, or whenever it was I was awake enough, perhaps the following day, um, this Indian lady came round, and she said, 'Now, do you understand why you had the Caesarean?' and she explained the baby was getting distressed [Yuh], so that was nice [Yuh], and she said, 'And you did do, you know, you did have a try' (Yuh), and so on, so it was nice that she bothered, you know, to come.

This other interpretation, that everything happened as it had to, 'for the best', depends on a trust in the medical authorities: this point comes up again when I describe coming round from the operation:

I was in quite a lot of pain [Yuh] I remember, and they gave me some injection for that. I remember, kind of, asking, 'How long will it take for this injection to [Yuh], to, to act?' and they said, sort of, 'Half an hour' [Yuh], so I thought, 'That's all right, I'm, just have to get through [Yuh, you can cope with that, can't you?], I have to be in this pain for half an hour, and then it will – ' [You hold them to their word, though, don't you? I think if the pain had lasted longer than half an hour, you tend to think, well,] Yes, yes [you know, their word's law, isn't it? When they say something to you,] Yes, yes [you, you believe them].

The climax of my story is the time in the middle of the night when the two 'stories' of my childbirth, the (failed) induction and the (postponed) Caesarian don't quite meet:

> So, well, I'm going to have a Caesarean, so they didn't top up the epidural anymore, because they said it hadn't worked enough to do a Caesarean, they'd have to give me a general anaesthetic [Anaesthetic, yuh] as well, so, and then they came and said, 'There's a queue for the theatre, there's someone who's had a retained placenta, we have to do that first', and it was a couple of hours, Greg says, in the middle of the night, that I was waiting, you know, and of course there I was having the pains [Yuh], because [The epidural had worn off], yes, because the epidural hasn't worked [Yuh], and I knew I was going to have this Caesarean anyway, so I was having these useless [All these pains, yuh], totally useless pains. [So what was happening, Tess, was, what, you just weren't dilating, the baby just wasn't opening] – I just wasn't dilating [Yuh], yes, [Yuh], I was, just contractions, not doing anything, so there was that awful bit in the middle of the night, it was all in the middle of the night.

There are logical, medical explanations that I can repeat for what happened, but an absurd situation is produced. This is the 'horrible bit' I told Beth. I also repeated to Janice the story of Greg being the first to welcome Alice, and of my first sight of Alice's face, with her eyes shut, though here I don't contrast this with 'wonderful' first recognition stories: these are part of Beth's culture, not Janice's.

Finally, I talk about my weakened state after the operation, both physically and mentally:

> I seemed very emotionally awful I think when [Yuh], and they kept coming with these painkillers, er, and one day the nurse was asking me, 'D'you want these painkillers?' and I said, 'Well, I don't really

think I'm in pain, but, but I just don't want to, kind of, feel [Yuh] anything'. So she just said, 'Well, you're going to have to feel it in the end' [Yuh]. It was nice talking to her [Yuh], she was a very nice [Yuh] midwife, and she, she then took me for this walk down to the end of the corridor, there's this lovely view of the mountains [Yuh], and said, 'You'll be walking up with Alice soon'.

Here, my emphasis is on the unexpected kindness of the medical personnel, not this time in furnishing a definite medical explanation, but in providing a story about life beyond the hospital, and beyond the experience of birth. The two women, the Indian doctor and the sympathetic midwife, provide for me positive ways out of the experience, one by a retrospective story that labels my experience as inevitable; one by a prospective story that points to an 'afterwards' that can disconnect me from the pain. My sense of self in my story is shaken by the experience of birth: I express both a sense of 'violation', and an unwillingness to return to full consciousness of what has happened and how I might feel about it. The sympathetic midwife helps me by pointing to a future, active self who will return later, but with the addition of my daughter, in her image of me climbing the mountains with Alice. Janice doesn't pick up on my story of the sympathetic midwife, but on my description of postnatal depression: '[Yuh that that kind of depression's something you're not prepared for]'. A conversation develops between us on postnatal depression at home. Walking in the mountains is a part of my culture, and not of hers.

My conversations with these other women offered various perspectives on my story, all making use of, but also questioning, existing ideologies. Beth's story didn't conform to any of the cultural stereotypes available to her, but her only form of self-assertion was to criticise the natural childbirth-stories she had been offered; Keiko used feminist language of co-operation and relationality to fashion a new version of her story, while also criticising hopeful 'natural' stories. Janice had never accepted the 'natural' stories: she alternated between criticism and acceptance of the medical story. All three women tell the story from their point of view, in their own voices, and convey the threat to selfhood that birth posed to them: Beth's 'healthy' self is challenged by her unruly body; Keiko's individualistic self-help ethic is challenged by the vulnerability and two-ness of the birthing body; what happens to Janice's body is never fully explained by the medical account. It is these disruptions that lead them to question the 'official' versions of the birth-story.

The various interpretations of my story, told to these different women at different times, illustrate the plasticity of oral narrative, the way it varies according to time, place and audience. Written accounts, perhaps falsely, 'freeze' one version of a story. Nevertheless, certain features, both 'facts' and feelings, remain constant, the 'I'll always remember' often signalling such a feature. Interpretations, however, can change: in my story there is the fact of the Caesarean, interpreted either as defeat or as life-saver; then the less stable 'facts' of the high blood pressure and the baby's distress; then my feelings of defeat and violation, interpretable as the results of mistreatment by the medical authorities, or as inevitable consequences of necessary intervention and postnatal depression; or as due to misleading expectations of natural birth.

> Was it all a botch, a defeat?
> Did I do it all wrong?
> Could we have argued more coherently,
> More rationally, against
> The induction, the epidural, the Caesarean?
> It's all a blur now, a horror
> In the middle of the night:
> Panic, fear, through the dark gates,
> Your reluctance
> To come out, eyes tight shut;
> Yet your impatience
> Controlling us all:
> 'Quick, quick, I want to be a Leo!'
> This is what matters now –
> That you began, that we began,
> Out of that pain and blood.

References

Anderson, K., S. Armitage, D. Jack and J. Wittner (1990), 'Beginning where we are, feminist methodology in oral history' in J. M. Nielsen (ed.), *Feminist Research Methods, Exemplary Readings in the Social Sciences*, London, Westview Press, 94–112.

Atwood, M. (1979), *Surfacing*, London, Virago (originally published in 1973).

Atwood, M. (1984), 'Giving Birth' in *Dancing Girls*, London, Virago (originally published in 1977).

Bagnold, E. (1987), *The Squire*, London, Virago (originally published in 1938).

Baines, E. (1983), *The Birth Machine*, London, Women's Press.

Betts, D. (1974), 'Still Life With Fruit' in S. Cahill (ed.) (1978), *Women And Fiction 2*, New York, Mentor, 337–54.

Bourne, G. (1975), *Pregnancy*, London, Pan.

Bowder, C. (1983), *Birth Rites*, Brighton, Harvester.

Brittain, V. (1936), *Honourable Estate, A Novel of Transition*, London, Gollancz.

Butler, C. (1978), 'Margaret Drabble, *The Millstone* and Wordsworth', *English Studies*, 59, 353–60.

Butler, J. (1990), *Gender Trouble, Feminism and the Subversion of Identity*, London and New York, Routledge.

Byatt, A. S. (1986), *Still Life*, Harmondsworth, Penguin (originally published in 1985).

Cixous, H. (1981), 'The laugh of the Medusa' in E. Marks and I. de Courtivron (eds.), *New French Feminisms*, Brighton, Harvester, 245–64.

Cixous, H. (1988), 'Extreme fidelity' in S. Sellars (ed.), *Writing Differences, Readings from the Seminar of Hélène Cixous*, Milton Keynes, Open University Press, 9–36.

Chester, L. (1975) 'Song of Being Born' in L. Chester (ed.) (1989b).

Chester, L. (1989a), 'The Stone Baby' in L. Chester (ed.) (1989b).

Chester, L. (ed.) (1989b), *Cradle and All, Women Writers on Pregnancy and Birth*, Boston and London, Faber & Faber.

Chodorow, N. (1978), *The Reproduction of Mothering, Psychoanalysis and the Sociology of Gender*, Berkeley and London, University of California Press.

Cosslett, T. (1988), *Woman to Woman, Female Friendship in Victorian Fiction*, Brighton, Harvester.

Couzyn, J. (ed.) (1985), *The Bloodaxe Book of Contemporary Women Poets*, Newcastle-upon-Tyne, Bloodaxe Books.

Derricote, T. (1983), 'Natural Birth' in L. Chester (ed.) (1989b).

Doane, M. A. (1990), 'Technophilia, technology, representation, and the feminine' in M. Jacobus, E. Fox Keller and S. Shuttleworth (eds.), *Body/Politics, Women and the Discourses of Science*, New York and London, Routledge, 163–176.

Donnison, J. (1977), *Midwives and Medical Men, A History of Inter-Professional Rivalry and Women's Rights*, London, Heinemann.

Doubiago, S. (1989), 'South America Mi Hija' in L. Chester (ed.) (1989b).

Drabble, M. (1968), *The Millstone*, Harmondsworth, Penguin (originally published in 1966).

Ehrenreich, B. and D. English (1979), *For Her Own Good*, London, Pluto Press.

Emecheta, B. (1985), *The Rape of Shavi*, London, Fontana (originally published in 1983).

Emecheta, B. (1987), *Second-Class Citizen*, London, Fontana (originally published in 1974).

Emecheta, B. (1988), *The Joys of Motherhood*, London, Fontana (originally published in 1979).

Freedman, L., and V. M. Ferguson (1950), 'The question of "painless childbirth" in primitive cultures', *American Journal of Orthopsychiatry*, 20, 363–72.

Gingher, M. (1988), 'Camouflage' in L. Chester (ed.) (1989b).

Giovanni, N. (1971), 'Don't Have A Baby Till You Read This' in L. Chester (ed.) (1989b).

Griffin, S. (1978), *Woman and Nature, The Roaring Inside Her*, New York, Harper and Row.

Hardin, N. S. (1973), 'Drabble's *The Millstone*, a fable for our times', *Critique*, 15, 1, 22–34.

Hindmarch, G. (1989), 'A Birth Account' in L. Chester (ed.) (1989b).

Hirsch, M. (1989), *The Mother/Daughter Plot, Narrative, Psychoanalysis, Feminism*, Bloomington, Indiana University Press.

Hobby, E. (1988), *Virtue of Necessity, English Women's Writing 1649–88*, London, Virago.

Hoffman, A. (1985), 'Fortune's Daughter' in L. Chester (ed.) (1989b).

Howie, P. (1977), 'Induction of labour' in T. Chard and M. Richards (eds.), *Benefits and Hazards of the New Obstetrics*, London, Heinemann, 83–99.

Huff, C. (1991), 'Delivery, the cultural re-presentation of childbirth', *Prose Studies*, 14, 2, 108–21.

Jong, E. (1983), 'The Birth of the Water Baby' in L. Chester (ed.) (1989b).

Jong, E. (1989), 'On the First Night' in L. Chester (ed.) (1989b).

Jordanova, L. (1989), *Sexual Visions, Images of Gender in Science and Medicine between the 18th and 20th Centuries*, Hemel Hempstead, Harvester.

Jouve, N. W. (1991), *White Woman Speaks with Forked Tongue, Criticism as Autobiography*, London, Routledge.

Karmel, M. (1959), *Babies Without Tears, A Mother's Experience of the Lamaze Method of Painless Childbirth*, London, Secker & Warburg.

Kitzinger, S. (1962), *The Experience of Childbirth*, London, Gollancz.

Kitzinger, S. (1984), *The Experience of Childbirth*, 5th edn., Harmondsworth, Penguin.

Kitzinger, S. (ed.) (1987), *Giving Birth, How it Really Feels*, London, Victor Gollancz.

Konek, C., and D. Walters (eds.) (1976), *I Hear My Sisters Saying, Poems by Twentieth Century Women*, New York, Thomas Y. Crowell.

Kreppel, M. C. (1984), 'Books I've read, crosscurrents in obstetrics and literary childbirth', *Atlantis*, 10, 1–11.

Kristeva, J. (1977), 'Maternité selon Giovanni Bellini', *Polylogue*, Paris, Édition de Seuil.

Kristeva, J. (1981), 'Woman can never be defined' in E. Marks and I. de Courtivron, *New French Feminisms*, Brighton, Harvester, 137–41.

Kristeva, J. (1986), 'Stabat Mater' in Toril Moi (ed.), *The Kristeva Reader*, Oxford, Basil Blackwell, 160–86.

Lamaze, F. (1958), *Painless Childbirth*, London, Burke.

Lazarre, J. (1976), 'The Mother Knot' in L. Chester (ed.) (1989b).

Lessing, D. (1977), *A Proper Marriage*, London, Granada (originally published in 1956).

Lessing, D. (1962), *The Golden Notebook*, London, Michael Joseph.

Lewis, J. (1980), *The Politics of Motherhood, Child and Maternal Welfare in England, 1900–1939*, London, Croom Helm.

Marlatt, D. (1980), 'Rings' in L. Chester (ed.) (1989b).

Martin, E. (1987), *The Woman in the Body, A Cultural Analysis of Reproduction*, Boston, Beacon Press.

Mead, M., and N. Newton (1967), 'Cultural patterning of perinatal behaviour' in S. Richardson and A. Guttmacher (eds.), *Childbearing, Its Social and Psychological Aspects*, Baltimore, Williams & Wilkins, 142–244.

References 177

Miller, J. B. (1978), *Towards A New Psychology of Women*, Harmondsworth, Penguin.

Mitford, J. (1992), *The American Way of Birth*, London, Gollancz.

Morrison, T. (1987), *Beloved*, London, Chatto & Windus.

Morrison, T. (1988), 'Telling our story, an interview with Toni Morrison', *Spare Rib*, 12–16.

Nielsen, J. M. (ed.) (1990), *Feminist Research Methods, Exemplary Readings in the Social Sciences*, London, Westview Press.

Oakley, A. (1981), *From Here To Maternity*, Harmondsworth, Pelican.

Oakley, A. (1983), 'Women and health policy' in J. Lewis (ed.), *Women's Welfare/Women's Rights*, London, Croom Helm, 103–29.

Oakley, A. (1984), *The Captured Womb, A History of the Medical Care of Pregnant Women*, Oxford, Blackwell.

Oates, J. C. (1988), 'A Touch of the Flu' in L. Chester (ed.) (1989b).

O'Driscoll, K., and D. Meagher (1980), *Active Management of Labour*, London, W. B. Saunders.

Ostriker, A. (1980), 'Propaganda Poem: Maybe for Some Young Mamas' in L. Chester (ed.) (1989b).

Olds, S. (1980), 'The Language of the Brag' in L. Chester (ed.) (1989b).

Palmer, P. (1989), *Contemporary Women's Fiction, Narrative Practice and Feminist Theory*, Hemel Hempstead, Harvester.

Plath, S. (1981), *Collected Poems*, London, Faber & Faber.

Poston, C. H. (1978), 'Childbirth in literature', *Feminist Studies*, 4, 18–31.

Read, G. D. (1933), *Natural Childbirth*, London, Heinemann.

Read, G. D. (1942), *Revelation of Childbirth*, London, Heinemann.

Read, G. D. (1954), *Childbirth Without Fear*, London, Heinemann.

Reddy, M. T. (1991), 'Motherhood, knowledge, and power', *Journal of Gender Studies* 1, 1, 81–5.

Rich, A. (1977), *Of Woman Born, Motherhood as Experience and Institution*, London, Virago.

Richards, M. (1975), 'Innovation in medical practice, obstetricians and the induction of labour in Britain', *Social Science and Medicine*, 9, 595–602.

Robinson, L. (1986), *Sex, Class, and Culture*, New York and London, Methuen.

Roberts, H. (ed.) (1981), *Doing Feminist Research*, London, Routledge & Kegan Paul.

Rosenthal, B. (1984), 'Baby Moves Inside' in L. Chester (ed.) (1989b).

Rothman, B. K. (1982), *In Labor, Women and Power in the Birthplace*, New York and London, Norton.

Schutt, C. (1989), 'Sisters' in L. Chester (ed.) (1989b).

Sebba, A. (1986), *Enid Bagnold, The Authorised Biography*, London, Weidenfeld & Nicholson.

Sebba, A. (1987), 'Introduction' in Enid Bagnold, *The Squire*, London, Virago, v–xxi.

Smith, P. (1988), *Discerning the Subject*, Minneapolis, University of Minnesota Press, xxxiv–xxxv.

Smith, S. (1991), 'The autobiographical manifesto, identities, temporalities, politics', *Prose Studies*, 14, 2, 186–212.

Spitzer, S. (1978), 'Fantasy and femaleness in Margaret Drabble's *The Millstone*', *Novel*, 11, 3 , 227–45.

Stanley, L. (ed.) (1990), *Feminist Praxis, Research, Theory and Epistemology in Feminist Sociology*, London, Routledge.

Stanley, L. (1992), *The Auto/Biographical I, The Theory and Practice of Feminist Auto/Biography*, Manchester, Manchester University Press.

Thomas, A. N. (1957), *Dr Courageous, The Story of Dr Grantly Dick Read*, London, Heinemann.

Thompson, J. (1987), 'Dreams of a New Mother' in L. Chester (ed.) (1989b).

Tompkins, J. (1991), 'Me and my shadow' in R. R. Warhol and D. P. Herndl (eds.), *Feminisms, An Anthology of Literary Theory and Criticism*, New Brunswick, Rutgers University Press, 1079–92.

Towler, J., and J. Bramall (1986), *Midwives in History and Society*, London, Croom Helm.

Treichler, P. (1990), 'Feminism, medicine, and the meaning of childbirth' in M. Jacobus, E. Fox Keller and S. Shuttleworth, *Body/Politics, Women and the Discourses of Science*, New York and London, Routledge, 113–38.

Waldman, A. (1983), 'Enceinte' in L. Chester (ed.) (1989b).

Walker, A. (1984), 'A writer because of, not in spite of, her children' in *In Search of Our Mothers' Gardens*, London, Women's Press, 66–70.

Walters, S. D. (1993), *Lives Together, Worlds Apart: Mothers and Daughters in Popular Culture*, Berkeley, University of California Press.

Waugh, P. (1989), *Feminine Fictions, Revisiting the Postmodern*, London, Routledge.

Weldon, F. (1980), *Puffball*, London, Hodder & Stoughton.

Wertz, D., and R. Wertz (1979), *Lying-In, A History of Childbirth in America*, New York, Schocken.

Williams, S. A. (1988), *Dessa Rose*, London, Macmillan.

Wordsworth, W. (1807), 'Ode, Intimations of Immortality from Recollections of Early Childhood' in T. Hutchinson (ed.) (1971), *Wordsworth. Poetical Works*, rev. Ernest de Selincourt, London, Oxford University Press, 460–2.

Index

Index

Cixous, H.,
'The laugh of the Medusa', 1
'Extreme fidelity', 120, 142
class, 4, 7, 39, 77, 80–1, 83, 89–109, 117
colonialism, 28, 33, 38, 42, 60
consultants, 50, 57, 61, 63; see also doctors; medical personnel; obstetricians
contraception, 64, 69
contractions, 16, 28, 31, 57, 67, 68, 116, 139–40, 142, 160, 163, 171
control, 3, 7, 12, 14–15, 17–18, 20, 29, 30–1, 34, 52, 54, 156–7, 159, 162, 164–5, 169
Cott, N., 4
Couzyn, J., *Bloodaxe Book of Women's Poetry*, 146
cultural
assumptions, 155
construct, 10
context, 154
contrasts, 162
origins, 22, 26, 27
practices, 10, 12, 23–5
see also social
culture, 10, 19, 23–4, 32, 37–40, 67, 102, 118, 172

daughters, 82, 111, 123–5, 129–31
death, birth as, 8, 152–6
Derricote, T., 'Natural Birth', 6, 29–30, 36–7, 39, 88, 92, 142, 151–2
devourment of mother, 8, 125, 127–31
Dickens, C., *Our Mutual Friend*, 92
discourses, 3, 4, 6–8, 20, 74, 77, 83, 87, 89, 109, 117–20, 133, 155; see also medical discourse; natural childbirth discourse; scientific discourse
Doane, M. A., 'Technophilia, technology, representation, and the feminine', 118–19
doctors, 2–3, 11, 13, 15–16, 20, 26, 30, 32, 52, 54, 61–3, 66, 95, 113, 121–2, 134, 140, 162, 170, 172; see also consultants; medical personnel; obstetricians
Donnison, J., *Midwives and Medical Men*, 5, 9, 32, 47
Doubiago, S., 'South America Mi Haja', 6, 21–2, 24, 32, 51

Drabble, M., *The Millstone*, 28, 61, 89, 91–2, 94–103, 106, 113–14, 131–2, 135, 137, 151
drugs, 54, 57, 88, 115, 137

Ehrenreich, B. and D. English, *For Her Own Good*, 89
embryo, 73, 145, see also foetus
Emecheta, B., 40, 100–7
Second-Class Citizen, 51, 89, 91, 94
The Joys of Motherhood, 40–2
The Rape of Shavi, 40–2
enema, 47, 49, 51, 78
epidural, 47, 75, 87, 158–9, 160–1, 168–9, 171
essentialism, 5, 7–8, 19
evolution, 10, 12
expertise, 55, 63, 110
experts, 5–6, 12, 15, 89, 109–10, 112–15

feminine mystique, 19, 81
feminist historians, 32
foetal monitoring, 32, 47, 52
foetus, 8, 64–5, 72–4, 117–19, 121, 123, 125–6, 143–50; see also embryo
forceps, 32, 68, 159
Fraser, K.,
'Poem Wondering if I am Pregnant', 121, 143
'Poem for the New', 121
Freedman, L. and V. M. Ferguson 'The question of "painless childbirth" in primitive cultures', 10
Freud, 12, 18

Gingher, M., 'Camouflage', 131–2, 151
Giovanni, N., 'Don't Have a Baby Till You Read This', 60
Gordon, M., 'The Unwanted', 128

Hardin, N., 'Drabble's *The Millstone*, a fable for our times', 95
heredity, 173
heterosexuality, 18, 85
Hindmarch, G., 'A Birth Account', 145
Hirsch, Marianne, *The Mother Daughter Plot*, 2, 131